99 Jumpstarts for Kids' Science Research

Peggy J. Whitley and Susan Williams Goodwin

LIBRARIES
UNLIMITED
A Member of the Greenwood Publishing Group

Westport, Connecticut • London

Library of Congress Cataloging-in-Publication Data

Whitley, Peggy.
99 jumpstarts for kids' science research / by Peggy J. Whitley and Susan Williams Goodwin.
    p. cm.
  Includes bibliographical references and index.
  ISBN 1-59158-261-X (pbk. : alk. paper)
    1. Science—Experiments—Juvenile literature. 2. Research—Juvenile literature. I. Goodwin,
Susan Williams. II. Title. III. Title: Ninety nine jumpstarts for kids' science research.

  Q182.3.W52 2006
  507.8—dc22   2005030845

British Library Cataloguing in Publication Data is available.

Library of Congress Catalog Card Number: 2005030845
ISBN: 1-59158-261-X

First published in 2006

Libraries Unlimited, 88 Post Road West, Westport, CT 06881
A Member of the Greenwood Publishing Group, Inc.
www.lu.com

Printed in the United States of America

The paper used in this book complies with the
Permanent Paper Standard issued by the National
Information Standards Organization (Z39.48–1984).

10 9 8 7 6 5 4 3 2 1

99 Jumpstarts for Kids' Science Research

Contents

ENERGY (*CONT.*)

THE ENVIRONMENT

GEOLOGY

THE HEAVENS

MATTER

MEDICINE AND HEALTH

TECHNOLOGY

TECHNOLOGY (*CONT.*)

WEATHER

Preface

In our previous books, *99 Jumpstarts to Research: Topic Guides for Finding Information on Current Issues* and *99 Jumpstarts for Kids: Getting Started in Research,* we focused on topics covering a variety of subjects from AIDS to the Boys Choir of Harlem. In *99 Jumpstarts for Kids' Science Research,* we have elected to examine 10 broad areas in science (animals, body parts, energy, the environment, geology, the heavens, matter, medical and health, technology, and weather) especially for students in grades 3 through 8. Each subject section has between 9 and 11 jumpstarts to help users gain a greater understanding of narrowing topics and selecting resources during the research process. Our goal in writing the 99 Jumpstarts series is to promote improved information literacy by encouraging beginning researchers to evaluate their topic and to examine a variety of materials.

Today's students have to deal with information overload, and this makes it difficult to select the best information—or even determine where the best information can be found. Do I look in the newspaper, in magazines, online, at videos, or in books? Each time these questions are asked, the answer may be different. So a little critical thinking about topics is an important starting point. We believe that systematic planning, by teacher, librarian, and student, will make all the difference in the quality of the final product—and the way the student feels about it. Help students get off to a good start, and you will reap the reward with well-organized papers and students who feel successful.

We continue to feel that the approach teachers take toward research deeply affects the way students (young or old) react to the process. This attitude toward the research process will influence students throughout their education. So enjoy the discovery process. Help develop the natural curiosity young students have.

As college librarians who were school librarians in our past lives, Susan and I especially want to thank school librarians everywhere for introducing students to the research process. Every day we see college students who are clueless about gathering information and writing short reports. So believe us, when you have taught it, we know and appreciate it. In our college library, we continue to encourage students to use a variety of formats—and to carefully evaluate the information they use. It is never too early to begin the process of critically analyzing information. If you have comments or suggestions, let us hear from you.

Illustrations for this book are by Susan, the Photoshop guru.

Peggy Whitley
Dean of Educational Services, Kingwood College
peggy.whitley@nhmccd.edu
kclibrary.nhmccd.edu

Susan Goodwin
Reference Librarian, Kingwood College
sue.goodwin@nhmccd.edu

Introduction: How This Book Is Organized

Each jumpstart is divided into the following sections:

- **New Words** introduces the students to words they will encounter when researching the topic.

- **What is _____ ?** is intended to give a short introduction to each topic. Students will feel encouraged to research a topic as they gain a better understanding of how it can be broken into parts, making it manageable for a short paper.

- **What Can I Write About?** includes several suggestions for the budding researcher. Most topics are too broad for a short paper. These suggestions break the topic down and give the interested student something he or she can handle.

- **Are There Books on _____?** lists three to five of the best books, both reference and circulating, on the topic. Students will use the books in their library. When writing about scientific topics, currency is important. This section can be used by librarians for collection development. All listed books have received positive reviews and are appropriate for grades 3–8.

- **Can the Internet Help?** sends the researcher to kid-friendly sites with appropriate reading levels. The information found on these selected sites can be trusted for use in a research paper. We have attempted to choose organization, education, and government sites, since they generally have the best staying power.

 **Ta Da!**

- **Create Your Own or _____ in Action!** includes Web sites students can use to do a little research of their own or enjoy a game or other activity on their topic.

- **Experiment** offers an online or home project that allows students to experiment hands-on with their chosen topics.

- **In the Classroom,** a section designed for the teacher, includes online lesson plans, experiments, enrichment activities, or sites for background information for teachers.

We have not added newspapers or journal full-text databases. We hope teachers and students will use them if they are available. They are very useful and often contain the newest and best information on a topic. They are generally reliable, and online full-text databases are important for student learning.

Finally, we hope that teachers will celebrate the completion of the big research project. Allow the students to make oral reports, encourage them to bring in experiments and posters to share with the class. If the Internet is available, let the students share with their classmates the site that was most helpful to them. Think back on your own learning—and provide the kind of environment that you remember as the best. Celebrating new knowledge allows the students to realize how important their curiosity is to learning.

Search Engines Especially for Kids

Several very good search engines are available for kids of all ages. They are filtered and touted to be safe from pornography and suggestive advertising. The ones we list are chosen for entertainment and enlightenment. Bookmark the ones you like best, and use more than one when searching. We have also listed specialized search engines that you may not find on your own, like ALA Great Websites for Kids (from the American Library Association) and FirstGov for Kids. These collections are generally hand-picked for their information and appropriateness for children. They may not have the high visibility of KidsClick! or Yahooligans—but we encourage you to use them.

Major Kids' Search Engines

KidsClick!
http://www.kidsclick.org/
KidsClick lists about 5,000 Web sites in various categories. Librarians back these sites, and they are maintained by Colorado State Library. A click will take the student to the library version, arranged by Dewey Decimal number. Though it is a small collection, we usually start our search here because of the quality of the selections.

Yahooligans
http://www.yahooligans.com/
Yahoo for kids, designed for ages 7 to 12. Sites are hand-picked to be appropriate for children. Yahooligans is the oldest major directory for children, launched in March 1996. It is arranged by subject headings and subheadings just like its grownup version.

Ask Jeeves For Kids
http://www.ajkids.com/
Ask Jeeves For Kids has been vetted for appropriateness. Sometimes the results are good. It may be best for more experienced searchers.

Looksmart's Kids Directory
http://search.netnanny.com/
The Kids Directory is a listing of more than 20,000 kid Web sites that were hand-picked by employees of *Looksmart* subsidiary Net Nanny and vetted for quality. Arranged by broad subject, this is a friendly Web site for the young. Family-safe.

Collections of Search Engines for Kids

Kids Search Engine Watch

http://searchenginewatch.com/links/article.php/2156191

This site, by Danny Sullivan, has a huge collection of search engines designed for young kids. The major ones (Yahooligans, KidsClick!, and Ask Jeeves) are listed first for easy access. Filtering options are next. Mr. Sullivan goes through each of the major search engines and tells parents whether or how to filter. The drawback is that each engine selection needs an extra click to start.

Kids' Search Tools

http://www.rcls.org/ksearch.htm

Dictionaries, encyclopedias, search engines, and Web sites for teachers and kids are on this search-friendly page. A keyword search line is right on the page. The collection is maintained by InfoPeople Project of California. Easy to use.

My Prowler

http://www.myprowler.com/kids.htm

This metasearcher finds and prioritizes sites on five of the major kids' search engines: KidsClick!, Awesome Library, Yahooligans, SearchEdu, and CyberSleuth Kids. Save a little time and use a metasearch engine. You can narrow your search to images, MP3, audio, U.S. Government, Weblogs, too—before you put in your search words. Recommended.

TekMom's Search Engines for Kids

http://www.tekmom.com/search/

Starting with the big four, TekMom then gives immediate access to specialized search engines by topic: General, Science, History, Authors, Biographies, Encyclopedias, Dictionaries, Images and Maps. Easy to use, and the search line is on the page.

Ivy's Search Engines for Kids

http://www.ivyjoy.com/rayne/kidssearch.html

Listed are Internet search engine links (the big four), links to Web guides for kids, some specialized search engine forms, and specialized search engine links of interest to kids. Also included under "family-friendly" are search engines similar to Ivy's and engines where the user can set the filter.

Other Search Engines We Enjoy Using

ALA Great Web Site for Kids

http://www.ala.org/greatsites

Collection of sites from the American Library Association. You can search by age or grade or browse through the subjects. Excellent site with strict guidelines for selection.

Librarian's Index

http://lii.org/search/file/history

You can trust these sites to be good ones for kids and adults alike. Carefully selected by librarians for researchers, these 16,000 + sites are annotated, and review dates are listed.

Kids' World
http://www.northvalley.net/kids/index.shtml

Kid's World has an excellent collection of topics by subject, from government to vacation. Viewers can suggest sites, which are carefully searched for appropriateness. Easy to use, colorful, and well organized. The only drawback is that the user has to search through the list of sites under broad subject. There is no keyword search. (An easy fix, which we hope they will add soon.)

Awesome Library
http://www.awesomelibrary.org/

Over 26,000 reviewed sites have been classified into a directory, specifically organized for teachers, students, and parents. Browse or search; the "search engines" section is worth your time. Awesome Library is aptly named.

Education World
http://www.education-world.com/

This site features over 500,000 sites of interest to educators. Browsable or searchable; users have the ability to narrow terms by appropriate grade level. Launched in spring 1996, this site is a an educator's resource. One problem is the number of ads on this page—and you will need an ad blocker to be able to use it.

FirstGov for Kids
http://www.kids.gov/

FirstGov provides links to federal kids' sites along with some of the best kids' sites from other organizations, all grouped by subject. You are invited to explore, learn, and have fun. The keyword search helps—but this site is great to browse for a topic you might like to learn about.

The Why Files from Google
http://whyfiles.org/search.html

A good place to search for answers. No filter, but the sites are some of the best.

Science Search Engine List
http://www.search-engine-index.co.uk/Reference/Science_Search/

A nice list for all ages. This is a directory of science topics that lead the user to smaller search engine collections.

How Stuff Works
http://howstuffworks.com

Not a search engine, but a great place to find basic science information. This site is separated by broad subjects (electronics, health, home, people, science, computer) and is easily searched. Use the suggested Table of Contents topics that come with your search. Excellent, current information from howstuffworks.com.

Kids'Health
http://kidshealth.org

Separate sections for parents, kids, and teens. These are well researched and worth using. White papers for kids. Well organized for browsing, or use your own search terms.

10 Suggestions for Better Searching

Entering your search terms may be enough. But the Internet is huge, and you can ensure that you find what you want by using these tips. Keep in mind that each search engine is different. Use their Help or Advanced Searching, too. These tips are generally good with all search engines.

1) Add as many appropriate search terms as you can think of. The Internet is so big that our problem is "too much information."

   Example: *camouflage conceal fish environment*

2) Use the word "kids" in your search—for safer and easier sites.

   Example: *animals impact environment kids.*

3) Prefixes often help your search. Do NOT put in spaces. If you do, this will not work.
   a. Definition:environment (find definitions of terms)
   b. URL:nhmccd (nhmccd will be part of the URL of all findings)
   c. Title:animal husbandry (the title is above the line or in title line of page.)
   d. Domain:edu

4) Use your math when adding and subtracting search words. Attach the + or – to the word.
   a. Use + to make sure your words are included in a search. You *will find* pages that have all of the words.

      Example: *animals +impact +environment +kids*

   b. Use – to exclude words from your pages. You *will not* find the word *kids* on your result pages.

      Example: *animals +impact +environment –kids*

   c. If you want to find words together, like a phrase, surround them with quotation marks. You *will find* the phrase words together.

      Example: *"hazardous materials" +solution +kids*

5) Use the asterisk to take the place of letters: *stress (distress) stress* (stressful)

6) Boolean searching helps exclude or include terms. Examples:
   a. *"hazardous materials"* **and** *solution and kids* (find all terms)
   b. *"hazardous materials"* **or** *hazmat* (find either one or the other term—helps poor spellers ☺)

    c.   *"hazardous materials"* **not** *kids* (do not find pages with "*kids*")

    d.   *animals* **near** *environment* (these terms will be within 10 to 25 words of each other, depending on the selected search engine).

7)   Use more than one search engine. We start with KidsClick!—but it is not always the most current and often has selected only two or three sites. Use another search engine—maybe one of the specialized ones we mentioned above.

8)   Be happy when you come across subject lists from which to choose. Start your search by using them, then search within the subject with your terms.

9)   Love any Web site that has its own search engine—one just for that site.

10)   Be discriminating. You do NOT have to look at every site. Use the descriptions and don't be afraid to go to page 2 or even page 10 of your search. Often, the search results are selected by popularity. A really good new site may not yet be popular.

99 Jumpstarts for Kids' Science Research

ANIMALS

Kids love to learn about animals. Our list covers features about animals, rather than specific animals. We have included Jane Goodall, chimpanzee expert. There are other famous animal researchers who may be interesting to write about. You choose. We encourage researchers to enjoy their research. It is fun! Find several formats for your resources, for example, books, the Internet, magazine articles, and interviews.

Cow Burps and Pig Stink.

ANIMALS AND THE ENVIRONMENT

New Words

Animal Waste, Manure
Ecotoxicology
Factory Farming
Farm Pollution
Methane

What About Animals and the Environment?

Cow burps, hyperactive fish, stupid frogs, farm pollution, and animal waste all affect our environment. There are over 2.2 billion tons of animal waste to dispose of each year. Cows and other cattle burp methane into the air, contributing to the greenhouse effect. Factory farming has caused pollution, both odorous and chemical. Are humans being harmed by animals in our environment? As you read about this topic, remember that people feel very strongly about animals, and the information you find will likely have a bias. It is your job to be fair.

What Can I Write About?

Write a paper about whether or not animals have an impact on the environment. Use examples.

Select a topic like animals and the greenhouse effect or the impact of moving animals to a new environment.

Write about factory farming and its effects on the environment. Try to cover both viewpoints.

Manure and its disposal would be a fun topic to write about.

Are There Books or Videos on Animals and the Environment?

Using the library catalog, search words may be *animals and environment*, *livestock*, *air quality*, and other terms you think will help you. Ask the librarian for assistance.

Cheeke, Peter. *Impacts of Livestock Production on Society, Diet, Health, and the Environment.* Danville, IL: Interstate, 1993.

Godish, Thad. *Air Quality*. 4th ed. Boca Raton, FL: Lewis, 2003.

Johnsen, Carolyn. *Raising a Stink: The Struggle over Hog Farms in Nebraska.* Lincoln, NE: Bison, 2003.

Midkiff, Ken. *The Meat You Eat: How Corporate Farming Has Endangered America's Food Supply.* New York: St. Martin's Press, 2004.

Wade, Mary Dodson. *Texas Plants and Animals.* Chicago: Heinemann, 2003.

Can the Internet Help?

Animals Rights and the Environment—http://www.animalrightsmalta.com/animalsenvironment.html. Read carefully, watch for bias.

Pollution and Animal Behavior—http://www.newscientist.com/article.ns?id=dn6343

Air Quality Issues and Animals—http://cattlefeeder.ab.ca/manure/airqualityindex.shtml. Recent reports.

How Animals Affect the Environment—http://library.thinkquest.org/10009/

Factory Farming Environmental Impact—http://www.factoryfarming.com/environment.htm or http://www.nrdc.org/water/pollution/factor/aafinx.asp

Animal Environment and Its Stressors—http://www2.hawaii.edu/ansc/News/95summer/envstres.htm. How we can keep the animals' environment safe.

The Manure Speech—http://www.nviro.com/JPN/animal.htm. Effects of animal waste on society.

Ecotoxicology—http://www.iet.msu.edu/Tox_for_Journ/ecotoxforcitizen.htm#top. Understandable article on adverse effects of poisons on animals.

Feral Feast—http://library.thinkquest.org/03oct/00128/en/main.htm. Impact of moving animals to a new environment.

 TA DA!

Get into Action!

Make Cow Manure Without the Cow—http://www.motherearthnews.com/arc/3662/

Tip Rosebud—http://www.littlejoe.org/cowtipping.htm

In the Classroom

Agriculture and Environment Lesson Plans—http://www.khake.com/page81.html

2

Hiding in Plain Sight.

CAMOUFLAGE

New Words

> Camouflage
> Concealing Coloration
> Disruptive Coloration
> Disguise—Mimicry
> Predator/Prey

What Is Camouflage?

Camouflage is the art of concealment. It involves hiding in plain sight through the use of some disguise. Animals all seem to find ways to adapt to their environment. Small animals that are vulnerable to larger prey wouldn't last long if they had no means of hiding themselves. Large animals use camouflage as well. Some animals, like the chameleon, use color as camouflage. Others use shape and behavior to camouflage themselves, so that they are mistaken for something else. The walking stick is an example of this type of camouflage. Humans use camouflage also. Can you think of times when they may need to "hide?" Is there anything else that uses camouflage for hiding? While you are studying this topic, consider how you would conceal yourself and then try it. Try several times, so you get good at it.

What Can I Write About?

Write about camouflage in general, the "who, where, what, when, why, and how" of it.

Discuss the four basic types of camouflage and how each works. Give examples.

Write about a single animal and its ability to hide from predators. Describe the kind of camouflage it uses to hide itself from its enemy. Show pictures.

Write about unexpected camouflaging, for instance, animals that live around the farm

Are There Books on Camouflage?

Goodman, Susan. *Claws, Coats, and Camouflage: The Way Animals Fit in Their World.* Brookfield, CT: Millbrook, 2001.

Perry, Phyllis. *Armor to Venom: Animal Defenses.* New York: Franklin Watts, 1997.

Purser, Bruce. *Jungle Bugs: Masters of Camouflage and Mimicry*. Toronto: Firefly, 2003.

Swinburne, Stephen R. *Lots and Lots of Zebra Stripes: Patterns in Nature*. Honesdale, PA: Boyds Mills Press, 1998.

Can the Internet Help?

How Stuff Works: Camouflage—http://science.howstuffworks.com/animal-camouflage.htm. Explains each type of camouflage, with pictures.

Animals' Secret Weapon—http://il.essortment.com/animalcamouflag_rezr.htm. Be sure to look at the next page as well. Good background.

Camouflage Field Guide—http://www.harcourtschool.com/activity/camouflage/camouflage.html

Frogs—http://www.exploratorium.edu/frogs/. An excellent page on adaptation, metamorphosis, and camouflage. The frog has it all.

Find the Critters—http://www.longhorn-cattle.com/camo.html. Even ranch animals hide from predators.

Camouflage Q&A—http://www.greenwing.org/teachersguide/fall00activity/fall00ma.html

 **TA DA!**

Camouflage Fun!

Nova—Seeing Through Camouflage—http://www.pbs.org/wgbh/nova/leopards/seeing.html. Games—spot animals using all four types of camouflage.

Try This Camouflage Art Project

- Find a cool picture of a mammal, insect, or reptile in a magazine and cut it out. Cut out more than one animal of a similar color if you want. You are going to try to hide them.
- Glue your animal on a similar-colored piece of construction paper.
- Draw and color, cut out from colored construction paper, or paint an environment that "camouflages" your animal. See if you can fool your friends.

In the Classroom

Marco Polo Search—http://www.marcopolosearch.org/mpsearch/basic_search.asp. Find lesson plans by grade level and topic. The search term *Camouflage* results in excellent links.

Hidden Picture (Johnny Appleseed)—http://www.niehs.nih.gov/kids/apples.htm#answerapples. There are other sites with hidden pictures on the Web as well. These are fun for younger students—and there are more difficult ones for older ones.

Disappearing Acts.

EXTINCTION

New Words

Anthropologic
Biological Diversity
Extinction/Pseudo-extinction
Extirpation
Populations

What Is Extinction?

Dead as the dodo. For all the animals that are alive today, numerous others have disappeared. We see evidence of extinction in natural history museums, at archeological digs, and at living museums. Complete extinction is when the animal completely disappears. Pseudo-extinction is when an animal completely disappears from a specific location. How do we know these animals existed? How can we guess what they looked like? Fascinating!

What Can I Write About?

Write about extinction as a general topic. What is it? Why does it happen? What animals have become extinct?

Write about the impact humans have on the extinction or near extinction of some animals. What are scientists doing to help?

Write about an endangered species that has become extinct in your lifetime (or your parent's.)

Write about an animal that has become pseudo-extinct. How do scientists try to bring it back?

Are There Books and Videos on Extinction?

Use your library catalog to find the books in your library. Unless you are writing about an animal that has been extinct for many years, try to get the newest books. Scientific techniques to keep animals from becoming extinct change rapidly, and some pseudo-extinct animals can be discussed in other areas. Check out the series Animals Under Threat from Heinemann Publishers. There are several books in the series about endangered animals.

Day, David. *The Doomsday Book of Animals: A Natural History of Vanished Species.* New York: Viking, 1981. (Yes, it is old, but very good.)

Endangered and Extinct Animals. [videorecording]. Wynnewood, PA: Schlessinger, 1999.

Extinct Species. 10 vol. Danbury, CT: Grolier, 2002.

Flannery, Tim, and Peter Schouten. *A Gap in Nature: Discovering the World's Extinct Animals.* New York: Atlantic Monthly, 2001.

Can the Internet Help?

Extinct in the Wild—http://www.bagheera.com/inthewild/ext_background.htm. Get your basic information and definitions at this excellent site.

Yahooligans' collection of links for extinct animals—http://yahooligans. yahoo.com/Science_and_Nature/Living_Things/Animals/Extinct_Animals/

Recently extinct animals—http://www.petermaas.nl/extinct/english.htm

Endangered Species—http://eelink.net/EndSpp/. Look for the threatened and extinct "links." Good information here.

Extinct Animals—http://www.zoos.50megs.com/extinct.htm. Human causes for extinction.

Extinction and Pseudoextinction—http://encyclopedia.lockergnome.com/s/b/ Extinction. Basic article. Don't let the links take you too far away.

 **TA DA!**

Extinction—Games!

ThinkQuest—http://library.thinkquest.org/J001504/. ThinkQuestis always good. Try the hangman and quizzes to learn about the dinosaurs.

Extinction Game—http://www.basd.net/technology/STEEP/Science/pdfs/ ExtinctionGame.pdf. Print and copy.

Experiment

Draw a map of your area. Make it as large as a poster board or drawing paper, leaving just a little room for other information. Illustrate your map with the animals that live nearby. What do they eat? Draw their food sources on the map. How do they "hide?" Are any endangered? Draw their means of camouflage on the map. You may need to call your local wildlife agency; they will gladly help you. They can help you discover endangered animals from your area. Keep your map and track the animals over time. Share your findings.

In the Classroom

CNN—http://cnnstudentnews.cnn.com/2000/fyi/lesson.plans/11/14/missing.fish/. A lesson plan of a fish in Florida that is becoming extinct. Excellent.

National Geographic lesson plans—http://www.nationalgeographic.com/xpeditions/ lessons/08/g68/preserve.html. Choose the grade level and specific lesson.

4

To Sleep, Perchance to Dream.

HIBERNATION

New Words

Deep Hibernators
Diapause
Dormancy
Estivation
Hibernaculu
Torpor Hibernators

What Is Hibernation?

Hibernation is a state of inactivity in an animal brought about by short day lengths, cold temperatures, and limitations of food. Hibernation is nature's survival strategy for some animals. Of course, not all animals hibernate. Some animals hibernate, some stay active, and some migrate. It is interesting to examine nature's plan for the continued existence of each species.

When we think about hibernation, we usually think about the bear. But who do you think is the most famous hibernator of all? We think it is the groundhog. He lets us know whether spring is on the way. He even has a day named after him. Did you guess? It will be fun to watch the movie *Groundhog Day* when you write your report.

What Can I Write About?

Write about hibernation and the body's ability to adapt to sleeping the winter away.

Write about the dangers to animals as they hibernate and how nature solves them.

Select any hibernating animal for your report. The bear may be the obvious one—but there are many others. Perhaps there is an animal or insect that lives in your area; that would be interesting. You may even include an experiment. Do not forget to write about its long preparation to hibernate.

Write about how the study of hibernation is helping doctors understand body part transplants in humans. This is a great topic for future doctors.

Discuss how the body changes during deep hibernation. What are the differences between deep hibernation and torpor hibernation?

Are There Books About Hibernation?

We can't begin to tell you the best books. There are many. Use your library catalog. Do not forget the reference area, where you can find statistics and specialized encyclopedias.

Facklam, Margery. *Do Not Disturb: The Mysteries of Animals and Sleep.* Boston: Little, Brown, 1989.

Matero, Robert. *Animals Asleep.* Brookfield, CT: Millbrook, 2000.

The Simon and Schuster Encyclopedia of Animals: A Visual Who's Who of the World's Creatures. New York: Simon & Schuster, 1998.

Can the Internet Help?

ThinkQuest—The Deep Sleep—http://library.thinkquest.org/TQ0312800/hibernate.htm

Hibernation—The Virtual Nature Trail project at Penn State—http://www.nk.psu.edu/naturetrail/Winter/hibernation.htm

The Day of the Shadow—http://www.geocities.com/Heartland/7134/Shadow/groundhog.htm. Learn about the famous hibernator, the groundhog.

Chillin' out—http://whyfiles.org/187hibernate/. Hibernation and its impact on transplants.

The Black Bear—Master Dozer, from PBS—http://www.pbs.org/wgbh/nova/satoyama/hibernation.html. Hibernation information..

 **TA DA!**

Create Your Own

Hibernate your own box turtle—http://www.boxturtlesite.org/hib.html. You can only do this if you live where it is very cold in the winter. Read the directions carefully and understand them before you begin. Tess Cook offers very clear directions.

A Time to Hibernate, from Scholastic—http://teacher.scholastic.com/products/instructor/timetosleep.htm. Experiments to try.

In the Classroom

Bears: Dialog for Kids—http://www.idahoptv.org/dialogue4kids/bears/howmanybears.html. An excellent classroom project that helps students understand survival.

Hibernation Report—http://www.teachervision.fen.com/lesson-plans/lesson-3856.html. You will have to sign in to get the entire lesson, but this one is worth it.

Living with the Chimps.

JANE GOODALL

New Words

Animal Behavior
Animal Welfare
Chimpanzees
Great Apes
Nonhuman Primates
Primatologist

Who Is Jane Goodall?

An interest in animals and animal behavior always stirred Jane Goodall. When she was very young, she sat for five hours in a chicken coop watching to see how hens laid eggs. Almost 20 years later, on the shores of Lake Tanganyika in Africa, she sat quietly watching chimpanzees. It took many months before they accepted her presence. When they did, she was able to see things that scientists up to that time hadn't thought possible. She observed that chimpanzees used tools, had emotions, took care of orphans, and even fought wars! Her research changed the way people view animals. Much of the animal welfare movement can be credited to her.

What Can I Write About?

Discuss Jane Goodall's childhood and what made her want to become a primatologist.

Describe some of Jane's observations about chimpanzees and explain their significance.

Discuss Jane's work and how it affected endangered species around the world.

Learn what you would have to do to become a primatologist like Jane Goodall.

Write about Jane Goodall's early work with Dr. Louis Leakey in Gombe National Park in Tanganyika (now Tanzania).

Discuss Goodall's role in raising awareness about animal welfare.

Are There Books on Jane Goodall?

Jane Goodall has written many books. Check your library catalog for books and films by and about her. You will also find information in reference books.

Goodall, Jane. *The Chimpanzee Family Book*. New York: North South Books, 1989.

Goodall, Jane. *My Life with the Chimpanzees*. New York: Simon & Schuster, 1988.

Jane Goodall's Wild Chimpanzees. [videorecording]. Burbank, CA: Slingshot, 2002.

Schlager, Neil, ed. *Science and Its Times: Understanding the Social Significance of Scientific Discovery*. Vol. 7, *1950–Present*. Detroit: Gale, 2000.

World Book Encyclopedia of Science. Chicago: World Book, 2001.

Can the Internet Help?

The Jane Goodall Institute—http://www.janegoodall.org/jane/study-corner/default.asp. Has her biography, careers in the field, and the state of chimpanzees.

PBS has a film on Jane Goodall—http://www.pbs.org/wnet/nature/goodall/. This site tells you about her life, work, and studies.

The JGI Center for Primate Studies—http://www.discoverchimpanzees.org/. A chimpanzee behavior site.

National Geographic—http://www.nationalgeographic.com/council/eir/bio_goodall.html. Gives you a brief biography of Jane Goodall.

Jane Goodall Organization—http://www.janegoodall.org/jane/. Biographical information about Jane's early studies of chimpanzees.

 TA DA!

Chimpanzees in Action!

Discover Chimpanzees—http://www.discoverchimpanzees.org/behaviors/top.php. View feeding, communication, play, and other chimpanzee behaviors on RealPlayer.

Experiment

Roots and Shoots (http://www.rootsandshoots.org/) is an organization for kids who are interested in Jane Goodall's work. See if there is a chapter in your area.

Try Jane Goodall's techniques yourself. Find a nature area where you can sit undisturbed for a long time and observe wildlife. Bring a camera to record your observations.

In the Classroom

The Jane Goodall Institute has its own Web site—http://www.janegoodall.org/. For a fee, your class could become a chimpanzee orphan guardian! Have your class make a giant peace dove and create your own September 21 celebration.

You Were Just a Little Tadpole When First I Knew You.

METAMORPHOSIS

New Words

Amphibian
Life Cycle
Metamorphosis (simple and complete)
Regeneration
Transformation

What Is Metamorphosis?

Metamorphosis means change in form. It refers to the change in shape or structure experienced by an organism as it undergoes a transition from one developmental stage in its life to another. Insects and amphibians are most known for their metamorphic life cycle. We are most familiar with are caterpillars morphing into butterflies and tadpoles into frogs. How terrific Mother Nature is to think up this exciting way to present these animals to us. Wow!

What Can I Write About?

Write about metamorphosis in general, finding good basic information.

Write about the stages of the life cycle (egg, larvae, pupa, and adult for the butterfly.)

Visit a butterfly museum (if there isn't one close by, visit one online, perhaps the Field Museum (www.fieldmuseum.org), and write about the life and habitat of these beautiful insects. Interview the curator via e-mail.

Experiment by raising your own tadpole to a frog, etc., and keep a log. Report on your own firsthand experience. Use books to get the facts straight. Show and tell your animal.

Select two metamorphic animals and compare their life cycles or compare two insects or amphibians, one with complete metamorphosis and one with simple or incomplete.

Are There Books and Videos on Metamorphosis?

Use your library catalog. *Metamorphosis* is a good general term, but to find more books look for the specific animal. Use a magazine database; this is a good topic for articles.

Animal Life Cycles. [videorecording]. Wynnewood, PA: Schlessinger Media, 1999.

Goor, Ron, and Nancy Goor. *Insect Metamorphosis: From Egg to Adult*. New York: Atheneum, 1990.

Russell, Sharman Apt. *An Obsession with Butterflies: Our Long Love Affair with a Singular Insect*. Cambridge, MA: Perseus, 2003.

Zim, Herbert Spencer. *Insects: A Guide to Familiar American Insects*. New York: St. Martin's Press, 2001.

Zim, Herbert Spencer. *Reptiles and Amphibians*. New York: St. Martin's Press, 2001.

Can the Internet Help?

About.com—http://animals.about.com/. Has excellent information and links if you use the keyword search from this point.

This information is from Professor Marty Shandland for his Biology 349 class at the University of Texas—http://www.esb.utexas.edu/shankland/BIO349/lc22meta.htm

Entomology for Beginners—http://www.bijlmakers.com/entomology/begin.htm#Metamorphosis. About insect metamorphosis.

Insects—Metamorphosis—http://www.uen.org/utahlink/activities/view_activity.cgi?activity_id=2024. General information, then links to many insects.

Encarta has an excellent article on amphibians—http://encarta.msn.com/encyclopedia_761574532/Amphibian_(animal).html. Use the links for more information.

Insects.org—http://www.insects.org/index.html. Search the site. The photographs are wonderful.

 **TA DA!**

Metamorphosis in Action!

A Bug's Life—http://extension.usu.edu/aitc/news/newspdf/fall/fall02_insect.pdf. A game to play with your classmates. This would be a great follow-up to your class reports. Show your friends how to play.

Experiment

This is a great topic to try an actual experiment. Read up on how to care for the animal you choose, then watch the metamorphosis—right in your own home or class. Excellent choices are caterpillars to butterflies and tadpoles to frogs.

In the Classroom

This excellent page has links to animal life cycles—http://www.uen.org/themepark/cycles/animal.shtml. At the bottom are teacher resources.

Excellent information about the monarch butterfly—http://www.smm.org/sln/monarchs/. Your class might raise them. Information is available at this site.

7

Shhh! Did You Hear That?

NIGHT CREATURES

New Words

Camouflage
Diurnal
Echolocation
Night Vision
Nocturnal

What Is a Night Animal?

Have you ever been out late at night, maybe camping in the woods, when suddenly something runs through the bush? You look over and see two eyes shining in the dark. Your heart pounds! Then something flies by. And you hear a howl in the distance. Well, there is a whole world of creatures that do their prowling at night. Nocturnal animals are active after we go to bed. They include the bat, owl, raccoon, and alligator. Some fish are nocturnal. There are even plants that bloom at night. Nocturnal animals use their senses to maneuver in the dark. Good topic.

What Can I Write About?

Write a paper in which you include a thorough description of nocturnal animals in general, describing some of the ways in which they are different from daytime animals. Create a table comparing diurnal (daytime) and nocturnal animals.

Choose a specific nocturnal animal or animal family to write about.

Describe and write about night animals in a certain region of the world—maybe the area where you live. (I often have raccoons and opossums on my deck at night. I'd like to know more about them.)

Explain night vision or the sound sense developed by the night animals. Try echolocation as a topic.

For plant lovers, write about the many plants that bloom at night. How are they different from the more familiar plants? What about photosynthesis? How do they help the environment?

Are There Books and Videos on Night Animals?

Search the catalog for the broad topic of night animals—or for specific animals—or even for animals in parts of the world (for example, *Animals of the Desert*)

Animal Adaptations. Animal Life in Action. [videorecording]. VHS FN6682 Wynnewood, PA: Schlessinger Media, 2000.

Davol, Marguerite. *Batwings and the Curtain of Night.* New York: Orchard, 1997.

Hickman, Pamela. *The Night Book: Exploring Nature after Dark with Activities, Experiments and Information.* Buffalo, NY: Kids Can, 1999.

Krautwurst, Terry. *Night Science for Kids: Exploring the World After Dark.* New York: Lark, 2003.

Can the Internet Help?

Night vision, from PBS—http://www.pbs.org/wgbh/nova/kalahari/nightvision.html. A video.

Backpacker Magazines' "Be a Night Crawler"—http://www.backpacker.com/technique/article/0,1026,173,00.html. Good article, especially about the senses.

ThinkQuest: Creatures of the Night and You—http://library.thinkquest.org/5135/. An award-winning site.

Bat Watching: Encounters with Masters of the Night—http://gorp.away.com/gorp/activity/wildlife/bats.htm

Nocturnal Animals in the Rain Forest—http://rainforest-australia.com/nocturnal_animals.htm. If you want to tie your research into the environment, this is an excellent page.

Nocturnal Animals—http://www.enchantedlearning.com/coloring/nocturnal.shtml. This is a terrific site; you may be surprised at some of the nocturnal animals.

 TA DA!

Night Animals in Action

Summer Night Lights—http://www.dnr.state.wi.us/org/caer/ce/eek/critter/insect/firefly.htm. A project that teaches you more about the firefly.

Look It Up

What animal other than the bat uses echolocation to help it maneuver at night?

In the Classroom

Mammals at Night—http://dnr.state.il.us/lands/education/CLASSRM/wild_mammals/pdf/unit1_3.pdf

Use *Nocturnal Animals and Classroom Nights* by Barbara Dondiego (see the bibliography) as a classroom resource. There is plenty of information here about night animals and projects for your classroom. Grades 4–8.

8

Looking for a Free Lunch.

PARASITES

New Words

Ectoparasite—Endoparasite
Mesoparasite
Parasite—Parasitology
Predator
Scavenger

What Is a Parasite?

When children jump into swimming pools and lakes in the summer, they are often sharing the water with harmful parasites and bacteria that can cause serious problems. When they go to school, they share parasites with their school chums. And these are not the only places we find parasites. Oh no, parasites are everywhere, and they take, take, take!

A parasite is an organism that grows, feeds, and is sheltered on or in a different organism while contributing nothing to the survival of its host. Parasites live in or on humans, animals, and plants. They range from tiny organisms seen only through a microscope to the large cow bird. Hookworms and head lice are parasites that particularly like children. Yuck!

What Can I Write About?

Write about parasites in general, finding information about the "who, where, what, when, why, and how" of them.

Choose a specific parasite for your research: blood-borne, intestinal track, or another type.

Write about the fleas, ticks, or mites that like your pet, or the head lice that prefer you.

Write about a parasite that has infected someone in your family or someone you know. Learn all about this parasite, especially the treatment.

Are There Books on Parasites?

Use your library catalog. Do not forget the reference area, where you can find background information and statistics. The librarian is your best resource.

Breidahl, Harry. *The Zoo on You: Life on Human Skin.* New York: Chelsea House, 2002.

Friedlander, Mark P., and Terry M. Phillips. *The Immune System: Your Body's Disease-Fighting Army.* Minneapolis, MN : Learner Publications, 1998.

Lerner, K. Lee, and Brenda Wilmoth Lerner, eds. *Gale Encyclopedia of Science.* 3d ed. Detroit: Gale, 2004.

Marshall Cavendish Encyclopedia of Health. Tarrytown, NY: Marshall Cavendish, 1995.

Can the Internet Help?

Parasites and Parasitism—http://www.aber.ac.uk/parasitology/Edu/Para_ism/PaIsmTxt.html. A good place to start and learn the vocabulary.

The World of Parasites—http://martin.parasitology.mcgill.ca/JIMSPAGE/WORLDOF.HTM. Find out about the parasites that live in your part of the world.

Parasitology Resources—http://www.edae.gr/parasitology.html. A long collection of links. Many are too difficult, but it may be worth looking here for your specific topic.

National Geographic Magazine—http://nationalgeographic.com/parasites/splashworm.html. The life cycle of parasites, and more.

Centers for Disease Control—http://www.dpd.cdc.gov/DPDx/HTML/Image_Library.htm. Microscopic images of parasites.

Why Lice Aren't Nice—http://kidshealth.org/kid/ill_injure/sick/lice.html. If you are writing about head lice, this is a great place to start.

Stalking the Mysterious Microbe—http://www.microbe.org. Important information for kids.

 **TA DA!**

Parasites in Action!

Download this Parasites game, but don't let the parasites get you!—http://www.acid-play.com/download/Parasites.php

Play online—http://www.headlice.org/kids/headgames/index.htm. Several Head Games. Lots of fun.

Experiment

Words can have many meanings. The word "parasite" has come to refer to a person who takes from another without giving back. Find five words that describe people as parasites. (*Sponge* is one.) How many can you list without looking them up?

In the Classroom

Teaching Notes from the Parasitology Department at Aberystwyth University, Wales—http://www.aber.ac.uk/parasitology/Edu/EduIndex.html

Cells Alive—http://www.cellsalive.com/. Use the search term "parasites" to find several plans. Excellent site to share.

9

Which Came First, the Chicken or the Egg?

REPRODUCTION

New Words

Breeding
DNA
Fetus
Genetics
Gestation
Zygote

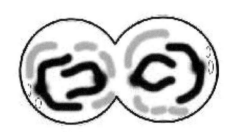

What Is Reproduction?

Reproduction, the way animals and people produce a new creature like themselves, can be so many things that you will have to narrow your topic. Most mammals give birth to a fully developed baby. Most birds, reptiles, and fish lay eggs. But even within the groups, there are variations. Platypuses lay eggs, and guppies give birth to live young. Among egg layers, some, such as birds, incubate their eggs by lying on them, keeping them warm. Reptiles are more likely to bury them and leave them to their own devices. Protozoa reproduce by cell division. Marsupial fetuses develop in an external pouch. Seahorse females lay their eggs in a male's pouch, where he broods and hatches up to 200 at a time. And while human babies develop inside their mothers for nine months, baby elephants take almost two years!

What Can I Write About?

Compare egg-laying to live-bearing animals and discuss the advantages and disadvantages.

Choose one animal and discuss its method of reproduction

Find pictures of the stages of development of a human or chicken embryo and describe the changes that take place.

Some creatures such as insects have hundreds of young at once. Others, like elephants, have only one every four or five years. Consider the reasons why these differences have evolved.

Are There Books on Reproduction?

We can't begin to tell you the best books. There are many. Use your library catalog. Do not forget the reference area, where you can find background information and statistics.

Encyclopedia of Family Health. New York: Marshall Cavendish, 1998.

Macmillan Health Encyclopedia. Vol. 6, *Sexuality and Reproduction.* New York: Macmillan, 1993.

Pearl, Mary Corliss. *Illustrated Encyclopedia of Wildlife.* Lakeville, CT: Grey Castle, 1991. Check the index by species.

Can the Internet Help?

PBS has an interactive flash program on animal breeding—http://www.pbs.org/wnet/nature/fun/baby_flash.html

Kids Genetics, by GlaxoSmithKline—http://www.genetics.gsk.com/kids/index_kids.htm

ThinkQuest Kids Genetic Site—http://www.thinkquest.org/library/site_sum.html?tname=3696&url=3696/

Cancer Research UK—http://www.icnet.uk/kids/cellsrus/cellsrus.html. Explains reproduction in simple terms.

Queensland Department of Primary Industries and Fisheries—http://www.dpi.qld.gov.au/beef/3138.html. Understanding genetics and reproduction.

TA DA!

Murdoch Children's Research Institute—http://www.genecrc.org/site/ko/index_ko.htm, Games to help you learn about genetics.'

See what happens when you crossbreed animals with another species—http://www.greenapple.com/~jorp/amzanim/crossesa.htm

Parents Place—http://www.parentsplace.com/first9months/main.html. A multimedia representation of the first nine months of development, from conception to birth.

Experiment

A Punnett Square helps you figure out heredity—http://www.usoe.k12.ut.us/curr/science/sciber00/7th/genetics/sciber/punnett.htm

GlaxoSmithKline—http://genetics.gsk.com/kids/heredity01.htm. A heredity game helps you understand the concepts.

In the Classroom

Links to sites about cells—http://dmoz.org/Kids_and_Teens/School_Time/Science/Living_Things/Cells/

Reproduction and Heredity, from the state of Utah—http://www.usoe.k12.ut.us/curr/science/sciber00/7th/genetics/sciber/intro.htm

The More, the Merrier.

SOCIAL INSECTS

New Words

Ants
Apiary
Bees, Wasps
Eusocial Insects
Hymenopteria
Pheromones

What Is a Social Insect?

If a colony of ants invades your space, you may be tempted to get out a can of insect spray and wipe them all out. Instead, why don't you take a few minutes to study them? Watch an ant follow a zig-zagged trail. The next ant, and the next, will follow the same trail. When one ant meets another coming from the other direction, they always touch each other for a moment before moving on. What is happening here?

While most animals live in small family groups or prefer to be alone, social insects—bees, ants, and some wasps—live together in complex societies. They communicate the location of food with elaborate dances and warn of danger with smells or pheromones. Just how do they communicate? Start an ant farm and watch them in action!

What Can I Write About?

Choose a certain social insect such as an army ant, a bumble bee, or a hornet and discuss its habitat, communication, and feeding. Why do we call it a social insect?

Look into humans' uses of insects, such as producing honey or controlling pests.

Social insects can become pests. Choose one such pest and look into methods to control its population. Some examples are fire ants, leaf cutter ants, and killer bees.

Discuss the role of the queen as she relates to the colony. What does *social* mean?

Write about eusocial insects. What are they, and what are their characteristics?

Are There Books on Social Insects?

We can't begin to tell you the best books. There are many. Use your library catalog. Do not forget the reference area, where you can find background information and statistics.

Grzimeks Animal Life Encyclopedia, Volume 3: Insects. 2d ed. Detroit: Gale, 2004.

Pearl, Mary Corliss. *Illustrated Encyclopedia of Wildlife.* Vol. 3, *Invertebrates.* Lakeville, CT: Grey Castle, 1991.

Can the Internet Help?

Social Insects World Wide Web from the American Museum of Natural History—http://research.amnh.org/entomology/social_insects/mainpage.html. Includes taxonomy, biology, habitat, and images of ants.

Ant Information from the University of Arizona—http://insected.arizona.edu/antinfo.htm

Bumblebee facts, species, behavior from the UK—http://www.bumblebee.org/

Take a Virtual Apiary Field Trip—http://www.vftn.org/projects/bryant/

Anatomy of a hive from PBS—http://www.pbs.org/wgbh/nova/bees/hive.html

Social insects learn from bad experiences—http://nationalzoo.si.edu/animals/invertebrates/news/default.cfm. Brief article, but very interesting.

Apiculture (Beekeeping) and Social Insects—http://www.ent.iastate.edu/list/directory/109. Good information if you follow the links.

 **TA DA!**

Social Insects in Action!

See a 15-second video of bees in their hive—http://www.draperbee.com/webcam/beecam.htm. Look closely—you might even see the queen!

In this video clip, the USDA experiments with natural predators in the fight against fire ants—http://www.ars.usda.gov/is/video/vnr/firepath.htm

Experiment

University of Arizona—http://insected.arizona.edu/antrear.htm. Make an ant farm and observe the ants' behavior yourself!

In the Classroom

National Biological Information Infrastructure—http://www.nbii.gov/education/insects.html. Lesson plans on insects.

Using Insects in the Classroom, from the University of Arizona—http://insected.arizona.edu/home.htm

BODY PARTS

There are many topics available for those who are writing a report about the body. We thought it would be fun to choose topics you may not have considered. Dr. Michael DeBakey is our person for this section. We ♡ him. Drawings, photographs, posters, and models are always helpful when you have to give an oral report to your class.

The Knee Bone's Connected to the Leg Bone . . .

BONES

New Words

Back
Fractures
Joints
Marrow
Osteo-
Spinal Cord

What Is the Skeletal System?

You have 206 bones in your body. The smallest, in your ear, is one-tenth of an inch long, and the longest, in your legs, can be up to two feet long. Because of bones, we can grow tall, hold our heads up high, lift things, and walk. Muscles alone couldn't do any of those things. They need the support of a skeleton. Just think of a slug! Bones also protect. Ribs form a protective cage around the heart and lungs. The skull encases the brain. Your spine is hollow in the middle to allow nerves to travel safely from the brain to the lower parts of your body.

What Can I Write About?

Consider the many functions that bones play in your body and write about them.

Discuss the causes and treatment of a bone disease such as osteoporosis, rickets, or spina bifida.

Think about what happens when you break a bone. Consider how it heals. Is it stronger or weaker after it is healed? How do you to keep it straight and strong while it's healing?

Write about the composition of your bones. What can you do to make them strong?

Compare and contrast vertebrate and invertebrate animals.

Are There Books on Bones?

Try *bones* or *skeletal system* as keywords. Do not forget the reference area, where you can find background information and statistics.

Beers, Mark H., et al. *Merck Manual of Medical Information.* 2d ed. Whitehouse Station, NJ: Merck, 2003.

Childcraft: The How and Why Library. Chicago: World Book, 2003.

Human Body. Eyewitness Book. New York: DK Publishing, 2004.

New Book of Popular Science. Danbury, CT: Grolier, 2004.

Simon, Seymour. *Bones: Our Skeletal System.* New York: HarperTrophy, 2000.

World Book Encyclopedia of Science. Vol. 7. *The Human Body.* Chicago: World Book, 2001.

Can the Internet Help?

National Institutes of Health—http://www.niams.nih.gov/hi/topics/osteoporosis/kidbones.htm. Kids and their bones. Includes nutrition, diseases.

Discovery Channel—http://yucky.kids.discovery.com/noflash/body/pg000124.html. Your skeletal system..

Kids Bones, from BBC Health & Fitness—http://www.bbc.co.uk/health/kids/bones.shtml

Better bones, from GotMilk.com—http://www.got-milk.com/better/

Skeletal system, from a seventh-grade science class—http://vilenski.org/science/humanbody/hb_html/skeleton.html

KidsHealth—http://kidshealth.org/kid/body/bones_noSW.html. Tells you all about your bones.

 **TA DA!**

Skeletal System in Action!

A Brainpop video tells you all about your skeleton—http://www.brainpop.com/health/skeletal/skeleton/index.weml

Videos from GotMilk—http://www.got-milk.com/fun/fun.html. Include games, Mr. Science.

Human Bones from QuizHub—http://kidshub.org/kids/bones.cfm. Matching game.

Experiment

KidWizard—http://www.kidwizard.com/Spells/BendingBones.asp. Make a bone soft enough to bend.

In the Classroom

BrainPop has videos, activities, and lesson plans—http://www.brainpop.com/. It does require a subscription, but you can browse the first time for free.

Lesson plans from the Community Learning Network—http://www.cln.org/themes_index.html

Remember That?

BRAINS

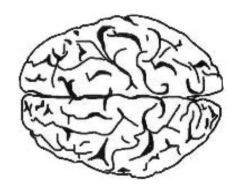

New Words

> Brain Stem
> Central Nervous System
> Cerebral Hemispheres
> Hippocampus—Dendrites
> Left Brain—Right Brain

What Does the Brain Control?

Scientists continuously detect more about how the brain works and which parts of the brain control different functions. It is fascinating to learn about this wonderful body part that helps us remember our thoughts and experiences and controls our nervous system. Try this. Without looking around your classroom, write down the names of everyone in your class. Did you look in your "mind's eye" and picture the room and the seating arrangement? Your wonderful brain is responsible for helping you remember. When we learn something new, our brain "attaches" it to similar things we already know. Wow!

What Can I Write About?

Identify the different parts of the brain and their function.

Do we have one brain or two? Write about the cerebral hemispheres. Which "side" of the brain controls speech, handwriting, language, etc? Write about right-brain or left-brain activities.

Find out about the brain and how memory works. Learn about the hippocampus and dendrites.

Write about brain disorders, including epilepsy, bipolar disorder, or cerebral palsy.

Are There Books or Videos on the Brain?

Do not forget the reference area, where you will find background information.

All About the Brain. The Human Body for Children. [videorecording]. Wynnewood, PA: Schlessinger, 2001.

The Brain and the Nervous Systems. Human Body in Action. [videorecording]. Wynnewood, PA: Schlessinger, 2001.

Bryan, Jenny. *Your Amazing Brain: A Fascinating See-Through View of How Our Brain Works.* New York: Random, 1996.

Curry, Don L. *How Does Your Brain Work?* New York: Children's Press, 2003.

Dubin, Mark. *How the Brain Works.* Malden, MA: Blackwell, 2002.

World Book Encyclopedia of Science. Vol. 7, *The Human Body.* Chicago: World Book, 2001.

Can the Internet Help?

Brain Connection—http://www.brainconnection.com/. Information about the brain and memory. Take time for the image gallery.

The Anatomy of the Brain—http://k-12.pisd.edu/schools/hughston/pace2/anatomybrain1.htm. What the brain is made of and the sections of the brain.

The Brain Is the Boss from KidsHealth—http://kidshealth.org/kid/body/brain_SW.html. An excellent site. All about brain functions.

The Brain Explorer is one of the best sites for explaining words with pictures—http://www.brainexplorer.org/brain_atlas/Brainatlas_index.shtml#image

Brain Dissection—http://www.exploratorium.edu/memory/braindissection/index.html. Learn about memory and how it works.

Neuroscience for Kids—http://faculty.washington.edu/chudler/split.html and http://faculty.washington.edu/chudler/introb.html#bb. All about the two parts of the brain.

 **TA DA!**

Brain Games!

Have fun with many brain games on this site—http://www.brainbashers.com/

Kids Games online—http://free-coloring-pages.com/game.html. Play the memory game, word games, and other memory joggers.

Experiment

Try the split brain experiments at nobelprize.org—http://nobelprize.org/medicine/educational/split-brain/index.html

In the Classroom

Brain Power!—http://school.discovery.com/lessonplans/programs/brainpower/ Lesson plans for grades 6–8.

Choose from a long list of Brain Booster activities—http://school.discovery.com/brainboosters/. For all ages.

Neuroscience—http://www.awesomelibrary.org/Classroom/Science/Biology/Neuroscience.html. Includes a few excellent "papers" for teacher information and background.

We ♡ You

MICHAEL DEBAKEY

New Words

Artificial Heart
Cardiovascular
Circulatory System
M.A.S.H.
Transplant

Who Is Dr. Michael DeBakey?

Dr. DeBakey is a pioneer in medicine who has won award after award. While there are many "firsts" for Dr. Michael DeBakey, we know him best for his innovations in open heart surgery. He performed the first 12 heart transplants. Born in 1908, Dr. Michael E. DeBakey, chancellor emeritus of Baylor College of Medicine in Houston, is the chairman of the Foundation for Biomedical Research. He last operated when he was 92 years old. Dr. DeBakey has been a lifelong scholar. He has contributed greatly to medical research. One of his accomplishments was the creation of the Mobile Army Surgical Hospital (M.A.S.H.) unit, used first during the Korean War.

What Can I Write About?

Why is Dr. DeBakey considered the "father of modern cardiovascular surgery"?

Write about the advances in medicine with which Dr. DeBakey is credited.

Discuss some of the early developments of Dr. DeBakey, such as the M.A.S.H. unit.

Write about some of Dr. DeBakey's contributions leading to healthy hearts. Include inventions he patented.

Dr. DeBakey has been a pioneering force in telemedicine. Write about it.

Are There Books on Dr. DeBakey?

Use your library catalog and your keywords to find the best books in the library. Medical and biographical encyclopedias will give you much of what you need.

> *Biography Today: Scientists & Inventors Series: Profiles of People of Interest to Young Readers.* Detroit: Omnigraphics, 1996– .

> DeBakey, Michael. *The New Living Heart.* Holbrook, MA: Adams Media, 1997.

Hoffman, Nancy. *Heart Transplants.* San Diego: Lucent, 2003.

Scientists at Work: Profiles of Today's Groundbreaking Scientists from "Science Times". New York: McGraw-Hill, 2000.

Can the Internet Help?

Interviews with Dr. DeBakey—http://www.laskerfoundation.org/awards/library/lumin_dm.html and http://www.tmc.edu/tmcnews/03_15_01/page_ 01.html

Michael E. DeBakey Veterans Affairs Medical Center—http://www.houston.med.va.gov/misc/DeBakey.html. Biographical information.

A recent news story, using the DeBakey Vad pump—http://www.med.umich.edu/opm/newspage/2003/DeBakey.htm

President's Medal of Freedom and the Congressional Medal of Honor presentation—http://www.medaloffreedom.com/MichaelDeBakey.htm

February 25, 2004, FDA's approval of DeBakey's VAD Child Left Ventricular Assist System—http://www.fda.gov/cdrh/ode/H030003sum.html

Biographical information—http://www.fbresearch.org/about/DeBakey.htm. Watch the interview on DeBakey's ninetieth birthday.

DeBakey receives the Congressional Gold Medal—http://www.congressionalgoldmedal.com/MichaelEllisDeBakey.htm

 **TA DA!**

Transplants in Action!

Visit this heart transplant site and see the surgery yourself—http://www.pbs.org/wgbh/nova/eheart/transplant.html

The Franklin Institute's Heart: An Online Exploration—http://www.fi.edu/biosci/heart.html

Are You Fit? How's Your Heart Rate?

Bodies in Motion by ThinkQuest—http://library.thinkquest.org/12153/. Find out how fit you are. Test your fitness and heart rate.

In the Classroom

NASA's "I Have the Heart of a Rocket"—http://www.nasaexplores.com/show2_articlea.php?id=01-005. Print the article; select the grade level plans.

Watch an episode of the TV show *M.A.S.H.* and discuss what it might have really been like for the doctors and nurses on the battlefield. DeBakey started M.A.S.H. units during the Korean War.

When a Pin Drops.

EARS AND NOSE

New Words

Ears:
-Otic
Otitis Media
Tinnitus

Nose:
Deviated Septum
Nasal
Nosebleeds

Speaking:
Balance
Decibels
Larynx
Vocal chords

What About the Ears and Nose?

It's not just coincidence! The ear is shaped like a funnel to help capture sound waves and direct them toward the ear drum. From there, bones help carry the vibrations to the brain. What a system! Did you know that ears also affect your balance? And think about your nose! Scientists are still trying to figure out just how a smell gets from its source to the part of your brain that can identify it. Is it the shape of the chemical molecule? Or does it give off a vibration? The ears and nose are connected in many ways. You can look at their interaction or research just one of them.

What Can I Write About?

Discuss the connection between smell and taste.

Think about hearing loss. You could write about the causes or the effects it would have on your life.

Explain how speech works. Include the many parts of the body that are involved.

Compare ears from different species. Rabbit ears are long, dog ears floppy, bird ears invisible. Why?

What might make you lose your sense of smell? How would that affect you?

Are There Books on the Ears and Nose?

We can't begin to tell you the best books. There are many. Use your library catalog. Do not forget the reference area, where you can find background information and statistics.

Beers, Mark H., et al. *Merck Manual of Medical Information.* 2d ed. Whitehouse Station, NJ: Merck, 2003.

Childcraft: The How and Why Library: About You. Chicago: World Book, 2003.

New Book of Popular Science. Vols. 2 and 3. Danbury, CT: Grolier, 2003.

Shin, Linda M., and Karen Bellenir. *Ear, Nose and Throat Disorders Sourcebook.* Detroit: Omnigraphics, 1998.

World Book Encyclopedia. Chicago: World Book, 2005.

Can the Internet Help?

KidsHealth—http://kidshealth.org/kid/body/ear_noSW.html. Explains how hearing works.

KidsHealth—http://kidshealth.org/kid/body/nose_noSW.html. Explains about the sense of smell.

Pfizer—http://www.kidsears.com/. Ear infections and the problems they can cause.

"The Yuckiest Site on the Internet" from The Discovery Channel—http://yucky.kids.discovery.com/noflash/body/pg000008.html. Includes bad breath, ear wax, spit, and boogers—but it also explains how your senses work.

University of Washington—http://faculty.washington.edu/chudler/bigear.html. Interesting site on how ears work, with the decibel levels of various sounds.

The Value of Having Two Ears, from the Howard Hughes Medical Institute—http://www.hhmi.org/senses/c220.html. For older students.

TA DA!

Your Ears in Action!

Blow up a balloon. Stretch the neck tightly side to side. Do you hear anything? Let a little air out. Now what do you hear? Watch the rubber closely. Do you notice that it vibrates when it gives off sound? That's basically how the vocal chords work.

Experiment

National Geographic—http://www.nationalgeographic.com/media/world/9703/nose/index.html. Test the sense of taste on a friend.

University of Washington—http://faculty.washington.edu/chudler/chhearing.html. Experiments that test your hearing.

In the Classroom

BrainPop has videos, activities, and lesson plans—http://www.brainpop.com/. The site does require a subscription, but you can browse the first time for free.

Community Learning Network—http://www.cln.org/themes/hearing.html Lesson plans focusing on hearing.

Windows to the World.

EYES

New Words

Astigmatism
Blindness
Color Blindness
Optic
Refraction

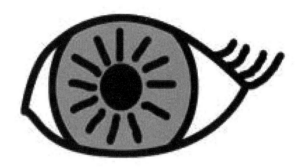

What Are Eyes?

If you had to pick only one sense that was the most valuable to you, which one would you pick? Most people would choose their sight. Eyes can take in so much of the world around you, from the print in this book to stars billions of miles away. They tell you when it's safe to cross the street, or when your mom has had enough and you'd better get serious. Your eyes are super-sensitive, super-important organs, so much so that your body has built a triple protection system around them: you have eyelids that close on reflex, a bony eye socket, and tears to keep your eyes moist.

What Can I Write About?

Write about the structure of the eyes and how they work.

There are many causes of blindness. Identify three of them and discuss how they develop, as well as any possible cures.

How does the eye focus? What happens when focusing is not precise—nearsightedness and farsightedness?

Discuss the pros and cons of LASIK (Laser-Assisted in Situ Keratomileussis) surgery. Sounds difficult, but it is very common.

Explain color blindness. Include why people get it, how it works, and what they see differently.

Are There Books on Eyes?

We can't begin to tell you the best books. There are many. Use your library catalog. Do not forget the reference area, where you can find background information and statistics.

Childcraft: The How and Why Library: About You. Chicago: World Book, 2003.

Lerner, K. Lee, and Brenda Wilmoth Lerner, eds. *New Gale Encyclopedia of Science.* 3d ed. Detroit: Gale, 2004.

New Book of Popular Science. Danbury, CT: Grolier, 2004.

World Book Encyclopedia. Chicago: World Book, 2005.

Can the Internet Help?

KidsHealth—http://kidshealth.org/kid/body/eye_noSW.html. Explains the basics of how the eye works.

Prevent Blindness Connecticut—http://www.optima-hyper.com/eyetests/kidsquiz/KIDSAFE.htm. A kids' eye safety guide.

The Eye and How We See, from Prevent Blindness America—http://www.preventblindness.org/resources/howwesee.html

Optical Research Associates—http://www.opticalres.com/kidoptx.html. Optics for kids.

HealthSure, UK—http://www.healthyeyes.org.uk/index.php?id=7. Offers information on how the eye works, history of eye research, optical illusions, and great artists with vision problems.

Howard Hughes Medical Institute—http://www.hhmi.org/senses/b110.html. How we see color. For older students.

Optometrists Network—http://www.children-special-needs.org/. Vision problems in children, such as wandering eye and double vision. For older students.

 **TA DA!**

Eyes in Action!

BrainPop—http://www.brainpop.com/health/senses/vision/index.weml. Animated video explaining how vision works.

Dialog for Kids, from the state of Idaho—http://idahoptv.org/dialogue4kids/stream.cfm. An educational program for kids that talks about eyes.

Experiment

University of Washington—http://faculty.washington.edu/chudler/chvision.html. Test your blind spot.

In the Classroom

BrainPop has videos, activities, and lesson plans—http://www.brainpop.com/. The site does require a subscription, but you can browse the first time for free.

Eye Anatomy and Physiology, from the University of Washington—http://faculty.washington.edu/chudler/eyetr.html

16

I Can't Stomach This.

GUTS

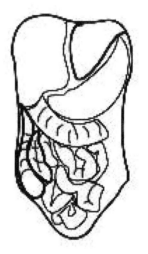

New Words

Digestive System
Epiglottis
Esophagus
Gall Bladder
Intestines
Stomach—Abdomen

How Does the Stomach Work?

What does your stomach tell you? "Please, don't give me any more French fries." "Please, send a little green veggies my way." "That's enough." "I'm hungry." If we learned to listen to our stomachs, we would be healthier. The stomach is part of our digestive system. Digestion begins in the mouth when we chew. When we swallow, we send lots of different shapes, sizes, and weights down through our body. Digestion is the process the body has for breaking down all these different foods so that the body can use them to build and nourish cells and provide energy.

What Can I Write About?

Select a single function or part of the digestive system, like the stomach, gall bladder, or intestines. What is its purpose, and how does it work within the whole system?

Many things can go wrong with the digestive system, from a stomach ache or a virus to gall bladder and liver problems. Research the causes of these problems.

It may be fun to write about all the noises the digestive system can make, and why!

Describe the digestive system. What happens to food from the time we put it into our mouths until it is gone?

Write about the nutrients provided by carbohydrates, fats, vitamins, water, salt, and sugars. Does the body need all of these things to survive? Learn more and write about it.

Are There Books on Guts and the Stomach?

Do not forget the reference area, where you can find background information. Ask the librarian.

Cromwell, Sharon. *Why Does My Tummy Rumble When I'm Hungry? And Other Questions about the Digestive System.* Des Plaines, IL: Rigby, 1998.

Parker, Steve. *Eyewitness: The Human Body.* New York: DK Publishing, 2004.

Silverstein, Alvin. *Digestive System (Human Body Systems.)* New York: Twenty-first Century, 1994.

Silverstein, Alvin. *Stomachaches.* New York: Franklin Watts, 2003.

Walker, Pam, and Elaine Wood. *The Digestive System.* San Diego, CA: Lucent, 2003.

Can the Internet Help?

The Digestive System from KidsHealth—http://kidshealth.org/kid/body/digest_noSW.html. Good basic information.

Inner Body's information about the digestive system—http://www.innerbody.com/image/digeov.html. Check out the overviews.

The Digestive System—http://www.tvdsb.on.ca/westmin/science/sbi3a1/digest/digest.htm. Follow this site through and you will be able to recognize all the parts.

Digestive System from the "Yuckiest Site on the Web"—Take a walk with Your Gross and Cool Body—http://yucky.kids.discovery.com/noflash/body/pg000126.html

Winner of the National Science Teachers Association—http://www.borg.com/~lubehawk/hdigsys.htm. All about digestion.

Your Digestive System and How It Works—http://digestive.niddk.nih.gov/ddiseases/pubs/yrdd/#top. Be sure to look at the list of digestive diseases.

Food and Nutrition—http://www.nutristrategy.com/digestion.htm. Follow food from the mouth to the large intestine.

 TA DA!

Iron Stomach!

Have a little fun after all your research is completed! Play iron stomach online—http://www.optonline.net/Games/GamesPlayer_Heavy?game=Iron+Stomach

Word Game—http://www.quia.com/ws/66042.html. See if you know all of the words relevant to digestion.

Experiment

Look at the live display the students made—http://www.marion.wilmsn.k12.il.us/bodywalk/page3.html. Taking a walk through the digestive system really helps you understand it. Make your own small model with posters and tubes.

In the Classroom

Blood and Guts—http://www.pacsci.org/education/sow/bag.html and http://hes.ucf.k12.pa.us/gclaypo/digestive_system.html. Units for fun and education in the classroom.

I'm Catching On!

HANDS AND FEET

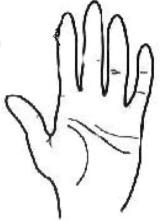

New Words

Arches
Metacarsal
Metatarsal
Phalange
Podiatry

What About the Hands and Feet?

Try your hand at something, learn firsthand, hands-on, it's in your hands, foot in your mouth, foot and mouth disease, handhold, foothold, on hand, shoot yourself in the foot, waiting on him hand and foot, and the shoe is on the other foot are just a few of the expressions we use that include "hands" or "feet." Why do you think there are so many? More than half of the bones in your body are found in your hands and feet. There are 27 in each hand and 26 in each foot. They are part of your skeletal framework. You can perform intricate tasks with both. Find out more by researching these essential parts of your body.

What Can I Write About?

Select either your hands or your feet to write about. Write about the bone structure.

Write about fingerprints and toeprints, which are unique and identifiable.

Write about diseases that can affect the hands or feet. Describe treatment. Describe prevention.

Write about how we use our hands (and other body parts) as part of our language.

What can we tell others simply by using our hands (in addition to sign language). Watch people and make a list of ways in which we communicate with our hands.

Are There Books or Videos About Hands and Feet?

We can't begin to tell you the best books. There are many. Use your library catalog. Do not forget the reference area, where you can find background information and statistics.

Parker, Steve. *Eyewitness: Skeleton.* New York: Dorling Kindersley, 2002.

Rourke, Arlene. *Hands and Feet.* Vero Beach, FL: Rourke, 1987.

Savage, Stephen. *Hands and Feet.* Adaptation for Survival. New York: Thompson, 1995.

Walker, Richard. *Eyewitness Visual Dictionary of the Skeleton.* New York: DK Publishing, 1995.

Whitfield, Paul. *The Human Body Explained: A Guide to Understanding the Incredible Living Machine.* New York: Henry Holt, 1995.

Can the Internet Help?

Hands and Feet—http://www.bbc.co.uk/science/humanbody/body/factfiles/handsandfeet/hand.shtml. The skeleton and basics.

American Podiatric Medical Association—http://www.apma.org/. Good information about care of the feet. Find the skeleton that names every part of the foot.

Healthopedia.com—http://www.healthopedia.com/hands-and-feet.html. Has many pages of information about diseases and medical conditions.

MEDtropolis—http://www.medtropolis.com/VBody.asp. Choose Skeleton and the KidsHealth (see under Health Sources).

It's in Your Hands—http://www.llrx.com/columns/guide11.htm. Using your hands to convey language.

Body Language: The Language Everybody Speaks—http://www.lichaamstaal.com/english/bodylanguage.html?quiz2.html. Excellent information, if this is your topic.

 **TA DA!**

Hands in Action!

Get a friend and learn to make the Cat's Cradle—http://www.ifyoulovetoread.com/book/chten_cats.htm. All you need are four hands and some string.

Find a pair of crutches and go without the use of one foot for an entire day.

Solo Sports

PBS for Kids—http://pbskids.org/itsmylife/body/solosports/article6.html. Has excellent information about bouldering, rock climbing, walking, running. Find a local scaling wall and test your skill with your feet and hands.

In the Classroom

Afghanistan and other countries cut off limbs as punishment—http://www.glennsmart.btinternet.co.uk/lessonplans/taliban.html. Is this right?

Artsonia is a collection of art projects for school, several using hands and feet—http://www.artsonia.com/teachers/projects/. (We love Trace a Hand, Trace a Foot.)

Math Forum—http://mathforum.org/arithmetic/arith.units.html. A feet-on math lesson for telling time, also hand squeeze teaching data collection.

And the Beat Goes On . . .

HEART

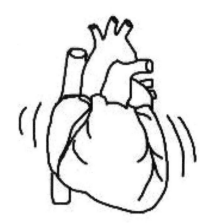

New Words

Aorta—Cardio-
Circulatory System
Heart Attack
Heart Murmur
Rheumatic Fever

What Is the Heart?

Your heart is a muscle about the size of your fist that pumps blood throughout your body. As you grow, your fist grows larger. So does your heart. The heart has four chambers. Both upper chambers take blood in, and both lower chambers push it out, but they're moving it to and from different places. Although they knew the heart was important, ancient people had different theories about its purpose. The ancient Chinese believed happiness resided in the heart. The Egyptians believed it was the source of intelligence. It wasn't until 1628 that a fairly accurate description of the circulatory system with the heart as the pump was developed.

What Can I Write About?

Discuss artificial hearts or heart transplants.

Learn about CPR (cardiopulmonary resuscitation). Describe how and why it works. Demonstrate it for your class.

Discuss the four chambers of the heart and how they function. Be sure to include a drawing of the heart

Choose one heart disease or problem and discuss the causes, treatment, and outcome.

Are There Books on the Heart?

We can't begin to tell you the best books. There are many. Use your library catalog. Do not forget the reference area, where you can find background information and statistics.

Beers, Mark H., et al. *Merck Manual of Medical Information.* 2d ed. Whitehouse Station, NJ: Merck, 2003.

Childcraft: The How and Why Library: About You. Chicago: World Book, 2003.

Lerner, K. Lee, and Brenda Wilmoth Lerner, eds. *New Gale Encyclopedia of Science.* 3d ed. Detroit: Gale, 2004.

New Book of Popular Science. Danbury, CT: Grolier, 2004.

Whitfield, Paul. *The Human Body Explained: A Guide to Understanding the Incredible Living Machine.* New York: Henry Holt: 1995.

Can the Internet Help?

KidsHealth—http://kidshealth.org/kid/body/heart_noSW.html. A great, basic site about how the heart works.

The Heart, from the Franklin Institute Online—http://sln.fi.edu/biosci/heart.html

PediHeart—http://www.pediheart.org/kidzone/index.html. Congenital heart conditions.

How Stuff Works—http://science.howstuffworks.com/heart.htm. Good information. Use the contents to find related topics.

Nova's Heart—http://www.pbs.org/wgbh/nova/heart. Easy to understand and enjoy. Includes pioneers in heart surgery, the healthy heart, and a map of the heart.

 **TA DA!**

The Heart in Action!

BrainPop—http://www.brainpop.com/health/seeall.weml. A cartoon movie shows and explains how the heart works..

Experiment

Check your pulse at rest, after walking, and after running. Think of some other activities. Make a chart and compare the results.

Health for Kids newsletter—http://www.aboutchildrenshealth.com/library/weekly/aa021001a.htm and http://www.teachers.net/lessons/posts/278.html (for teachers, also). Watch your heart beat! .

In the Classroom

BrainPop—http://www.brainpop.com/. Has videos, activities, and lesson plans. It does require a subscription, but you can browse the first time for free.

The Musical Health Show Guide to Slim Goodbody—http://www.slimgoodbody.com/TeacherResources.htm. Has experiments that can be used with or without the video.

Lesson plans on the human body.—http://www.teach-nology.com/teachers/lesson_plans/science/anatomy/

I'm Caged In!

LUNGS

New Words

Asthma
Capacity
Diaphragm
Inhale—Exhale
Respiratory System
Spirometry

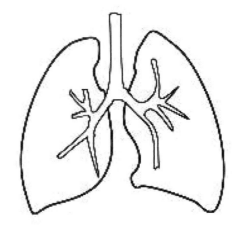

What Do the Lungs Do?

If we are unable to breath, we cannot stay alive. Our lungs are large and in charge when it comes to breathing. They are one of the largest organs in our body, and they work with the respiratory system to help us breath fresh air in and bad air out. They are important for talking. Who knew?

By the time we are 70 years old, we will have taken over 600 million breaths. So, we could say the lungs are hard working, never take a vacation, and don't mind working overtime. If this is so, we should probably learn more about how they work, so that we can take better care of them.

What Can I Write About?

How do the lungs work as part of the respiratory system? Describe the system and include diagrams.

What role do the lungs play when we talk? Write all about it.

Write about some of the things that can go wrong with the lungs and respiratory system. Asthma, pneumonia, and bronchitis are all diseases of the respiratory system.

Write about the effects of smoking or pollution on the lungs.

Write about ways we can keep our lungs healthy throughout our lives.

Are There Books on the Lungs and Respiratory System?

Use your library catalog. Do not forget the reference area, where you can find background information and statistics.

Ballard, Carol. *Lungs: Injury, Illness, and Health.* Chicago: Heinemann-Raintree, 2003.

Furgang, Kathy. *My Lungs.* New York: PowerKids, 2001.

Hayhurst, Chris. *The Lungs: Learning How We Breath.* New York: Rosen Group, 2002.

LeVert, Suzanne. *The Lungs.* New York: Marshall Cavendish, 2002.

Parker, Steve. *The Lungs and Respiratory System.* Austin, TX: Raintree Steck-Vaughn, 1997.

Can the Internet Help?

KidsHealth.org—http://www.kidshealth.org/kid/body/lungs_noSW.html. Information about lungs—their function—good basic information.

Asthma Tutorial for Parents and Children—http://www.healthsystem.virginia.edu/internet/pediatrics/patients/Tutorials/asthma/

Oxygen Delivery System—http://sln.fi.edu/biosci/systems/respiration.html. Explains how the respiratory system works.

Lungs and Respiratory System: Inside the Human Body—http://kidshealth.org/parent/general/body_basics/lungs.html

American Lung Association—http://www.lungusa.org/site/pp.asp?c=dvLUK9O0E&b=22542. This site contains good up-to-date research for older students.

How Stuff Works—http://science.howstuffworks.com/lung.htm. The basics about how we breath, where air goes, and more.

 **TA DA!**

Games or Activities

Respiratory system—http://www.lung.ca/children/grades4_6/respiratory/. Games to play and learn. (Click on your grade level.)

Plants and Oxygen—Breathing Easy—http://www.tnrcc.state.tx.us/air/monops/lessons/breathingeasylesson.html. Try this experiment to watch plants breath.

Experiment

Fill a bucket with 13 pints of water. Show it to your class. Your body breaths in 13 pints of air every minute.

Look at Canada's plan for R2000 housing (http://www.lung.ca/children/grades7_12/air_pollution/r2000.html). Find other sites about it. Is this a good concept for housing in your area? What can you do to help decrease pollution in your area?

In the Classroom

The Human Body's Respiratory System—http://www.cln.org/themes/respiratory.html. Good background, plans, and activities

Teacher's Resources—http://www.lung.ca/children/teachers/resources7_12.html. Choose your grade level.

I'm Covered Up.

SKIN

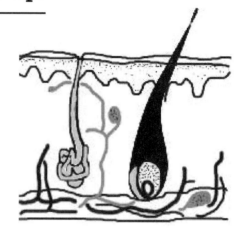

New Words

Epidermis
Hair Follicle
Melanin
Oil Glands
Sebaceous Glands
Sweat Glands
Ultraviolet Rays

What Is Skin All About?

The skin is there to prevent the loss of body fluids and to protect the body from harmful chemicals and accidents. It is a part of our body's temperature system, plays a role in keeping us immune from organisms, and (importantly) keeps us all together. The skin is the largest organ of the body, and its cells are continuously replaced as they are lost to normal wear and tear. Have a cut? Burn? Mole? Freckle? Zit? Pimple? Eczema? Hives? Wart? Rash? Spot? Itch? Fungus? Yes, our skin may occasionally have a few problems. Learn about the part our skin plays and how we can best take care of it.

What Can I Write About?

Identify and describe the layers of the skin and their role.

Write about the role your skin plays as the largest organ of your body.

Write about one or more (compare) skin diseases or skin problems.

Discuss sun damage and UV rays. Or write about acne, that plague of teen years.

Find out what makes each person's skin different. Why are we various shades? Race? Genes?

Are There Books About Our Skin?

Be sure to look for books on the human body, if you can't find enough on skin. Do not forget the reference area. Ask the librarian for help if you need it.

Elgin, Kathleen. *The Human Body: The Skin.* New York: Franklin Watts, 1970.

McNally, Robert. *Skin Health Information for Teens: Health Tips About Dermatological Concerns and Skin Cancer Risks.* Detroit: Omnigraphics, 2003.

Parker, Steve. *Skin, Muscles, and Bones.* Milwaukee, WI: Gareth Stevens, 2004.

Williams, Julie. *Skin & Nails: Care Tips for Girls.* Middleton, WI: American Girl, 2003.

World Book Encyclopedia of Science. Vol. 7. *The Human Body.* Chicago: World Book, 2001.

Can the Internet Help?

The Whole Story of Skin—http://kidshealth.org/kid/body/skin_noSW.html. Written especially for kids.

National Skin Center—http://www.nsc.gov.sg/. Good information about skin diseases and cures. (See *Handbook of Common Skin Diseases.*)

About.com collection of information about the skin—http://dermatology.about.com/cs/skinanatomy/a/anatomy.htm. Good site for the basics.

Electronic Textbook, Anatomy of the Skin—http://www.telemedicine.org/anatomy.htm#functions. Good information.

Two sites to help you understand sun or burn damage—http://www.lorealv2.com/_en/_ww/sunprotectionorg/focus-sunprotection.aspx and http://www.quickcare.org/skin/burns.html

American Academy of Dermatology—Kids Connection—http://www.aad.org/public/Parentskids/kids.htm. Contains basic information.

Skin Color—http://en.wikipedia.org/wiki/Human_skin_color. What makes our skin different shades and colors.

 **TA DA!**

Action!

First study the skin; then see if you can label the parts of the skin using this information and printout—http://www.enchantedlearning.com/subjects/anatomy/skin/

Experiment

Experiment with the power of sunblock. Put sunblock on one of your arms and none on the other. After a few hours in the sun, see whether the sunblock is doing its job. Read about ultraviolet (UV) rays to find out more.

In the Classroom

An excellent lesson plan for grades 7–9 on the skin and the sense of touch—http://www.atozteacherstuff.com/go/jump1.cgi?ID=2161. Good experiments.

For grades 3–6, this plan includes black masters that can be very useful—http://www.healthyhands.com/educator/grades_3_6/lesson_2_4.htm

ENERGY

Energy is everywhere. It takes energy to blow up a balloon, to play a trombone, to walk up stairs, to wave at friends. It takes energy to start your car, to maintain the magnets on your refrigerator, to pedal your bike, or to run the motor of your remote cars. These topics are very interesting—and you may be surprised at a few we have selected.

21

On and On and On . . .

ALTERNATIVE ENERGY

New Words

Biodiesel
Geothermal
Hydroelectric power
Solar Energy
Wind Power

What Is Alternative Energy?

As more and more people discover the comfort of air conditioning instead of open windows, the convenience of riding in a car instead of on a bicycle, and the excitement of television and the Internet, increased fuel is needed to power the electricity and engines of modern life. Oil, the most common fuel, is rapidly becoming harder to find, and before too long, there will be very little left. To continue our lifestyle, we will need to develop other sources of energy. Some people fuel their cars with used cooking oil from fast food restaurants. Others heat and cool their houses with power from the sun. Energy is all around us, in the wind, in the water, in the sun, and in the vegetation. We need to learn how to use it.

What Can I Write About?

Identify several sources of alternative energy and compare their benefits and drawbacks.

Choose one source of energy. Learn all you can about it, and discuss it.

Compare one or more sources of alternative energy to oil power.

Choose one source of energy. Plan a power plant or battery using your energy, from raw material to the end user.

Experiment with one alternative energy source. Explain your experiment and evaluate your results.

Are There Books on Alternative Energy?

Use your library catalog. Do not forget the reference area, where you can find background information and statistics.

Engelbert, Phillis. *Technology in Action: Science Applied to Everyday Life.* Detroit: UXL, 1999.

Lerner, K. Lee, and Brenda Wilmoth Lerner, eds. *Gale Encyclopedia of Science.* 3d ed. Detroit: Gale, 2004.

New Book of Popular Science. Vols. 2 and 3. Danbury, CT: Grolier, 2004.

Can the Internet Help?

U.S. Department of Energy—http://www.eere.energy.gov/afdc/altfuel/altfuels. html. Gives data on and comparisons of alternative fuels.

Danish Wind Energy organization—http://www.windpower.org/en/kids/index. htm. Take a crash course in wind energy. .

Edugreen in India—http://edugreen.teri.res.in/explore/renew/hydel.htm. Hydropower from rivers and oceans..

Classroom Project from Arlington, Virginia, schools—http://www.arlington. k12.va.us/schools/gunston/library/students/links/energy. Has good links to many sources of energy.

Alternative Energy—http://www.rtsd26.org/trails/LearningCenter/altenergy.htm. Many selected sites are especially for kids. Find the best links.

**TA DA!**

Multimedia

Geothermal Education Office—http://geothermal.marin.org/GEOpresentation/. View a slide show about geothermal energy.

U.S. Department of Energy—http://www.eere.energy.gov/consumerinfo/ animations.html. Animations of wind power and Distributed Energy Resources.

Experiment

Florida Solar Energy Center—http://www.fsec.ucf.edu/ed/sm/ch4-solarthermal/ hotcoldcolors_student.htm. Experiment to see which colors absorb the most solar energy.

Windpower.org—http://www.windpower.org/en/kids/choose/rotor/model.htm. Build a small wind turbine.

U.S. Department of Energy—http://www.eere.energy.gov/consumerinfo/factsheets/ solar.html. Make a solar air heater.

In the Classroom

Links to teaching materials of all sorts—http://www.eere.energy.gov/afdc/ resources/curr_68.html (Department of Energy) and http://idahoptv.org/ dialogue4kids/stream.cfm (from Idaho).

Fueling the Future, from the National Energy Foundation—http://www.nef1. org/ftf/. Activities for the classroom.

22

Portable Power.

BATTERIES

New Words

> Alessandro Volta
> Potential Energy
> Primary and Secondary Batteries

What Are Batteries?

Video games, CD players, automobiles, and smoke alarms: What do they have in common? They all need batteries. A battery stores energy until it is needed. Some batteries get used up, while others, like a car battery or a wireless telephone battery, can be recharged again and again. Potential energy, energy that is waiting to be tapped, is everywhere. You can find it in plants, metals, and moving water. You can even make a battery yourself from a lemon or a potato with enough power to light a bulb or run a clock.

What Can I Write About?

Research how a battery works. Include primary batteries and secondary batteries.

Look into the history of batteries. Think about the problems the inventors were trying to solve and analyze their success.

Consider the different materials used in batteries and discuss their advantages and disadvantages.

Analyze different conductors. Discuss the benefits and drawbacks of each.

Compare and contrast rechargeable batteries with disposable batteries.

Are There Books on Batteries?

We can't begin to tell you the best books. There are many. Use your library catalog. Do not forget the reference area, where you can find background information and statistics.

Bender, Lionel. *Invention.* Eyewitness Books. New York: Knopf, 1991.

Considine, Glenn D. *Van Nostrand's Scientific Encyclopedia.* New York: Wiley-Interscience, 2002.

Lerner, K. Lee, and Brenda Wilmoth Lerner, eds. *Gale Encyclopedia of Science.* 3d ed. Detroit: Gale, 2004.

McGrath, Kimberly A., ed. *World of Invention.* 2d ed. Detroit: Gale, 1999.

Newton, David E., et al. *UXL Encyclopedia of Science.* Detroit: UXL, 1997.

Schmittroth, Linda, Mary Reilly McCall, and Bridget Travers. *Eureka!* New York: UXL, 1995.

Can the Internet Help?

Panasonic's World of Science—http://www.discovery.panasonic.co.jp/en/lab/lab10bat/. How batteries work, and their history.

Enchanted Learning—http://www.enchantedlearning.com/inventors/page/b/battery.shtml. Brief history of batteries.

How Stuff Works—http://electronics.howstuffworks.com/battery.htm. How batteries work.

BBC—http://www.open2.net/science/roughscience/library/batteries.htm. How batteries work.

Santee Electric Company—http://santee.apogee.net/kids/lewc_ifrm.aspx. Conductors and insulators.

 **TA DA!**

Batteries in Action!

Energizer Batteries—http://www.energizer.com/learning/howbatterieswork.asp. Animated demonstration of how batteries work.

Experiment

NASA—http://whyfiles.larc.nasa.gov/text/kids/D_Lab/activities/battery_4-5.html. Make your own batteries from lemons.

PBS—http://pbskids.org/zoom/activities/sci/steadinesstester.html. Try out different conductors.

In the Classroom

Teach-nology—http://www.teach-nology.com/teachers/lesson_plans/science/physics/electricity/. Lesson plans for batteries and magnets.

U.S. Department of Energy—http://www.netl.doe.gov/coolscience/teacher/lesson-plans/lesson6.html. Fuel cell technology lesson plans for older students.

"Charge Up to Recycle"—Rechargable Battery Recycling Program and National Geographic—http://www.rbrc.org/graphics/PDF/Rb272.pdf

Seeing Red!

COLOR

New Words

Color Blindness
Color Spectrum
Electromagnetic Radiation
Photons
Reflection—Refraction
RGB

What Is Color?

What makes a ruby red? What makes the sky blue? Imagine a world without color. Color plays a vital role in the world in which we live. It can affect the way the think and our reactions to different things. Color can make us feel happy or sad. It can hurt our eyes or be soothing. It can be used to save energy. Color sends messages, it helps us remember, and it can act as camouflage. Color is very powerful. Learn more about it.

What Can I Write About?

What is color? Why are things colored? How does light affect the colors we see?

Choose a single color to write about. What colors are put together to allow us to see it? (Or is it a primary color?) How does it make us feel?

Explain how the eye sees color.

Write about color blindness: what it is, how it works, and dangers of being color blind.

Write about skin colors (pigment.) Include information about the effects of the sun.

Are There Books on Color?

We can't begin to tell you the best books. There are many. Use your library catalog. Do not forget the reference area, where you can find background information and statistics.

Ballard, Carol. *How Do Our Eyes See?* Austin, TX: Raintree Steck-Vaughn, 1998.

Burton, Jane, and Kim Taylor. *The Nature and Science of Colors.* Milwaukee, WI: Gareth Stevens, 1998.

Doherty, Paul, and Don Rathjan. *The Magic Wand and Other Bright Experiments on Light and Color.* Chichester; New York: Wiley, 1995.

Lauber, Patricia. *What Do You See and How Do You See It?: Exploring Light, Color, and Vision.* New York: Crown, 1994.

Woodford, Chris. *Light.* Routes of Science. Detroit: Blackbirch, 2004.

Can the Internet Help?

Light and Color—http://micro.magnet.fsu.edu/optics/lightandcolor/index.html. Discusses the many aspects of color and light.

The Skinny on White—http://www.discovery.com/area/skinnyon/skinnyon971003/skinnyon.html. If you choose one color, white is a great one! Who knew?

Causes of Color—http://webexhibits.org/causesofcolor/index.html. An excellent exhibit. See it all the way through to understand color and light.

Color Matters—http://www.colormatters.com/. The science of color. Excellent information and interesting.

Color Blindness—http://www.toledo-bend.com/colorblind/aboutCB.html. About it, tests for color blindness, why and how it happens.

Psychology of Color—http://www.infoplease.com/spot/colors1.html. How color makes us feel. Follow the links to other information.

Understanding Color—http://www.rgbworld.com/color.html. The RGB world.

Color and Light—the Physics Classroom—http://www.glenbrook.k12.il.us/gbssci/phys/Class/light/u12l2e.html. Several excellent lessons about color.

 TA DA!

Science of Light—http://www.learner.org/teacherslab/science/light/color/. Fun activities to help you understand color and light.

Physics Optics Experiments—http://physics.about.com/od/opticsexperiments/. Why is the sky blue? Measure the speed of light—with chocolate.

Experiment

Catch a Rainbow—http://www.kidzone.ws/science/rainbow.htm. Something we all want to do . . .

In the Classroom

The Science of Light, from Annenberg/CPB—http://www.learner.org/teacherslab/science/light/. An excellent lesson; includes activities.

Homeschooling—Light and Color links—http://homeschooling.gomilpitas.com/explore/optics.htm. Excellent collection for the classroom.

That's Shocking!

ELECTRICITY

New Words

Alternating Current (AC)
Direct Current (DC)
Volts
Amperes
Ohms

What Is Electricity?

Electricity has been around for a long time, probably since the beginning of the universe. Static electricity was described back as far as 600 BC. (See jumpstart 31, "Static Electricity.") But it wasn't until relatively recent times (the seventeenth century) that scientists started trying to harness electricity to be used when it was needed. Just what is electricity? It is the movement of electrons. As long as an atom has the right number of electrons, it's stable. But if one of those electrons gets loose, watch out! It bounces around trying to find a home, that is, an atom in need of an electron. In the process, it transmits energy.

What Can I Write About?

Explain how electricity works. Be sure to include conduction and resistance.

Find out several ways electricity can be generated. Compare them.

Research and report on one of the scientists who was instrumental in the discovery of electricity. Some possibilities are Benjamin Franklin, Alessandro Volta, G. S. Ohm, Michael Faraday, Heinrich Hertz, Thomas Edison, George Westinghouse, and Nikolas Tesla.

Compare alternating current to direct current.

Discuss the changes electricity has made in our lives since it became commonplace in the twentieth century.

Are There Books on Electricity?

Use your library catalog. Do not forget the reference area. The librarian will help.

Lerner, K. Lee, and Brenda Wilmoth Lerner, eds. *Gale Encyclopedia of Science.* 3d ed. Detroit: Gale, 2004.

Macaulay, David. *The New Way Things Work.* Boston: Houghton Mifflin, 1998.

New Book of Popular Science. Vols. 2 and 3. Danbury, CT: Grolier, 2004.

Parker, Steve. *Eyewitness: Electricity.* New York: Dorling Kindersley, 2000.

Richards, Elise. *Turned on by Electricity.* Mahwah, NJ: Troll, 1997.

Can the Internet Help?

What Is Electricity? From the U.S. Department of Energy—http://www.eia.doe.gov/kids/energyfacts/sources/electricity.html. For kids.

The Electric Universe, from Cipco—http://cipco.electricuniverse.com/flash/eu/education/frontier/index.html

Internet Plasma Physics Experience—http://ippex.pppl.gov/interactive/electricity/. Learn the basics of electricity.

Fact Monster—http://www.factmonster.com/ce6/sci/A0857938.html. History of the discovery of electricity, and the basics of how electricity works.

How Stuff Works—http://science.howstuffworks.com/electricity.htm. How electricity works.

NC Public Power—http://www.ncpublicpower.com/children_how.html. More basic explanation of how electricity works.

Electrical Safety World—http://www.safeelectricity.org/esw_v1_1/science/index.html. Electricity basics and safety.

42 Explore—http://www.42explore.com/electric.htm. Learn the basics and follow the links to everything about electricity.

 **TA DA!**

Electricity in Action!

NASA—http://whyfiles.larc.nasa.gov/kids/Problem_Board/problems/electricity/treehouse.html. Game to help you understand electricity.

Experiment

Simple Circuits from TEAMS Distance Learning—http://teams.lacoe.edu/documentation/classrooms/gary/electricity/activities/circuits/circuit.html. Shows you how to make an electrical circuit to light a bulb.

In the Classroom

Southern Energy—http://www.southernco.com/learningpower/. Lesson plans, experiments, and guides to understanding electricity.

Teach-nology—http://www.teach-nology.com/teachers/subject_matter/science/physics/magnets/. Links to Web sites on electricity and magnetism.

Some Like It Hot!

HEAT TRANSFER

New Words

Conduction
Convection
Joules
Radiation
Thermal Energy—Thermodynamics

What Is Heat Transfer?

If heat from the sun stayed at the sun, heat from a fire remained in the flame, and heat in a radiator didn't penetrate the pipe, the earth would be a cold and uninviting place. But we are fortunate. The sun shines down on the earth, radiating heat energy. You can feel it on your skin on a sunny day. If you stand near a fire or a hot oven, you don't need to touch it to feel the heat. It spreads through the air. When you touch the back of your television set, it's warm and conducts that warmth to your hand. If you check the temperature of a room near the floor and again near the ceiling, as long as you stay away from sources of heat or air conditioning, the floor will almost always be cooler. What are the three methods of heat transfer? You have probably already figured that out. They are radiation, convection, and conduction.

What Can I Write About?

Choose one method of heat transfer—convection, radiation, or conduction—and explain how it works.

Describe the interaction among the three methods of heat transfer.

Consider one of the ways humans have harnessed heat energy and describe how it is used. Examples are a heating system or a microwave oven, but you can think of others.

Discuss heat transfer, especially convection, in relation to the weather.

Are There Books on Heat Transfer?

We can't begin to tell you the best books. There are many. Use your library catalog. Do not forget the reference area, where you can find background information and statistics.

Considine, Glenn D. *Van Nostrand's Scientific Encyclopedia.* New York: Wiley-Interscience, 2002.

Lerner, K. Lee, and Brenda Wilmoth Lerner, eds. *Gale Encyclopedia of Science.* 3d ed. Vol. 5. Detroit: Gale, 2004.

New Book of Popular Science. Vol. 3. Danbury, CT: Grolier, 2004.

Newton, David E., Rob Nagel, and Bridget Travers. "Radiation." In *UXL Encyclopedia of Science.* Detroit: UXL, 1998.

Can the Internet Help?

Science Fair Projects—http://www.all-science-fair-projects.com/science_fair_projects_encyclopedia/Heat. Explains how heat moves.

Cartage.org—http://www.cartage.org.lb/en/kids/science/Physics/Thermodynamics/Heat%20transfer.htm. Simple explanations of heat transfer, to get you started.

Wikipedia and kids.net.au—http://www.kids.net.au/encyclopedia/?p=he/Heat. Heat transfer.

How Stuff Works—http://www.howstuffworks.com/thermos.htm. Gives a great introduction to heat transfer by explaining how thermoses work.

Thermodynamics and the study of heat—http://www.cartage.org.lb/en/kids/science/Physics/Thermodynamics/mainpage.htm. Look at each of the short essays.

 **TA DA!**

Radiation and Conduction in Action!

Energy for Children: All About Heat. [videorecording]. Wynnewood, PA: Schlessinger Video Library, 2000—http://www.libraryvideo.com/ssl/energy_for_children.asp. Choose the *All About Heat* video and watch a three-minute video clip.

Experiment

University Corporation for Atmospheric Research—http://www.ucar.edu/40th/webweather/tstorms/tstorms.htm. Demonstrates convection currents.

PBS Kids—http://pbskids.org/dragonflytv/doit_conductioncountdown.html. Try this experiment with conduction.

California Energy Commission—http://www.energyquest.ca.gov/projects/solardogs.html. Build a solar-powered hot dog cooker.

In the Classroom

Chariho Regional School District—http://www.chariho.k12.ri.us/faculty/kkvre/units/2002/ashfour/heatenergy.html. Heat transfer lesson for grade 4.

The Argyle Center—http://argyll.epsb.ca/jreed/bookmark/science9.htm. Lessons plans on controlling heat.

California Energy Commission—http://www.energyquest.ca.gov/projects/index.html. Interesting science projects. .

We're Catching On!

MAGNETISM

New Words

Electromagnets
Magnetic Field
Magnetosphere
North and South Poles
Repel—Attract

What Is a Magnet?

You have probably enjoyed using magnets since before first grade. Natural magnets have north and south poles; like poles repel, opposite poles attract. Magnetic field lines flow from north to south. We know all of this, but still, there is much more to learn about magnets and magnetism. You might learn about the magnetosphere (the earth's magnetic field), how the compass works, more about magnetic north, or more about electromagnets. Go beyond the basics, and be sure you have experiments to show the class.

What Can I Write About?

Write a general report about the magnet and how it works.

Write about the earth's magnetic field and magnetic north.

Learn more about the electromagnet. What big jobs does it do? You might see how these magnets are used in the MRI or another important use.

Take a look at magnetic therapy. What is it? How does it work? Is it effective?

Are There Books or Videos on Magnets?

We can't begin to tell you the best books. There are many. Use your library catalog. Do not forget the reference area, where you can find background information and statistics.

Fleisher, Paul. *Waves: Principles of Light, Electricity, and Magnetism.* Minneapolis, MN: Lerner, 2002.

Magnetism. Physical Science in Action. [DVD]. DVD FV8876. Wynnewood, PA: Schlessinger Media, 2000.

Null, Gary. *Healing with Magnets.* New York: Carroll & Graf, 1998.

Parker, Steve. *Electricity and Magnetism.* New York: Chelsea House, 2004.

Weilbacher, Mike. *The Magnetism Exploration Kit: Discover One of Nature's Most Astonishing Forces.* Philadelphia: Running Press, 1993.

Can the Internet Help?

Earth's Magnetic Field—information from NASA—http://liftoff.msfc.nasa.gov/academy/space/mag_field.html

Magnets from Canada Science and Technology Museum—http://www.sciencetech.technomuses.ca/english/schoolzone/Info_Magnets.cfm. Good basics.

Magnetic Compass and how it works—http://science.howstuffworks.com/compass1.htm. Use search screen for electromagnets and magnets.

Magnetism Information with quiz and links—http://www.school-for-champions.com/science/magnetism.htm

Excellent information on magnetism from South Dakota State—http://www.state.sd.us/deca/DDN4Learning/ThemeUnits/magnet/general.htm

Discovering Magnetic North—http://www.ruf.rice.edu/~feegi/magnet.html

Magnetic Therapy—http://healing.about.com/od/magnets/. Find out how magnets work in holistic medicine.

Beginner's Guide to the Magnetosphere, the earth's magnet—http://en.wikipedia.org/wiki/Magnetosphere

 **TA DA!**

Magnets in Action!

A series of experiments creating magnets—http://www.exploratorium.edu/snacks/iconmagnetism.html

Something Different

Create a Saturday Science Lab for your family and friends. Use one of the experiment Web sites (listed above or below) or a book with science experiments and set up a lab so that lab partners can work through several magnet projects. Have at least six experiments with all of the equipment ready. Provide written directions at each station. Be ready to give an introduction to your lab.

Also, do you like to go antiquing with Mom? Take along a magnet to check metals. Gold or silver won't stick to your magnet! Mom will be impressed when you help her get a good price.

In the Classroom

Experiments for the classroom—http://www.state.sd.us/deca/DDN4Learning/ThemeUnits/magnet/lesson.htm and http://wow.osu.edu/Magnetism/maglist.htm

I Hear a Symphony.

MUSICAL INSTRUMENTS

New Words

Brass
Frequency
Percussion
Pitch
Strings
Woodwinds

What Does Music Have to Do with Science?

How do wood, strings, and a horse's tail come together to make beautiful music? As long as 3,000 years ago, people figured out that they could make pleasing sounds by plucking a string. Thicker or thinner strings, longer or shorter strings, changed the sound. In time, stringed instruments such as harps, violins, and guitars were born. A hollow log may well have been the first drum. A simple whistle uses the movement of air through a small opening to create sound. Most instruments we now use had been developed by the early 1800s. Musical families include strings, woodwinds, brass, and percussion. The instruments are varied, but they all have one thing in common. They all use physics to create sound.

What Can I Write About?

Choose a musical instrument and explain how it works.

Look into the history and development of a particular instrument.

Explain the development of the musical scale and the math behind it.

Compare and contrast two instruments from different families.

Create an instrument of your own. Explain how it works and play a song for your class.

Are There Books on Musical Instruments?

We can't begin to tell you the best books. There are many. Use your library catalog. Do not forget the reference area, where you can find background information and statistics.

Cooper, Christopher. *Physics Matters: Sound.* Vol. 5. Danbury, CT: Grolier, 2001.

Dearling, Robert. *The Encyclopedia of Musical Instruments.* 5 vols. Philadelphia: Chelsea, 2001.

Witman, Kathleen L., Kyung Lim Kolasky, and Neil Schlage. *CDs, Super Glue and Salsa.* Series 2. Detroit: UXL, 1996.

World Book Encyclopedia. Chicago: World Book, 2005.

Can the Internet Help?

How Stuff Works—http://www.howstuffworks.com/guitar.htm. How acoustic guitars work. Search other instruments here.

Physics Classroom—http://www.physicsclassroom.com/Class/sound/soundtoc. html. Sound waves and music, for older students.

Exploratorium—http://www.exploratorium.edu/music/. Explores the science of music.

Sibelius Academy—http://www2.siba.fi/Kulttuuripalvelut/instruments.html. Sibelius has collected links for every type of instrument.

ThinkQuest page on history and how instruments work.—http://library. thinkquest.org/11315/instrum.htm

 **TA DA!**

Music in Action!

New England Panflute Academy—http://www.panflutejedi.com/academypage. html. Video clip lessons on how to play the pan flute.

Folk of the Woods—http://www.folkofthewood.com/page2523.htm. Has video samplers of several different acoustical guitars.

Experiment

Houghton Mifflin—http://www.eduplace.com/kids/hmr/4/4/instr.html. Invites you to make your own guitar!

The New York Philharmonic Orchestra—http://www.nyphilkids.org/lab/ make-your-own/. Helps you make your own instrument.

In the Classroom

Rice University—http://cnx.rice.edu/content/m11063/latest/. Sound and music activities for grades 3–6.

Rice University—http://cnx.rice.edu/content/m12364/latest/. Wind instrument basics for middle school.

Rice University—http://cnx.rice.edu/content/m12589/latest/. Standing waves and wind instruments.

Up and Down!

ROLLER COASTERS

New Words

Amusement Parks
Centripetal Force
Gravity
Inertia
Potential Energy—Kinetic Energy
Roller Coaster

What Is a Roller Coaster?

Most kids (young and old) love roller coasters. When you were young, you could hardly wait to stand in front of the measuring stick and be proclaimed tall enough to ride the big coaster. It takes your breath away, scares you, and yet you want to ride again. Why, scream machines have been popular for over 200 years. Find out about the history of roller coasters—and the science that allows them to run without an engine.

What Can I Write About?

Write about the history and physics of the roller coaster, like at Coney Island. Include a time line.

Several people (LaMarcus Thompson, John Miller, Harry Traver, John Allen, Ron Toomer, and others) were involved in the development of the coaster throughout the years. Write about their contributions and how they came about. Include a time line.

Explain scientifically how roller coasters work. Explain the physics of why the roller coaster stays in forward motion up and down the track.

Describe the differences between the two types of coasters, wooden and tubular steel. Be sure to compare the records for height, speed, drop, length, and angle of descent. Try to include a graph or chart that compares these roller coaster types.

Are There Books or Videos on Roller Coasters?

Use your library catalog. Do not forget the reference area for encyclopedias and science books.

Bennett, David. *Roller Coasters: Wooden and Steel Coasters, Twisters, and Cork-screws.* Edison, NJ: Cartwell, 1998

Cook, Nick. *Roller Coasters: Or, I Had So Much Fun I Almost Puked.* Minneapolis, MN: Carolrhoda, 2004.

Roller Coaster Physics. [videorecording]. Bethesda, MD: Discovery Channel School, 2004.

Rutherford, Scott. *The American Roller Coaster.* Osceola, WI: MBI, 2000.

Wiese, Jim. *Roller Coaster Science: 50 Wet, Wacky, Wild, Dizzy Experiments About Things Kids Like Best.* New York: Wiley, 1994.

Can the Internet Help?

Roller Coaster Data Base—http://www.rcdb.com/. Statistics and pictures of the world's roller coasters—great for comparison charts.

How Roller-Coasters Work—http://www.howstuffworks.com/roller-coaster.htm

Roller Coaster History from the Ultimate Rollercoaster pages—http://www.ultimaterollercoaster.com/coasters/history/

Great Roller Coaster—http://www.greatcoasters.com/. A company that designs and makes coasters. Look at the many styles.

Learner Org—http://www.learner.org/exhibits/parkphysics/. Gives amusement parks physics.

The Ultimate Rollercoaster Pages—http://www.ultimaterollercoaster.com/coasters/records/. Records of roller coasters.

Centripetal Force—http://www.stevespanglerscience.com/experiment/00000054. Try this experiment. It will help you understand this force.

**TA DA!**

Coasters in Action!

Download a roller coaster game—http://www.atari.com/rollercoastertycoon/us/downloads. Be sure toto view the videos—take a few virtual rides.

Experiment

Design your own coaster and check it for safety—http://www.learner.org/exhibits/parkphysics/coaster/ and http://www.funderstanding.com/k12/coaster/

In the Classroom

Roller Coaster Lesson Plans—http://school.discovery.com/lessonplans/programs/rollercoaster/. Includes activities, history, information, and links.

We Are Combustible.

SMALL ENGINES

New Words

Combustion
Connecting Rod
Cylinder
Engines
Overhead Valves—Piston

What Is a Small Engine?

Small engines are all around us, powering lawn mowers, leaf blowers, chain saws, generators, motorcycles, boats, and many other handy tools and toys. Some are powered by battery, some are electric, and some are fuel driven. How do they work? They are actually pretty simple. Read about them. It would make your research much more fun if you can build a simple engine. Maybe your dad has a broken house appliance he will help you take apart. I'd ask first if I were you. (☺)

What Can I Write About?

Describe how a small engine works. Be sure to provide a drawing, labeling all the parts you describe.

Write about small engine emissions. How are small engines affecting the environment? What can be done to reduce the effects?

Write about the early steam engines. How did they work? Build one yourself to show.

Compare two engine types. Explain their workings. Bring in examples.

Repair a small engine at home. Write up your work and bring it to class to show and discuss.

Write about your job if you became a small engines mechanic. What are some of the things you would do? What training would you need? Where might you work?

Are There Books or Videos on Engines?

Use your library catalog. Do not forget the reference area, where you can find encyclopedias.

London, Daniel. *Small Engine Care & Repair.* Chanhassen, MN: Creative, 2003.

Maxwell, Jeffrey. *Engines and How They Work.* New York: Franklin Watts, 2000.

Olney, Ross Robert. *The Internal Combustion Engine.* New York: Lippincott, 1982.

Stephenson, James. *Farm Engines and How to Run Them.* Guilford, CT: Lyons, 2004. (Originally published in 1903.)

Warm It Up (Start Your Engines): Small Engines 2. Minneapolis: University of Minnesota Press, 2000.

Can the Internet Help?

Bob Vila's Small Engine Fix-it Club page—http://www.bobvila.com/FixItClub/Task/Repairing/FIG_SmallEngines.html

DIY Network (Do it Yourself)—http://www.diynet.com/diy/ab_small_engines/. Many small machines and how to repair them.

How Stuff Works: Engines and Electric Motors—http://auto.howstuffworks. com/engine.htm or http://electronics.howstuffworks.com/motor.htm. Search other topics also.

Pratt-Whitney—http://www.pratt-whitney.com/how.htm. See how engines work.

All about steam engines, their history, and how they work—http://www.steamboats. com/engineroom.html

Lawn mower man's repair hints for small engines—http://www. lawnmowerman.tv/

Small Engines—from the U.S. Department of Labor—http://www.bls.gov/oco/ocos198.htm. About the job of small engines mechanic.

Small Engine Emissions—http://www.egr.msu.edu/erl/emiss/emiss.htm

 **TA DA!**

Engines in Action!

Have a little fun with Thomas the Tank Engine & Friends—http://www. hitentertainment.com/thomasandfriends/. Games and activities.

Experience

Building an aster steam locomotive kit—http://www.machinetoys.com/kits. html. Try it yourself.

Build a steam engine—http://www.neatstuff.net/wilesco-steam.html

In the Classroom

Small engines, simple motors, and machines—http://www.ext.nodak.edu/county/cass/fourh/4HKids/4HProjectInfo/4HMachineResources.htm. Resources for kids' projects.

Motors—http://www.educationcoffeehouse.com/voc/automotive.htm. A few lesson plans and other links.

30

Seeing Is Believing!

SOUND AND LIGHT WAVES

New Words

Light Waves
Radiation
Electromagnetic Spectrum
Wave Motion
Diffraction
Photoelectric Effect

What Are Light and Sound Waves?

Stars are billions of miles away, and yet we can see them. How does the light get from the star to our eyes? Light can be waves, but in a dual effect it can also travel in particles. Sound too travels in waves, but the waves can travel through the air or through objects, such as telephone wires or even water. If both sound and light are transmitted through waves, why is it that something that will block light, such as a sheet of metal, will help sound travel? And why can light travel millions of miles while sound rarely goes over half a mile?

You're going to have to concentrate hard to learn more about this fascinating topic.

What Can I Write About?

Compare and contrast sound and light waves.

Describe possible communication with distant planets using sound or light waves.

How does a radio work?

Pick a musical instrument and discuss how it works, using wave theory.

Are There Books on Light and Sound Waves?

Use *electromagnetic spectrum* and *waves* to search the library catalog and reference books. Reference books offer good basic information.

Considine, Glenn D. *Van Nostrand's Scientific Encyclopedia.* New York: Wiley-Interscience, 2002.

Engelberg, Phillis. *Technology in Action: Science Applied to Everyday Life.* Vol. 2. Detroit: UXL, 1999.

Lerner, K. Lee, and Brenda Wilmoth Lerner, eds. *Gale Encyclopedia of Science.* 3d ed. Vol. 5. Detroit: Gale, 2004.

Newton, David E., Rob Nagel, and Bridget Travers. *UXL Encyclopedia of Science.* Detroit: UXL, 1998.

Can the Internet Help?

University of New South Wales—http://www.phys.unsw.edu.au/music/. An excellent site that demonstrates the interaction between music and physics.

Optical Research Associates presents Optics for Kids—http://www.opticalres.com/kidoptx.html. About understanding and controlling light.

The Science Fair Project Encyclopedia—http://www.all-science-fair-projects.com/science_fair_projects_encyclopedia/Radio_frequency. Gives radio frequencies and the electromagnetic spectrum.

World Almanac for Kids—http://www.worldalmanacforkids.com/explore/space/radioastro.html. Could radio help us to detect life in other galaxies? World Almanac for Kids has some facts.

Johns Hopkins University—http://fuse.pha.jhu.edu/~wpb/spectroscopy/basics.html. The basics of light.

Waves and Vibrations from Physical Science Topics—http://www.svsu.edu/mathsci-center/ePS_Waves.htm. Excellent information for all levels.

 **TA DA!**

Electromagnetic Waves in Action!

Zooish—http://www.zooish.com/Sounds.htm. Sounds, from an elephant to thunder.

Experiment

University of New South Wales—http://www.phys.unsw.edu.au/~jw/hearing.html. Test your hearing using this Web site and a good set of headphones.

In the Classroom

CBEL presents Physics for Kids—http://www.cbel.com/physics_for_kids/

Wavelength demonstrations for middle school kids—http://cmb.physics.wisc.edu/tutorial/demos.html

Teach-nology—http://www.teach-nology.com/teachers/lesson_plans/science/physics/waves/. Presents lesson plans using waves, sound, and optics.

It's Shocking!

STATIC ELECTRICITY

New Words

Attraction and Repulsion
Friction—Induction
Positive and Negative Charges
Spark, Charge, Voltage
Van de Graaff Generator

What Is Static Electricity?

You walk across the floor, ring the doorbell, and get a shock. You pull your hat off and your hair stands up. You touch your friend and Ouch! And, even worse—you have static cling, a black sock hangs on the back of your shirt. On cold winter days, static electricity builds up in our bodies and causes a spark that jumps from us to another person or piece of metal. Static electricity is where electrical charges build up on the surface of a material. It is called "static" because there is no current flowing, as in AC or DC electricity. This is a great topic if you want to bring in experiments to show your classmates.

What Can I Write About?

What is static electricity? What causes it? Give examples.

Explain why we get a charge in dry cold weather. Provide examples. Can we avoid this?

How can static electricity be useful? Describe some of its uses in the workplace.

Explain the Van de Graaff generator. What does this generator do? How does it work?

Explain some of the causes of static electricity. In what situations can it be good; when might it be hazardous? How can it be removed?

Are There Books or Videos on Static Electricity?

Do not forget the reference area, where you can find science dictionaries and encyclopedias.

Adams, Charles K. *Nature's Electricity.* New York: McGraw-Hill, 1986.

Ford, R.A. *Homemade Lightning: Creative Experiments in Electricity.* 3d ed. New York: McGraw-Hill, 2002.

Moore, A. D. *Electrostatics: Exploring, Controlling, and Using Static Electricity.* Morgan Hill, CA: Laplacian, 1997.

Parker, Steve. *Eyewitness: Electricity.* New York: Dorling Kindersley, 2000.

Richards, Elise. *Turned on by Electricity.* Mahwah, NJ: Troll, 1997.

Sootin, Harry. *Experiments with Static Electricity.* New York: Norton, 1969.

Can the Internet Help?

What Is Static Electricity?—http://www.sciencemadesimple.com/static.html

Basics of Static Electricity—http://www.school-for-champions.com/science/static.htm, http://www.school-for-champions.com/science/staticcont.htm, and http://www.school-for-champions.com/science/staticexpl.htm. There are several lessons. Very good explanations.

Misconceptions about Static Electricity—http://www.amasci.com/emotor/stmiscon.html

The Physics Classroom—Static Electricity—http://www.physicsclassroom.com/mmedia/estatics/itsn.html

Electrostatics—http://www.electrostatics.com/. Causes, uses, and remedies.

How Van de Graaff Generators Work—http://science.howstuffworks.com/vdg1.htm

 TA DA!

Electricity in Action!

Van de Graaff Generator—http://amasci.com/emotor/vdg.html. All about it.

Experiment

If you are really into this topic, take a look at this collection of Web sites. There are many projects and experiments you can see and try for yourself. The articles may also help with your research.

http://www.eskimo.com/~billb/emotor/statelec.html

The Atoms Family—http://www.miamisci.org/af/sln/frankenstein/index.html. Enjoy a few experiments on your own.

In the Classroom

Links for Static Electricity—http://www.amasci.com/emotor/statelec.html or http://www.mos.org/sln/toe/staticmenu.html. Includes teacher background and activities.

Scientific American's *"The Amateur Scientist,"* Science Fair Edition, [CD-ROM], is worth purchasing for the classroom. (Available through amazon.com.)

THE ENVIRONMENT

The environment is all around us. Caring citizens are concerned about keeping it safe for ourselves and future generations. The more we know about the environment, from biomes to recycling, the better we are able to work toward improving our small part of the world. Rachel Carson and Jacques Cousteau were environmentalist who had an impact on the world's thinking. You may think of others. Learning about the environment helps us to understand how important relationships are—between people, animals, and the earth.

Falls Down Slowly
Seeps into the Ground . . .

ACID RAIN

New Words

Air Pollution
Alkalinity
Clean Air Act
Nitrogen Oxide
Sulfur Dioxide

What Is Acid Rain?

When smoke goes up into the air, it soon spreads out and fades. You might think that's the end of it. It seems to have evaporated. But in reality, the compounds in the smoke, nitrogen oxide and sulfur dioxide, are still there in the air. They mix with water, oxygen, and other chemicals to make acidic pollutants. They move with the trade winds, across continents and sometimes across oceans. Eventually, they come down again in the form of rain, fog, or snow—called acid rain.

What Can I Write About?

Explain the cycle that creates acid rain. Draw a helpful diagram.

Examine several solutions to the acid rain problem. Compare and contrast them.

Discuss the effect of acid rain on buildings and monuments. Include antiquities.

Evaluate the harm acid rain can do to nature areas such as forests and lakes.

Consider acid rain from a human health standpoint.

Are There Books on Acid Rain?

Use your library catalog. Do not forget the reference area, where you can find background information and statistics.

Childcraft: The How and Why Library. Chicago: World Book, 2003.

Lerner, K. Lee, and Brenda Wilmoth Lerner, eds. *Gale Encyclopedia of Science.* 3d ed. Vol. 1. Detroit: Gale, 2004.

Mongillo, John, and Linda Zierdt-Warshaw. *Encyclopedia of Environmental Science.* Phoenix, AZ: Oryx, 2000.

New Book of Popular Science. Vol. 2. Danbury, CT: Grolier, 2004.

Newton, David E., Rob Nagel, and Bridget Travers. *UXL Encyclopedia of Science.* Vol. 1. Detroit: UXL, 1998.

Can the Internet Help?

Environment Canada—http://www.ec.gc.ca/acidrain/acidfact.html. Explains acid rain, its sources, and levels in the United States and Canada.

The Environmental Protection Agency—http://www.epa.gov/acidrain/site_students/. Explains the types of acid rain and solutions to it.

ENVIS in India—http://envis.tropmet.res.in/kidacidraineffect.htm. A brief overview of the effects of acid rain.

History of the Clean Air Act, from the American Meteorological Society—http://www.ametsoc.org/sloan/cleanair/index.html

Science Learning Network—http://www.jsf.or.jp/sln/acid_e/index.html. See the effects of acid rain on outdoor monuments.

 **TA DA!**

Acid Rain in Action!

Environmental Protection Agency—http://www.epa.gov/acidrain/site_kids/. Interactive story and games about acid rain.

Watch an Environmental Protection Agency animation about acid rain—http://www.epa.gov/acidrain/site_students/acid_anim.html

Experiment

Discovery Kids—http://www.discoverykids.ca/gross/experiments/experimentsDetail. asp?id=69. See the effects of acid rain on growing plants! This experiment will need adult supervision.

The Kids Ecology Corps—http://www.kidsecology.org/activity_4.html. Create acid rain in your kitchen.

In the Classroom

The Educators Toolkit—http://www.eagle.ca/~matink/themes/Environ/acidrain. html. Links to lesson plans and activities on acid rain.

Thirteen Ed Online—http://www.thirteen.org/edonline/wue/air2_procedures. html. A class project on acid rain.

The Foundation for Clean Air Progress—http://www.cleanairprogress.org/classroom/teachers.asp. Offers resources and links for teachers.

33

Everything Is Related.

BIOMES AND ECOSYSTEMS

New Words

> Biodiversity
> Ecosystem and Biome
> Food Chain
> Microorganisms
> Producers, Consumers, Recyclers

What Is a Biome or Ecosystem?

A biome is a major region of distinctive plant and animal groups. Each biome has similar rainfall, elevation, temperature, and soil. Ecosystems are interactions among plants, animals, and microorganisms and their environment. They work together as a unit. Many ecosystems survive within each biome. Everything in an ecosystem is related to everything else, so ecosystems will fail if they do not remain in balance. Each species needs food, water, and shelter. If you are interested in the environment, this will be a great topic. Go broad and describe different biomes or go narrow for ecosystems.

What Can I Write About?

Explain and describe what a biome is. Name and describe several world biomes.

Compare biomes and ecosystems. Or choose a type of biome and discuss it, for example, wetlands. What is the climate like? What animals and plants live there?

Describe the ecosystem in your neighborhood. Is it large? Small? Tell about the food chain that supports your ecosystem.

Are the ecosystems in your area surviving? Are they being degraded because of development or for another reason? Make a phone call and ask questions of a local environmental agency. Write about it.

Are There Books or Videos About Biomes and Ecosystems?

We can't begin to tell you the best books. There are many. Use your library catalog.

Erickson, Jon. *Environmental Geology: Facing the Challenges of Our Changing Earth.* New York: Facts on File, 2002.

Kalman, Bobbie. *What Is a Biome?* New York: Crabtree, 1998.

Richardson, Gillian. *Ecosystems: Species, Spaces, and Relationships.* Chicago: Raintree, 2003.

U-X-L Encyclopedia of Biomes. Detroit: UXL, 2003.

Walker, Pam. *Ecosystem Science Fair Projects Using Worms, Leaves, Crickets and Other Stuff.* Berkeley Heights, NJ: Enslow, 2004.

Can the Internet Help?

Ecosystems—http://library.thinkquest.org/11353/ecosystems.htm. What is the difference between ecosystems and biomes?

What Is an Ecosystem?—http://www.nres.uiuc.edu/outreach/esm_il_lo/intro-es.htm

Food Chains—http://www.planetpals.com/foodchain.html

Houston Habitat Alteration—http://www.harc.edu/4site/4siteFCRhal.html. Find your own area by searching: *city name, ecosystem.*

Biomes—http://www.cotf.edu/ete/modules/msese/earthsysflr/biomes.html. Excellent place to start.

Think Quest—http://library.thinkquest.org/TQ0310225/. Survival in the different biomes.

Biomes and Ecosystems—http://mbgnet.mobot.org

 **TA DA!**

Ecosystems in Action!

Environmental Protection Agency—http://www.epa.gov/students/ecosyste.htm. Links to great projects you can participate in to help the environment.

Kids Did This Hotlist—http://sln.fi.edu/tfi/hotlists/kid-sci.html. Science projects by kids.

Experiment

Create an ecosystem in your backyard. Keep a journal and describe it. What worked? What did not? Why?

In the Classroom

Schoolyard Habitats—http://www.nwf.org/schoolyardhabitats/index.cfm. Have your class create and certify your schoolyard habitat.

Introduction to Biomes—http://www.teachersfirst.com/lessons/biomes/#. Bibliography, activities, background information.

Where Have All the Songbirds Gone?

RACHEL CARSON

New Words

Food Chain
Environmental Movement
DDT
Pesticides
Ecology

Who Is Rachel Carson?

As a child, Rachel Carson was quiet and shy. She spent most of her time either with books or out of doors enjoying nature. Her very first publication, in *St. Nicholas Literary Magazine for Children*, was when she was 10 years old. As she grew up, she continued to enjoy both writing and nature. She started college as an English major but graduated with a degree in zoology. Around that time, the government was spraying wide areas with pesticides to kill off harmful insects like mosquitoes and fire ants. Rachel noticed that wherever the spraying occurred, other creatures were deformed or dying. She realized that the birds and mammals who ate insects received the poison also, and she wrote a book, *Silent Spring*, to warn people about the danger. Chemical companies and even the government attacked her, but many people read her book, and they believed her. The environmental protection movement was begun.

What Can I Write About?

Describe Rachel Carson's observations about the food chain.

Discuss how Rachel Carson's early life influenced her ideas as an adult.

Compare the use of DDT with other means of controlling harmful insects. Discuss why Ms. Carson warned against the use of DDT.

Explain Rachel Carson's legacy by writing about her impact on the beginnings of the environmental movement.

Read *Silent Spring* and describe Rachel Carson's main ideas.

Are There Books on Rachel Carson?

You can find the influential books she has written as well as books about Rachel Carson.

Carson, Rachel. *The Sea Around Us.* New York: Oxford, 1951.

Carson, Rachel. *The Sense of Wonder.* New York: Harper & Row, 1965.

Carson, Rachel. *Silent Spring.* Boston: Houghton Mifflin, 2002. First published in 1962.

Landau, Elaine. *Rachel Carson and the Environmental Movement.* New York: Children's Press, 2004.

Roth, Anna. *Current Biography 1951.* New York: Wilson, 1951.

Saari, Peggy, ed. *Prominent Women of the 20th Century.* UXL, 1996.

Can the Internet Help?

This Web site devoted to Rachel Carson includes her biography, legacy, and links to other environmental sites—http://www.rachelcarson.org/

PBS—http://www.pbs.org/wgbh/aso/databank/entries/btcars.html. Gves a brief summary of Rachel Carson's accomplishments.

The National Institutes of Health—http://www.niehs.nih.gov/oc/factsheets/fskids.htm. Discusses current research on the effects on kids of pesticides and other environmental hazards.

The Boston Research Center—http://www.brc21.org/carson/carson_long.html. Tells of Rachel's accomplishments and of those who followed her.

National Geographic article about the environmental movement—http://news.nationalgeographic.com/news/2002/04/0419_020419_rachelcarson.html. Excellent resource.

 **TA DA!**

Ecology in Action!

PBS—http://www.pbs.org/wgbh/aso/ontheedge/ecology/. View an online comic book, *Ecology Is Hep!*

Experiment

The Chemical Heritage Foundation—http://chem.lapeer.org/Chem1Docs/EggshellTitration.html. See what acid can do to an eggshell! Try acid/base titration of an eggshell.

In the Classroom

The Discovery Channel—http://school.discovery.com/lessonplans/programs/championsofland/. Environmental lesson plans.

Environmental Protection Agency—http://www.epa.gov/safewater/kids/exper.html. Classroom activities and experiments on water purity.

Under the Sea.

JACQUES COUSTEAU

New Words

Environmentalist
Marine Biologist, Oceanographer
Self-Contained Underwater Breathing Apparatus (scuba)

Who Is Jacques Cousteau?

French oceanographer Jacques Cousteau explored undersea from the Amazon River to the Antarctic ice shelf. He created television documentaries and wrote books about his research undersea. He introduced viewers to a world of sharks, whales, dolphins, sunken treasure, and coral reefs. Cousteau worked as an environmentalist, looking after the health of the ocean environment. His inventions—the Aqua-Lung™, the underwater camera, and the one-man submarine—led to a new era of underwater discovery. Cousteau enjoyed many things and was able to fight for the environment he loved. If you love marine life, write about Jacques Cousteau.

What Can I Write About?

Write a biography of Cousteau's life. Choose one part of his life, so you won't have so much to cover. Maybe you could write about his youth, or his "ocean lab work."

Write about the work Cousteau did on the *Calypso*. It would be very interesting to describe the *Calypso* and its labs. (Be sure to attach a picture to your report—or bring one to class.)

Write about some of Cousteau's inventions. His Aqua-Lung was used after World War II to find unexploded water mines. It paved the way for scuba gear as we know it today.

Are There Books or Videos on Cousteau?

Use your library catalog. Ask the librarian to help with reference books.

Bankston, John. *Jacques-Yves Cousteau: His Story Under the Sea.* Bear, DE: Mitchell-Lane, 2003.

Cousteau, Jacques. *The Ocean World.* New York: Abradale, 1985.

Cousteau, Jacques. *The Silent World*. Washington, DC: National Geographic, 2004 (or any previous edition; first published in 1953).

Cousteau, Jacques-Yves. *Jacques Cousteau's Calypso*. New York: Harry N. Abrams, 1983.

DuTemple, Lesley A. *Jacques Cousteau*. A&E Biography. Minneapolis: Lerner, 2000.

Hopping, Lorraine Jean. *Jacques Cousteau: Saving Our Seas*. New York: McGraw-Hill, 2000.

Can the Internet Help?

Aquatic Network: Jacques Cousteau—http://www.aquanet.com/features/cousteau/cousteau.htm. This site links to very good information.

Obituary on CNN—http://www.cnn.com/WORLD/9706/25/cousteau.obit/index.html. Hear Jean Michael Cousteau talk about his father, Jacques Cousteau.

The Cousteau Organization—http://cousteau.org/. Videos, information, papers. Be sure to ride the submarine.

Scuba Diving History—http://scuba.about.com/od/history/

Wikipedia's biography and information about Cousteau—http://en.wikipedia.org/wiki/Jacques-Yves_Cousteau. Lots of links to other information.

 **TA DA!**

Cousteau in Action!

Play "fish" games free online or download—http://www.digifish.us/

Find a John Denver album and teach your classmates the lyrics to "Calypso," dedicated to Cousteau—http://www.dweller.com/musicofjd.html (Denver singing)—http://home.wanadoo.nl/mtenbrug/denver/calypso/denver_6.htm (Lyrics and salute)

Online Summer Games—http://www.kidsdomain.com/games/summer.html. Several involve underwater activities.

Experiment

Find out what a diving bell is and make one to show your classmates—http://www.seagrant.wisc.edu/madisonjason11/experiment_divebell.html. Explore the cool science on this Web site.

In the Classroom

Enjoy *Jacques Cousteau: The Ocean World* or another of his books for your own reading pleasure. Show *The Silent World* or one of the documentaries from his series, *The Undersea World of Jacques Cousteau*.

CNN lesson plans—Cousteau—http://cnnstudentnews.cnn.com/2002/fyi/lesson.plans/05/09/nat.sound/

36

There's a Fungus Among Us!

FUNGI

New Words

Cell Wall—Spores
Fungus—Fungi
Mycologists
Organisms
Penicillin

What Are Fungi?

Are you planning to become a mycologist? If so, you will spend your time studying fungi. The kingdom Fungi includes some of the most important organisms, both in terms of our environment and their economic roles. In fungi, we have both the good guys and the bad guys. Fungi break down dead organic material. This helps continue the cycle of nutrients our ecosystems need. Most of us think of mushrooms when we mention fungi, but the topic is broader than that. There are fungal diseases, and don't forget mold and yeast. They are fungi, too. If you have ever had a fungus, it may be interesting to find out what caused it, and be sure to add your own experience to your report.

What Can I Write About?

Describe the kingdom Fungi. What is it? Name and describe a few of its inhabitants.

What role do fungi play in our ecosystems? Do we need them? How do they help or harm? Don't forget examples and descriptions.

Describe the friendly fungi—and fungi enemies. Make a comparison table as part of your report.

Discuss the fungi that cause animal and human diseases (ringworm, athlete's foot, yuck!) Or discuss the fungi that cause plant diseases (leaf, root, and stem rot.) Choose one single fungus or a group.

Select one fungus to discuss. I would choose the truffle because it is SO expensive. (Look it up.)

Are There Books About Fungi?

We can't begin to tell you the best books. There are many. Use your library catalog. Do not forget the reference area, where you can find background information and statistics.

Allen, Missy. *Dangerous Plants and Mushrooms.* New York: Chelsea House, 1993.

Silverman, Buffy. *Molds and Fungi.* San Diego, CA: Kidshaven, 2005.

Silverstein, Alvin, Virginia Silverstein, and Robert Silverstein. *Fungi.* New York: Twenty-first Century, 1996.

Souza, D. M. *What Is a Fungus?* New York: Franklin Watts, 2002.

Viegas, Jennifer. *Fungi and Molds.* New York: Rosen, 2004.

Can the Internet Help?

Learn and have fun with Sam Sleuth—http://www.microbe.org/. Good basic information about fungi.

Dr. Fungus—http://www.doctorfungus.org/thefungi/index.htm. A little difficult, but there is a lot here.

The Amazing Kingdom of Fungi—http://waynesword.palomar.edu/ww0504.htm

FAQs about truffling—http://www.natruffling.org/faq.htm

How Fungi May Effect Other Organisms—http://www.ajhslibrary.org/fungi_may_affect_other_organ.htm. Good links to follow.

Kingdom Fungi: Mushrooms, Molds, Yeast—http://www.geocities.com/RainForest/6243/diversity3.html. Excellent site with links.

 **TA DA!**

Fungi in Action!

Try this experiment—http://pbskids.org/zoom/activities/sci/yeast.html or http://pbskids.org/zoom/activities/sci/yeastpartii.html. Report your findings on the Internet at PBSKIDS.

Experiment with Mold—http://www.kidzone.ws/science/mold.htm or http://www.exploratorium.edu/science_explorer/mold.html

Experiment

Science fair coming soon?—http://www.mycomasters.com/Science-fair-projects.html. Here are a few projects using mushrooms and other fungi.

In the Classroom

Fun Facts about Fungi—http://www.herbarium.usu.edu/fungi/funfacts/factindx.htm and http://www.dmturner.org/Teacher/Library/5thText/SimplePart2.html. Includes games and teaching activities.

37

Eternal Summer

GLOBAL WARMING

New Words

Climate
Degree
Greenhouse Effect
Ice Age
Temperature

What Is Global Warming?

Over the past 100 years, the average temperature on Earth has risen one degree. That doesn't sound like much. You probably can't tell the difference between a 76 degree day and a 77 degree day. But if the average temperature continues to rise, it could cause some real problems. For instance, the ice in the polar ice caps could melt, making the sea level rise. That could flood coastal areas. There might be a climate change, bringing drought to now fertile climates. Some plant and animal species might not be able to adapt. Scientists don't know for sure what will happen, but they do know that even though 1 degree doesn't seem too important, the average temperature in the Ice Age was only 7 degrees colder than it is now.

What Can I Write About?

Discuss the possible causes of global warming. Can we help reverse it?

Consider the problems and the benefits of global warming.

Explain several of the methods scientists use to monitor the changes in the climate.

Explain the greenhouse effect.

Are There Books on Global Warming?

We can't begin to tell you the best books. There are many. Use your library catalog. Do not forget the reference area, where you can find background information and statistics.

Lerner, K. Lee, and Brenda Wilmoth Lerner, eds. *Gale Encyclopedia of Science.* 3d ed. Vol. 3. Detroit: Gale, 2004.

Mongillo, John, and Linda Zierdt-Warshaw. *Encyclopedia of Environmental Science.* Phoenix, AZ: Oryx, 2000.

New Book of Popular Science. Vol. 2. Danbury, CT: Grolier, 2004.

Newton, David E., Rob Nagel, and Bridget Travers. *UXL Encyclopedia of Science.* Vol. 5. Detroit: UXL, 1998.

Can the Internet Help?

Environmental Protection Agency—http://www.epa.gov/globalwarming/kids/. Explains the causes and effects of global warming.

PEW Center—http://www.pewclimate.org/global-warming-basics/kidspage.cfm. Discusses global warming and what you can do to help prevent it.

ThinkQuest—http://library.thinkquest.org/CR0215471/global_warming.htm. Explains global warming, including what the government is doing to combat it.

Green Facts Organization—http://www.greenfacts.org/studies/climate_change/. Answers questions about global warming and climate change.

Carnegie Mellon University—http://www.gcrio.org/gwcc/. Discusses the impact of global warming.

The Ozone Hole Tour from Cambridge University—http://www.atm.ch.cam.ac.uk/tour/. Especially for kids.

The Knaurer Group's site on global warming—http://globalwarming.enviroweb.org/. Explore how natural processes have, and human activity can, change the environment.

 **TA DA!**

Global Warming in Action!

View an animation and games and activities on your topic—http://www.epa.gov/globalwarming/kids/animations.html (EPA) or http://shand.saskpower.com/greenhouse/kids/activities/activities.shtml (Sask Power).

Experiment

Energy Quest—http://www.energyquest.ca.gov/projects/greenhouse.html. Re-create the greenhouse effect in this experiment.

In the Classroom

The Greenhouse Effect in a Jar from the Franklin Institute—http://www.fi.edu/tfi/activity/earth/earth-5.html

USA Today—http://www.usatoday.com/weather/resources/climate/climate-sci-resources.htm. Links to articles about climate change and global warming.

Teachers' Information Sheet on the Greenhouse Effect from ARIC—http://www.ace.mmu.ac.uk/Resources/Teaching_Packs/Key_Stage_4/Climate_Change/01t.php

Danger, Will Robinson! Danger!

HAZARDOUS WASTE

New Words

Contamination—Safe Disposal
Emergency Response Teams
Environmental Protection Agency and
    Department of Energy
Landfill
Reduce—Recycle

What Is Hazard Waste?

You watch a few drops of gasoline fall to the ground as your dad fills the lawn mower. Your mom sprays her hair so it will look nice all day long. Ants invade, and your mom puts out poison. Paints, pesticides, and many other products in your home may be poisonous. These and other hazardous materials (HAZMAT) are dangerous to humans, animals, and plants. When large quantities of hazardous materials spill, whole communities may have to be vacated. The EPA and local agencies are actively working to make sure the environment is safe for future generations. Learn more—and find out what you can do to help.

What Can I Write About?

Write about the steps your community takes to control the disposal of hazardous waste.

Write about household hazardous waste. What are the dangers of improper disposal?

Write about the Superfund. Describe a project that has been worked on under this fund.

Explain what a hazardous waste fill is. What is done to protect the environment?

Report on a large spill, like the *Exxon Valdez*, or a pollution crisis, like Love Canal. How did it happen? What was the impact on the environment? How was it cleaned up?

Are There Books or Videos on Hazardous Waste?

Use your library catalog. Do not forget the reference area and environmental encyclopedias.

Bang, Molly. *Chattanooga Sludge: Cleaning Toxic Sludge*. San Diego, CA: Harcourt, 1996.

Bryan, Nichol. *Love Canal: Pollution Crisis.* Milwaukee, WI: World Almanac, 2004.

Cothran, Helen, ed. *Garbage and Recycling: Opposing Viewpoints.* San Diego, CA: Greenhaven, 2003.

Kellert, Stephen, ed. *Macmillan Encyclopedia of the Environment.* New York: Macmillan, 1997.

Marsh, Carole. *Heroes & Helpers Adventure Diaries: "Haz" Matt, Hazardous Materials Worker!* Peachtree City, GA: Gallopade, 2002.

Can the Internet Help?

Garbage: How Can My Community Reduce Waste?—http://www.learner.org/exhibits/garbage/intro.html

Waste Management Information from the Department of Energy—http://web.em.doe.gov/em30/

Hazardous Waste from Newton's Apple—http://www.ktca.org/newtons/13/hazmat.html

Superfund for Kids—http://www.epa.gov/superfund/kids/index.htm and http://www.epa.gov/superfund/. Be sure to read the stories.

ETC Hazardous Waste—http://www.etc.org/index.cfm. Be sure to see "What is a hazardous waste landfill?"

Household Hazardous Waste—http://www.metrokc.gov/dnr/kidsweb/haz_waste_main.htm and http://www.epa.gov/epaoswer/non-hw/househld/hhw.htm

Oil Spills—Especially for Kids—http://response.restoration.noaa.gov/kids/kids.html

Hazardous Materials in Schools—http://www.edfacilities.org/rl/hazardous_materials.cfm. Articles on problems schools should watch for.

**TA DA!**

Students in Action against HAZMAT!

Especially for Kids—http://response.restoration.noaa.gov/kids/kids.html. This page has everything, including several experiments.

Visit the Virtual House—http://www.epa.gov/grtlakes/seahome/housewaste/house/house.htm. Find the products that are hazardous and their effects on you.

Experience

Publish a newsletter that includes a list of hazardous materials in the home and their antidotes, warning symbols, local statistics, and local agencies that will help in an emergency.

In the Classroom

See the University of Missouri list of resources for all grade levels or the National Geographic lesson plan—http://muextension.missouri.edu/explore/wasteman/wm5003.htm or http://www.nationalgeographic.com/xpeditions/lessons/14/g912/tghazardous.html

It's Not Easy Being Green.

PHOTOSYNTHESIS

New Words

Carbon Dioxide
Carbon Cycle
Chlorophyll
Osmosis
Oxygen
Transpiration

What Is Photosynthesis?

To grow and develop, plants use a process called photosynthesis. The word itself comes from *photo*, meaning "light," and *synthesis*, which means "putting together." Originally, scientists thought that plants took their energy from the soil, but they now know that what plants need are energy from the sun, water from the ground, and carbon dioxide from the air. Plants use photosynthesis to put carbohydrates together out of carbon dioxide and water, using the light energy of the sun. In addition to giving us food, plants give us air to breathe. As a plant takes in the carbon dioxide, it gives off oxygen. Improve your green thumb by learning more about plants.

What Can I Write About?

Explain how the photosynthesis process works.

Describe why leaves change color in the autumn.

Discuss the role of photosynthesis in the carbon cycle.

Write about the scientific discoveries that led to the understanding of photosynthesis.

Are There Books on Photosynthesis?

We can't begin to tell you the best books. There are many. Use your library catalog. Do not forget the reference area, where you can find background information and statistics.

Lerner, K. Lee, and Brenda Wilmoth Lerner, eds. *Gale Encyclopedia of Science.* 3d ed. Vol.5. Detroit: Gale, 2004.

New Book of Popular Science. Vol. 4. Danbury, CT: Grolier, 2004.

Newton, David E., Rob Nagel, and Bridget Travers. *UXL Encyclopedia of Science.* Vol. 7. Detroit: UXL, 1998.

Tanacredi, John T., and John Loret, eds. *Experiment Central.* Vol.3. Detroit: UXL, 2000.

Tocci, Salvatore. *Chemistry Around You.* New York: Arco, 1985.

World Book Student Discovery Encyclopedia. Chicago: World Book, 2003.

Can the Internet Help?

Cornwall Wildlife Trust—http://www.cornwallwildlifetrust.org.uk/educate/ kids/photsyn.htm. A very basic explanation of photosynthesis.

Real Trees—http://www.realtrees4kids.org/sixeight/letseat.htm. Explains photosynthesis and tree growth.

Science Master—http://www.sciencemaster.com/jump/life/leaves.php. How leaves change color.

Ribbons of Green—http://www.mcjags.com/rog/greenspaces.html. Explains the benefits of photosynthesis.

 **TA DA!**

Photosynthesis in Action!

Science Isn't Hard—http://www.scienceisnthard.com/Photosynthesis.htm. Watch a silly video on photosynthesis.

Experiment

U.S. Department of Education—http://www.ed.gov/pubs/parents/Science/ celery.html. Demonstrate osmosis in plants using celery.

Fun Science—http://www.funsci.com/fun3_en/exper1/exper1.htm#photosynthesis. Experiments in environmental education, including photosynthesis. You may need an adult to help you with some of them.

In the Classroom

ProTeacher—http://www.proteacher.com/110013.shtml. Lesson plans for plants, photosynthesis, and transpiration.

The National Biological Information Infrastructure—http://www.nbii.gov/education/ botany.html. Collects several sites with good information on photosynthesis, transpiration, and botany by grade level.

Education World—http://www.education-world.com/a_lesson/lesson024.shtml. Has lessons and activities demonstrating photosynthesis.

40

An Ecosystem of Your Own.

POND LIFE

New Words

Amphibious
Biomes
Emergent and Submergent Plants
Food Chain
Interdependence
Microorganisms
Unicellular

What Is Special About Pond Life?

One of the wonderful things about ponds, even the small pond in your backyard, is that each contains a whole ecosystem. When you study life in a pond, you begin to understand the cycle of nature and how it is all interrelated. There you will find everything from unicellular organisms to amphibious animals like frogs. Not only that, but land and air animals contribute to life in a pond as well. And the pond can't do without plant life. Since a pond is fresh water, it will be easy to create and maintain your own pond, if you don't already have one.

What Can I Write About?

Research what a pond really is. How does it compare with a lake? What relationship does it have to a river?

How does a pond form in nature to create a small ecosystem? What is needed?

Write about the microbe animals that are part of a pond. Explain why they are important.

Write about the critters that live in a pond. The frog is always fun, since it starts life as a tadpole.

Interested in plants? Study the plants that grow in a pond. What is their role?

Are There Books on Pond Life?

Don't forget the reference area, where you can get background information and statistics.

Cooper, Ann. *Around the Pond.* Niwot, CO: Roberts Rinehart, 1998.

Nadeau, Isaac. *Food Chains in a Pond Habitat.* New York: PowerKids, 2002.

Reid, George K. *Pond Life: A Guide to Common Plants and Animals of North American Ponds and Lakes.* Rev. ed. New York: St. Martin's Press, 2001.

Sayre, April Pulley. *Lake and Pond.* New York: Twenty-First Century, 1996.

Can the Internet Help?

The Microbe Zoo—http://commtechlab.msu.edu/sites/dlc-me/zoo/zwpmain.html. Microscopic animals that live in a pond.

Lakes and Ponds—http://mbgnet.mobot.org/fresh/lakes/index.htm. Good background information. The links here are some of the best.

The Smallest Page on the Web—http://www.microscopy-uk.org.uk/mag/wimsmall/smal1.html. What is in a small drop of water? Find out here.

Pond Life Animals—http://www.enchantedlearning.com/biomes/pond/pondlife.shtml. Good site for background or specific pond life.

42explore—Pond Life—http://www.42explore.com/pond.htm. Ideas for research and exploration of your own.

Microscopic Pond Life Identification Guide—http://www.microscopy-uk.org.uk/index.html? and http://www.microscopy-uk.org.uk/pond/. Take the virtual pond dip.

 **TA DA!**

Create Your Own

Create your own pond. Half-Barrel Pondlife—http://www.jeffcook.com/hbpond.shtml, Explore a Pond—http://octopus.gma.org/turtles/pond.html, Populate your virtual pond—http://www.uen.org/utahlink/pond/virtpond2.cgi

Experiment

Ponds are a fantastic source of microbes, which are easy to see with the proper magnification. Scoop up some pond water in a jar and examine the water using a magnifying glass or a microscope. How many different types of microbes can you see? Compare the types of microbes you find at the top of the pond with those you find near the bottom of the pond. Why are the microbes near the surface different from those at deeper levels? (This activity is from the University of Michigan, Digital Learning Center, http://commtechlab.msu.edu/sites/dlc-me/zoo/zwpmain.html)

In the Classroom

Lesson Planet—http://www.lessonplanet.com/search/search/?keywords=pond+life. Keyword "pond life." Excellent selections to use in the classroom.

Read *Life in a Pond* by Karen Secules and use the lesson plan here—http://www.lessonplanspage.com/ScienceLALifeInAPond3.htm. Good links and ideas.

Pond Action——http://www.uen.org/utahlink/pond/action.html. Links the teacher to a huge collection, by discipline, e.g., Pond Math.

Nine Lives.

RECYCLING

New Words

Compost
Natural Resources
Solid Waste

What Is Recycling?

Five hundred million tons of trash and garbage are thrown away in the United States every year. That's a lot of garbage! We need to think of ways to reduce the amount. Much of it could be recycled and used in different ways. Newspapers can be used to make compost or new paper; aluminum, glass, and plastic can be melted down to make new containers. Old computers and cell phones can be taken apart so that the pieces can be reused. Not only does recycling save landfill space and natural resources, it saves energy. Twenty aluminum cans could be made from recycled aluminum for the energy that it would take to make one new can. Remember the three R's: reduce, reuse, recycle.

What Can I Write About?

Choose one recyclable material, such as aluminum, yard waste, plastic, paper, or glass, and discuss the recycling process.

Write about landfills, including problems, benefits, and how they work.

Compare and contrast recycling one material with producing it new.

Think of at least three ways to dispose of garbage and compare them.

Think of a recycling plan for your family or your classroom. Be sure to find out where to recycle materials and how to store them. Report on the results.

Are There Books on Recycling?

We can't begin to tell you the best books. There are many. Use your library catalog. Do not forget the reference area, where you can find background information and statistics.

Childcraft: The How and Why Library. Chicago: World Book, 2003.

Lerner, K. Lee, and Brenda Wilmoth Lerner, eds. *Gale Encyclopedia of Science.* 3d ed. Vol. 5. Detroit: Gale, 2004.

Mongillo, John, and Linda Zierdt-Warshaw. *Encyclopedia of Environmental Science*. Phoenix, AZ: Oryx, 2000.

World Book Student Discovery Encyclopedia. Chicago: World Book, 2003.

Can the Internet Help?

Put in your zip code to see what recycling opportunities are in your neighborhood—http://www.epa.gov/epahome/commsearch.htm

The Environmental Protection Agency's Student Center—http://www.epa.gov/students/waste.htm. Shows about solid waste management and hazardous waste.

The Washington State Department of Ecology—http://www.ecy.wa.gov/programs/swfa/kidspage/. Tells how materials are recycled.

The Steel Recycling Institute—http://www.recycle-steel.org/. Explains recycling cans and cars.

U.S. Geological Survey—http://pubs.usgs.gov/fs/fs060-01/. Recycling computers—is it worth it? U.S.

Tufts University—http://www.tufts.edu/tuftsrecycles/more/USstats.html. Offers a time line of recycling history and information about landfills.

 **TA DA!**

Recycling in Action!

The EPA's Recycle City—http://www.epa.gov/recyclecity/. This interactive virtual town shows the advantages of recycling as well as what happens when nothing is recycled.

Experiment

Texas A&M University—http://aggie-horticulture.tamu.edu/sustainable/slidesets/kidscompost/cover.html. Recycle your yard waste into compost and use it in your garden.

EcoKids—http://www.ecokidsonline.com/pub/fun_n_games/printables/activities/assets/science_nature/paper_making.pdf. Make your own recycled paper.

In the Classroom

Use the EPA's Recycle City in your classroom—http://www.epa.gov/recyclecity/activity.htm

Use your classroom for a model of recycling, following the Tools for Zero Waste in Schools—http://www.kidsrecycle.org/index.php

GEOLOGY

Geology is the science of the origin, history, and structure of the earth. Studying the earth today reveals life long ago. It helps us understand life and its evolution better. It is hard to fathom what the earth was like thousands or millions of years ago, but our studies of geology help us envision it. Learn more on this topic at the library. Better still, go on a dig of your own to discover the past.

What Color Is Your Aura?

ATMOSPHERE

New Words

Atmospheric Gases
Meteorology
Troposphere, Stratosphere, Mesosphere,
    Thermosphere
Nitrogen and Oxygen
Clean Air Act

What Is the Atmosphere?

When we talk about the atmosphere, we mean the air we breathe, the breeze that blows, the clouds that form, the gases that surround us, and the weather. The atmosphere surrounds us in layers of gases like a blanket. These gases make up exactly what we need to breathe. How does Earth's atmosphere determine climate? Or seasons? How do we impact the atmosphere? Are the gases in the atmosphere better today than before the Clean Air Act? Read about the atmosphere and its importance to us. Find out more!

What Can I Write About?

What is the earth's atmosphere? What impact does the atmosphere have on the earth?

Write about the layers of the atmosphere. What is the role of each?

Explain how the atmosphere is made up of nitrogen and oxygen and other gases.

Report on one of the effects of what is happening in the atmosphere today: air pollution, greenhouse effect, or ozone depletion.

Learn about the Clean Air Act. Be sure to include some of the changes that have been made and whether or not they have improved our atmosphere.

Write about a company or organization near you that is doing something to improve the earth's atmosphere. See if you can get an interview with someone who works there.

Are There Books About the Atmosphere?

Use the library catalog. Reference books will be helpful. Ask the librarian.

Asimov, Isaac. *How Did We Find Out About the Atmosphere?* New York: Walker, 1985.

Dickinson, Terence. *Exploring the Sky by Day: The Equinox Guide to Weather and the Atmosphere.* Camden East, ON: Camden House, 1988.

Earth. E. Explore Series. London: Dorling Kindersley, 2004.

Gallant, Roy A. *Atmosphere: Sea of Air.* New York: Benchmark, 2003.

Luhr, James, ed. *Earth.* New York: DK Publishing, 2003.

Can the Internet Help?

Atmosphere—http://sunshine.chpc.utah.edu/labs/atmosphere/atmosphere_main.html. An excellent basic explanation with graphics.

Global Climate—http://www.exploratorium.edu/climate/. Choose Atmosphere to learn about the effects of atmosphere on climate.

The Atmosphere, from NASA—http://liftoff.msfc.nasa.gov/academy/space/atmosphere.html

Enchanted Learning—http://www.enchantedlearning.com/subjects/astronomy/planets/earth/Atmosphere.shtml. Be sure to look at the other topics that have to do with the atmosphere.

The earth's atmosphere layers—http://www.windows.ucar.edu/tour/link=/earth/Atmosphere/layers.html&edu=elem. For beginner, intermediate, and advanced learners.

The Atmosphere—http://www.mardiros.net/atmosphere/index.html. What keeps us alive.

The Clean Air Act and information about it—http://www.cleanairprogress.org/classroom/index.asp

TA DA!

The Atmosphere in Action!

Atmospheric Optics—http://www.sundog.clara.co.uk/atoptics/phenom.htm. Use the index—and enjoy these beautiful images with explanations. Use your own digital camera and take a few photographs of your own.

Experiment

Look at these experiments showing how NASA studies air. You try, too—http://kids.earth.nasa.gov/air.htm

In the Classroom

Lesson Plans and Activities for the Classroom—http://www.windows.ucar.edu/tour/link=/teacher_resources/activity.html#aw2. Lots of them.

Teacher's Troposphere—http://pao.cnmoc.navy.mil/Educate/zeus/teacher/teacher.htm. Everything you need to make an exciting unit.

Let's Go Spelunking!

CAVES

New Words

Cavern, Grotto
Cavers/Spelunkers
Formations
Hollow, Recess, Cavity, Core, Chambers
Speleology

What Are Caves?

Some of us believe that caves can be creep crawly places. Many are. But there are many caves around the world where visitors can safely go with guides; these are wondrous places. Not everyone likes to go into the earth, but cavers (and speleologists) love to explore these fascinating spots. They will travel all over the world to find unexplored caves. You can explore them, too, because of the great pictures that cavers share online. This is called being an armchair traveler. So, grab your hard hat, boots, and a couple of flashlights, and let's go to the library or get online and find out more about spelunking!

What Can I Write About?

What are caves? How are they formed? Who explores them? What lives there?

Describe several formations found in caves, for example, stalagactites, stalagmites, flowstone.

Write about a type of cave: lava tube caves, solution caves, sea caves, or erosional caves.

There are caves in almost every state. Write about a cave where you live. What made the tunnel? What kind of rock? Describe some of the rooms. Include pictures.

Like history? Write about the caveman. Include the implements he used to stay alive, the food he ate, and how he lived. Yes, describe the science of living BC.

Are There Books or Videos on Caves?

Here are a few suggestions. Use the catalog to find more.

Brimner, Larry Dane. *Caves.* True Book. New York: Children's, 2000.

Courbon, Paul. *Atlas of the Great Caves of the World.* St. Louis, MO: Cave, 1989.

Geology of Caves and Caverns. [videorecording]. Maumee, OH: Instructional, 2000.

Gurnee, R. H. *Gurnee Guide to American Caves: A Comprehensive Guide to the Caves in the United States Open to the Public.* Teaneck, NJ: Zephyrus, 1979.

Harrison, David L. *Caves: Mysteries Beneath Our Feet.* Honesdale, PA: Boyds Mills, 2001.

Moore, George W. *Speleology: Caves and the Cave Environment.* St. Louis, MO: Cave, 1997.

Can the Internet Help?

Encarta's Caves—http://encarta.msn.com/encyclopedia_761561626/Cave.html. Good basic information to begin your search.

Virtual Cave—http://www.goodearthgraphics.com/virtcave/index.html. Explore the four kinds of caves and learn about them. This is one of the best sites with the most complete information for your report. Spend time exploring.

Good basic information—http://www.bridalcave.com/kidspage/. Do rocks grow? Who lives in a cave? What's it like in there?

Describes several formations found in caves—http://www.cumberlandadventures. com/cave/form.html. Stalagactites, stalagmites, popcorn, rimstone.

The Armchair Caver—http://web.ukonline.co.uk/arthur.vause/. Enjoy the cave without the climb—and creepy crawly things.

The Life and Times of Early Man—http://members.aol.com/Donnclass/ EarlyMan.html

Caves from ThinkQuest—http://library.thinkquest.org/J0112123/lavamain.htm

The National Speleological Society—http://www.caves.org/. Conservation, music, art, more.

Caves Theme Page—Gander Academy—http://www.cdli.ca/CITE/cave.htm. Excellent glossary and links

 **TA DA!**

Caves in Action!

Games, virtual tour, and activities for fun—http://www.caveofthewinds.com/ test/kidpage.html

Experiment

Homeschooling page for caves—http://homeschooling.gomilpitas.com/explore/ caves.htm. Good links and activities.

In the Classroom

Three lesson plans: Cavern Geology, Cavern Life, People and Caverns— http://www.caverntours.com/Lessonplans.htm

Not My Fault.

EARTHQUAKES

New Words

Aftershock
Magnitude
Richter Scale
Seismic Waves—Seismologists

What Is an Earthquake?

You are fast asleep. The bed moves, your games and toys fall out of cupboards, and your books fall on the floor. What can it be? If you live in an area that has tremors and earthquakes, you know exactly what is happening. Earthquakes are frightening because we have no control over them; they are a force of nature. Learn more about earthquakes and what causes them.

What Can I Write About?

Write about tracking earthquakes. Who does it? What instruments do they use? Explain how they work. Bring report examples to class.

Write about faults. Describe the four basic kinds of faults and how they happen.

If you live in an area where earthquakes are likely to happen, you may want to write about being prepared for an earthquake and the organizations that help earthquake survivors. (FEMA and Red Cross or Salvation Army.)

Write about earthquake resistant buildings that are being built in the earthquake prone areas. Explain what architects and specialists are doing to keep them safe.

Read about the 2005 earthquake in Pakistan. Discuss the quake and its aftereffects.

Are There Books or Videos on Earthquakes?

Use your library catalog. Do not forget the reference area, where you can find more information and statistics.

George, Linda. *Plate Tectonics*. San Diego, CA: Kidhaven, 2003.

Simon, Seymour. *Earthquakes*. New York: HarperTrophy, 1995.

Sutherland, Lin. *Earthquakes and Volcanoes*. Pleasantville, New York: Reader's Digest Children's Publishing, 2000.

Tanaka, Shelley. *Earthquake! On a Peaceful Morning Disaster Strikes San Francisco.* New York: Hyperion, 2004.

Trueit, Trudi Strain. *Earthquakes!* New York: Franklin Watts, 2003.

Van Rose, Susanna. *Volcanoes and Earthquakes* Eyewitness Books. New York: DK Publishing, 2004.

Can the Internet Help?

History since 1906 and two excellent animations that help you understand earthquakes—http://www.crustal.ucsb.edu/ics/understanding/

Four basic types of faults—http://www.tinynet.com/faults.html and http://www.iris.edu/gifs/animations/faults.htm

Earthquake Preparedness Handbook—http://www.lafd.org/eqindex.htm

Links to information about preparing for an earthquake and organizations that will help—http://earthquake.usgs.gov/hazards/prepare.html

Forces of Nature—http://www.nationalgeographic.com/forcesofnature/. Choose Earthquakes. Go through all seven parts and you will learn a lot.

Savage Earth—http://www.pbs.org/wnet/savageearth/. Excellent earthquake information with short videos.

The Tech organization exhibit—http://www.thetech.org/exhibits_events/online/quakes/overview/. Go through it all. Very easy to understand, with good images.

Earthquake Resistant Building, with excellent links—http://www.build4earthquake.com/link.html

 **TA DA!**

Earthquakes in Action!

Make Your Own Earthquake—http://dsc.discovery.com/unsolvedhistory/earthquake/interactive/interactive.html and http://www.msnucleus.org/membership/html/k-6/pt/hazards/6/pth6_2a.html

Have Fun

Earthquakes for Kids—http://earthquake.usgs.gov/4kids/. Word games and other activities to enjoy.

In the Classroom

Earthquake ABCs—http://pasadena.wr.usgs.gov/ABC/index.html. With lesson plans, excellent dictionary for parents and teachers.

Footsteps of the Past.

FOSSILS

New Words

Paleontology
Geologic Time
Sedimentary Rock
Amber
Paleontologist

What Are Fossils?

You may have found a rock with the skeleton of an animal or the shape of a leaf embedded in it. Did you wonder how it got there? A fossil can be left from a living thing billions of years ago, or it might be far more recent. If you just want to see fossils, the best ones are usually in a museum. You might find fossils yourself if you keep an eye out when you are hiking in an area with sedimentary rock. Who knows? You might even find some in your own back yard.

What Can I Write About?

Learn about some of the oldest fossils and report on what has been learned from them.

Discuss the formation of fossils.

Compare and contrast fossils found in rocks with those found in amber.

Explain what a paleontologist does. Include the training and tools that are needed.

Discuss the methods used to determine when and where a fossil originated.

Are There Books on Fossils?

We can't begin to tell you the best books. There are many. Use your library catalog. Do not forget the reference area, where you can find background information and statistics.

Childcraft: The How and Why Library. Chicago: World Book, 2003.

Lerner, K. Lee, and Brenda Wilmoth Lerner, eds. *Gale Encyclopedia of Science.* 3d ed. Vol. 3. Detroit: Gale, 2004.

New Book of Popular Science. Vol. 1. Danbury, CT: Grolier, 2004.

Newton, David E., Rob Nagel, and Bridget Travers. *UXL Encyclopedia of Science.* Vol. 4. Detroit: UXL, 1998.

World Book Student Discovery Encyclopedia. Chicago: World Book, 2003.

Can the Internet Help?

The San Diego Museum of Natural History—http://www.sdnhm.org/kids/fossils/. Explains what fossils are and where to find them.

Fossils, Rocks and Time, from the U.S. Geologic Survey—http://pubs.usgs.gov/gip/fossils/contents.html

Eocine fossil specimens from Colorado Mountain College—http://www.coloradomtn.edu/campus_rfl/staff_rfl/kohls/eocene.html

NOVA presents *The Curse of T. Rex*—http://www.pbs.org/wgbh/nova/trex/. About dinosaurs and the living things from the same time, as evidenced by fossils.

Oceans of Kansas—http://www.oceansofkansas.com/. A virtual journey back in time, for older students.

Discovery Centre (Canada)—http://www.rom.on.ca/quiz/fossil/. Helps us understand fossils. How are they formed? Where do we find them? Who studies them? How are they prepared for study? Simple and good.

 **TA DA!**

Fossils in Action!

PBS has a video, *Becoming a Fossil*—http://www.pbs.org/wgbh/evolution/library/04/3/l_043_01.html

Experiment

PremDesign—http://www.premdesign.com/fosfaq.html. Go fossil hunting! You will have to learn the best fossil hunting places in your area, but you can get some tips from this Web site.

Fossils of Arkansas—http://rockhoundingar.com/pebblepups/makefossil.html. Make your own fossil.

In the Classroom

Learning from the Fossil Record, from UCMP Berkeley and Shell Offshore—http://www.ucmp.berkeley.edu/fosrec/index.html. Offers a variety of activities and resources.

Teach-nology links to paleontology Web sites for teachers—http://www.teach-nology.com/teachers/subject_matter/science/paleontology/

You Only See the Tip.

ICEBERGS AND ICE CAPS

New Words

- Antarctica
- Castle Bergs
- Glaciers
- Greenland

What Are Icebergs and Ice Caps?

Millions of years ago, during the Ice Age, ice covered much of the earth. As the earth warmed, that ice cap began to melt, break apart, and drift. Large glaciers scooped up forests and redeposited them thousands of miles away. They carved out valleys and melted into lakes. Glaciers still exist in the far north. Ice caps still cover the North Pole and Antarctica. An iceberg is a large chunk of floating ice that breaks off an ice cap or glacier. To be considered an iceberg, the floating ice must be at least 17 feet above sea level. The largest iceberg reported by the U.S. Coast Guard loomed 550 feet above the water. In the last hundred years, the atmosphere has warmed up 1 degree. That doesn't sound like much, but scientists are worried that it may be enough to melt the ice caps.

What Can I Write About?

Discuss where and how icebergs are formed.

Write about the Ice Age. You should include its effects on plant and animal life.

Find some examples of icebergs causing shipwrecks. Describe methods used to avoid similar problems today.

Compare and contrast glaciers and icebergs.

Discuss the melting of the polar ice cap and how it affects the rest of the earth.

Are There Books on Icebergs and Polar Caps?

Use your library catalog. Do not forget the reference area, where you can find background information and statistics.

Lerner, K. Lee, and Brenda Wilmoth Lerner, eds. *Gale Encyclopedia of Science.* 3d ed. Vol. 3. Detroit: Gale, 2004.

New Book of Popular Science. Vol. 2. Danbury, CT: Grolier, 2004.

Newton, David E., Rob Nagel, and Bridget Travers. *UXL Encyclopedia of Science.* Vol. 5. Detroit: UXL, 1998.

Seymour, Simon. *Icebergs and Glaciers.* New York: HarperTrophy, 1999.

Can the Internet Help?

Ocean World, from Texas A&M University—http://oceanworld.tamu.edu/students/iceberg/. Explains icebergs for students.

USA Today—http://www.usatoday.com/weather/research/wiceberg.htm. Has graphic illustrations of the anatomy of an iceberg.

National Ice and Snow Data Center—http://nsidc.org/iceshelves/. Icebergs and ice shelves.

Ronald Kramer—http://www.geocities.com/Yosemite/Rapids/4233/floating.htm. Formation of the Greenland Ice Cap and the anatomy of an iceberg.

The U.S. Coast Guard's International Ice Patrol—http://www.uscg.mil/lantarea/iip/Students/Default.htm. Tells kids about the life of an iceberg.

Secrets of the Ice—http://www.secretsoftheice.org/icecore/formation.html. Ice formation and flow in Antarctica.

The Ice Cap and the First Icebergs—http://www.geocities.com/Yosemite/Rapids/4233/ijsbergen.htm. Good information about how icebergs form.

 **TA DA!**

Icebergs in Action!

NASA—http://www.secretsoftheice.org/icecore/index.html. A quicktime movie on the melting of the Antarctic icecap.

Experiment

CG Kids—http://www.cgkids.ca/cgkids/files/geeology/experiment16.asp. Make your own floating iceberg.

National Park Service—http://www.nps.gov/lacl/kids/glacierslide.htm. Experiment with a glacier!

In the Classroom

Discovery—http://school.discovery.com/lessonplans/programs/iceberg/. Glacier and iceberg lesson plan.

Ocean World at Texas A&M University—http://oceanworld.tamu.edu/educators/lesson_activities.htm. Lesson plans.

It's All Wet!

OCEANS

New Words

Continental Shelf
Continental Slope
Hydrothermal Vents
Oceanic Zone—Zonation
Oceanographer

What Is an Ocean?

Covering three-quarters of the earth's surface, oceans are as diverse as they are large. They are their own biome, and their food chains range from plankton to the largest whale. Questions: If fresh water runs into (and out of) the sea, why is the sea still salty? Why is the ocean blue? What causes tides? What are some of the uses of the oceans? What is life under the sea like? What lives under the ocean and what food chains are there? What land forms would we see if we studied the ocean floor? What instruments do oceanographers use? How is a wave created?

What Can I Write About?

Write about the ocean zones—sunlit, twilight, and midnight. How are they different? What survives in each zone? Or write more in more depth about one single zone.

Think about the questions written above and answer one or more (tides, waves, uses of the ocean, animals of the sea, ocean floor, chemicals that make up sea water).

If you decided to become an oceanographer, what are the career paths you might take? Education? See a terms dictionary at http://library.thinkquest.org/18828/data/glossary.html

Write about weather and the ocean. Consider El Niòo, the ring of fire, or tsunamis, or write about how the ocean is helpful in predicting weather in advance.

Are There Books or Videos on Oceans?

Do not forget the reference area, where you can find background information.

Berger, Melvin, and Gilda Berger. *What Makes an Ocean Wave?: Questions and Answers About Oceans and Ocean Life.* New York: Scholastic, 2001.

Gray, Samantha. *Ocean.* New York: Dorling Kindersley, 2001.

Lambert, David. *Kingfisher Young People's Book of Oceans.* Boston: Houghton Mifflin, 2001.

National Geographic Concise Atlas of the World. Washington, DC: National Geographic, 2003.

Oceans of the World Set. 5 vols. Cleveland, OH: World Almanac, 2004.

Can the Internet Help?

Temperate Oceans—http://mbgnet.mobot.org/salt/oceans/. The Atlantic and Pacific Oceans and other basic information.

Ocean AdVENTure—http://library.thinkquest.org/18828/. Looking at hydrothermal vents—ocean research.

Enchanted Learning—The Oceans—http://www.enchantedlearning.com/subjects/ocean/. Good place to start.

Ocean Quest—Education modules from Navy Meteorology and Oceanography Command—http://pao.cnmoc.navy.mil/educate/neptune/quest/quest.htm

UN Atlas of the Oceans—http://www.oceansatlas.org/index.jsp

Careers in Oceanography—http://pao.cnmoc.navy.mil/PAO/Educate/career-o.htm

Pacific Ocean—http://library.thinkquest.org/15931/. The largest; contains good information about weather and oceans.

The Anatomy of a Wave from Boatsafe.com, Nautical Know-How —http://www.boatsafe.com/nauticalknowhow/waves.htm

Scripps Institute of Oceanography—http://scripps.ucsd.edu/. This group studies the ocean. Look at their experiments.

 **TA DA!**

Oceans in Action!

Word games and puzzles about the sea—http://sln.fi.edu/fellows/fellow8/dec98/intera.html and http://www.mbayaq.org/lc/activities.asp. Have a little fun.

Experiment

Make your own wave—http://www.mos.org/oceans/motion/wind.html. Why does it work?

In the Classroom

Celebrate the Year of the Ocean in your Classroom—http://www.education-world.com/a_lesson/lesson060.shtml or http://www.libsci.sc.edu/miller/Ocean.htm or http://www.fi.edu/fellows/fellow8/dec98/

48

Liquid Gold.

OIL AND GAS

New Words

Fossil Fuel
Gasoline
Hydrocarbons
Petroleum

What Is Oil?

Oil started as organic life such as plants and animals millions of years ago. Deep under the ground and under the ocean it gradually changed. When petroleum or crude oil is harvested from the ground, it is refined to make gasoline, natural gas, tar, and many other products that may surprise you. We need oil; we can't live without our automobiles, heaters, and air conditioners, and petroleum products are needed to fuel them. But oil has caused many problems, including air pollution and oil spills. In addition, it is a finite resource. One of these days, we will run out!

What Can I Write About?

Explore the formation of petroleum. You might want to compare it to other fossil fuels.

Consider the effects of oil spills on wildlife and the methods of cleanup. Choose a specific animal.

Discuss the world oil reserves. Include how much remains, methods of locating it, and what will happen when it is depleted.

Compare and contrast fossil fuels with other sources of energy.

Examine other uses of petroleum besides as a fuel source. Or explain how we get gas for cars.

Are There Books on Petroleum?

Use your library catalog. Do not forget the reference area, where you can find background information and statistics.

New Book of Popular Science. Vol. 2. Danbury, CT: Grolier, 2004.

Newton, David E., Rob Nagel, and Bridget Travers. *UXL Encyclopedia of Science.* Vol. 7. Detroit: UXL, 1998.

Smith, Roland. *Sea Otter Rescue: The Aftermath of an Oil Spill.* New York: Puffin, 1999.

World Book Encyclopedia. Chicago: World Book, 2005.

World Book Student Discovery Encyclopedia. Chicago: World Book, 2003.

Zemlicka, Shannon. *From Oil to Gas.* Minneapolis, MN: Lerner, 2002.

Can the Internet Help?

U.S. Department of Energy—http://www.eia.doe.gov/kids/energyfacts/sources/non-renewable/oil.html. Explains where petroleum comes from and how it's processed.

United Kingdom Offshore Operators Association—http://www.oilandgas.org.uk/education/students/intro.htm. Explores the formation of oil and gas, extraction, and exploration.

The Story on Oil Spills, from the National Oceanic and Atmospheric Administration—http://response.restoration.noaa.gov/kids/spills.html

A Young Person's Guide to Oil and Gas, from the Institute of Petroleum—http://www.world-petroleum.org/education/ip1/ip1.html

U.S. Geological Survey—http://energy.er.usgs.gov/products/papers/World_oil/oil/. A map of the world's oil reserves.

Gasoline and You, from the American Petroleum Institute—http://www.gasolineandyou.com/. About gasoline and other fuels, where they come from, and what influences prices.

How Oil Refining Works, from How Stuff Works—http://science.howstuffworks.com/oil-refining.htm

 **TA DA!**

Petroleum in Action!

Adventures in Energy, from the American Petroleum Institute—http://www.adventuresinenergy.org/. A flash animation showing how gasoline goes from petroleum reserves to the pump.

Experiment

Environmental Protection Agency—http://www.epa.gov/oilspill/labintro.htm. Try one of these experiments to learn about cleaning up oil spills.

In the Classroom

Classroom Energy, a Web site from the American Petroleum Institute—http://www.classroom-energy.org/teachers/. Lesson plans and links to Web sites on energy resources.

National Geographic—http://www.nationalgeographic.com/xpeditions/lessons/01/g68/iraqoil.html. A lesson plan for oil and water in the Middle East.

49

Hang Ten!

TSUNAMI

New Words

Amplification
DART
Earthquake
Tectonic Force
Wave Maker

TSUNAMI INFORMATION

IN CASE OF EARTHQUAKE, GO TO HIGH GROUND OR INLAND

What Is a Tsunami?

A tsunami (pronounced soo-nahm-ee) is a series of huge waves that happen under the ocean after an earthquake or volcanic eruption. In the past we called them tidal waves. Imagine a wave that can travel as fast as a jet and can be 12 stories high! Usually, they aren't THAT fast or big; but they can be extremely destructive. In the United States, Hawaii, California, and Alaska have tsunamis every seven to eight years. In Asia, in December 2004, more than 150,000 were killed in one of the biggest tsunamis in history. It is hard to imagine something from nature that can be so destructive. It will be interesting to find out what causes a tsunami.

What Can I Write About?

What are tsunamis? What causes them? Can we predict them? Write about the basics so that your readers understand what a tsunami is.

Write about the research teams that study tsunamis. Who are they? What is DART? How is a wave-making machine used in research?

Describe the differences between wind-generated waves and a tsunami.

Describe a specific tsunami. How do the survivors live after the tsunami? Show pictures.

Are There Books on Tsunamis?

Reference books about geology and weather will be helpful for this topic.

Associated Press Library of Disasters. Vol. 1, *Earthquakes and Tsunamis.* Danbury, CT: Grolier, 1998.

Englebert, Phillis. *Dangerous Planet: The Science of Natural Disasters.* Detroit: UXL, 2001.

Kampion, Drew. *Waves: From Surfing to Tsunami.* Layton, UT: Gibbs Smith, 2005.

National Research Council. *Living on an Active Earth: Perspectives on Earthquake Science.* Washington, DC: National Academy, 1999.

Tsunami: Killer Wave. [videorecording]. Washington, DC: National Geographic, 1997.

Wade, Mary Dodson. *Tsunami: Monster Waves.* Berkeley Heights, NJ: Enslow, 2002.

Can the Internet Help?

Tsunami Research at U.S. Geological Survey—http://walrus.wr.usgs.gov/tsunami/. Excellent video and virtual reality clips.

Tsunami sites selected for kids—http://www.pmel.noaa.gov/tsunami-hazard/kids.html

Tsunami Warning—http://www.fema.gov/kids/tsunami/. Preparation for a tsunami, written especially for kids.

Tsunami Links Selected for Home Schoolers—and you—http:// homeschooling. gomilpitas.com/explore/tsunami.htm

Learn about researching a tsunami—http://www.pmel.noaa.gov/tsunami/ and http://www.nacse.org/neesSiteSpecs/incoming/21/siteDescr/Tsunami_Basin_5-page_description.pdf

Surviving a Tsunami—http://pubs.usgs.gov/circ/c1187/. Excellent.

The Savage Earth: Tsunami—from PBS—http://www.pbs.org/wnet/savageearth/tsunami/index.html. Good basic info and pictures.

 ## TA DA!

Tsunamis in Action!

Put together a disaster supply kit for your family—http://www.fema.gov/kids/tsunami.htm

Experience

This page of tsunami visualizations can help you experience what it must be like—http://serc.carleton.edu/NAGTWorkshops/visualization/collections/tsunami.html. Write about it.

In the Classroom

Kehret, Peg. *Escaping the Giant Wave.* New York: Simon & Schuster, 2004. This is an excellent book for reading aloud to middle schoolers.

Lesson Plans for Tsunami—http://school.discovery.com/teachers/tsunami/, http://lvillage.education.vic.gov.au/lv/beps/hp.nsf/PreviewHomePages/tsunamis, http://www.fema.gov/hazards/tsunamis/tsunamif.shtm (FEMA's fact sheet—for classroom prep), and http://www.cln.org/themes/tsunamis.html

50

Belching Fire!

VOLCANOES

New Words

Basalt
Dormant
Lava
Magma
Tectonic Plates

What Are Volcanoes?

When oceanic plates move, they converge and diverge. Between them, magma, or molten rock, begins to build up. It creates more and more pressure until it erupts, spewing forth lava. Boiling and bubbling its way up through the earth's crust, the magma cools, turns to lava, and becomes part of the earth's crust itself. Once, when the earth was forming, volcanoes were everywhere. They helped to form the continents, the islands, and the ocean. Even now there are about 600 active volcanoes. Almost half of them are in what is called the "Ring of Fire" rimming the Pacific Ocean.

What Can I Write About?

Describe the life cycle of a volcanic island.

Discuss the differences among composite volcanoes, strata volcanoes, and shield volcanoes. Or choose one of them and describe it in detail.

Explain the movement of tectonic plates and its relation to volcanoes.

Discuss some volcano relatives, hot springs and geysers.

Examine the composition of magma. Compare and contrast the different content.

Are There Books on Volcanoes?

We can't begin to tell you the best books. There are many. Use your library catalog. Do not forget the reference area, where you can find background information and statistics.

Buckwalter, Stephanie. *Volcanoes: Disaster & Survival.* Berkeley Heights, NJ: Enslow, 2005.

New Book of Popular Science. Vol. 2. Danbury, CT: Grolier, 2004.

Newton, David Ed, Rob Nagel, and Bridget Travers, eds. *UXL Encyclopedia of Science.* Vol. 9. Detroit: Gale, 1998.

Visual Dictionary of the Earth. London: Dorling Kindersley, 1993.

World Book Encyclopedia of Science. Vol. 4, *The Planet Earth.* Chicago: World Book, 2001.

Can the Internet Help?

Volcano facts from FEMA, including the Volcano Explosivity Index—http://www.fema.gov/kids/volcano.htm

Volcanologist John Search gives you facts about the most active, highest, and most deadly volcanoes—http://www.volcanolive.com/contents.html

Hawaiian Volcanoes from the American Park Network—http://www.americanparknetwork.com/parkinfo/hv/activities/kidspage.html. History, geology, and flora and fauna are especially interesting to the "researcher."

University of North Dakota's Volcano World—http://volcano.und.nodak.edu/vw.html. Excellent information, pictures, and media.

 **TA DA!**

Volcanoes in Action!

National Geographic Explorer—http://magma.nationalgeographic.com/ngexplorer/0405/quickflicks/. Quick Fliks, video clips, including one on volcanoes.

National Park Service—http://www.nps.gov/yell/oldfaithfulcam.htm. See the geyser, Old Faithful, on a live Webcam.

U.S. Department of Agriculture, Forest Service—http://www.fs.fed.us/gpnf/volcanocams/msh/. Shows Mount St. Helens on videocam.

Experiment

Reeko's Mad Scientist Lab—http://www.spartechsoftware.com/reeko/Experiments/volcano.htm. Shows you how to make your own erupting volcano!

Volcano World—http://volcano.und.nodak.edu/vwdocs/volc_models/models.html. Several volcano models at different skill levels.

In the Classroom

Teacher's Guide to the Geology of Hawaii Volcanoes National Park—http://volcano.und.nodak.edu/vwdocs/vwlessons/atg.html

The U.S. Geological Survey—http://interactive2.usgs.gov/learningweb/teachers/volcanoes.htm. Lesson plans and an introduction to volcanoes.

Volcano World—Teaching and Learning—http://volcano.und.edu/learning.html

THE HEAVENS

From our first song, "Twinkle, twinkle, little star" to myths about the stars, humans have always wondered about the heavens. There are many old stories and myths about the stars and sun. In the 1960s we finally reached the moon. Our space explorations have taught us much about the heavens. But we want to know more about this uncharted territory. Reach for the stars—write your research paper about our vast heavens.

Twinkle, Twinkle, Little Star.

CONSTELLATIONS

New Words

Constellations—Galaxies
Globular Cluster
Nebulae
Right Ascension (aka RA) and Declination (Dec)

What Is a Constellation?

The constellations are totally imaginary. Really! People have named the "constellations" in order to help us tell which stars are which. We look in the sky and say, "Oh, there is Little Bear. There is Leo. There is the Big Dipper." On a very dark night, you can see about 1,000 to 1,500 stars. You can see that it would all look like a blur if we didn't have ways to identify groups of stars. Make a family excursion away from the city lights, where you can enjoy the stars even more.

What Can I Write About?

What is a constellation? Why do we have them? How do they help us? Give two or three examples and tell a little about each.

Write about one of the constellation families, like Ursa Major or Zodiacal. This is an excellent way to break your report down so you can handle the information you find.

Write about stars. Why do they twinkle? Why do they change colors? How do they get named? Why are some brighter than others? Why do we see more in the country than in the city?

Write about telescopes. Do we need a large one to view the stars? What is the world's largest? Most powerful? Radio telescopes? What have we learned from powerful telescopes like the Hubble? (You could write a whole report on the Hubble telescope.)

Are There Books on the Constellations?

The library reference section has several astronomy books that will help. Here are a few.

Heifetz, Milton D., and Wil Tirion. *A Walk Through the Heavens: A Guide to the Stars and Constellations and Their Legends.* Cambridge, UK: Cambridge University Press, 1998.

Melcher, Gary. *The Audubon Society First Field Guide: Night Sky*. New York: Scholastic, 1999.

Mosley, John. *The Ultimate Guide to the Sky: How to Find Constellations and Read the Night Sky Like a Pro*. Los Angeles: Lowell, 1997.

Rey, Hans Augusto. *Find the Constellations*. Boston: Houghton Mifflin, 1976.

Rey, Hans Augusto. *The Stars: A New Way to See Them*. Boston: Houghton Mifflin, 1976.

Sanford, John. *Observing the Constellations*. Old Tappan, NJ: Fireside, 1989.

Can the Internet Help?

Chris Dolan's Constellation Pages—http://www.astro.wisc.edu/~dolan/constellations/ constellations.html. Pictures, FAQs, basic explanations, links. Excellent.

Peoria's Astronomical Society—http://www.astronomical.org/. Glossary, special topics, information about each constellation. Be sure to go through the beginning and intermediate lessons. WOW!

Winter Constellations—http://hometown.aol.com/ckckside/reports/constellation/ astro.htm. Created for a classroom, this information is very helpful for beginners.

The constellations and the constellation families—http://www.seds. org/Maps/Const/constS.html. Be sure to look at the constellation photos.

Kid's Astronomy—Telescopes—http://www.kidsastronomy.com/telescopes.htm. Learn all about them.

How the Hubble Space Telescope Works—http://science.howstuffworks. com/hubble.htm. Look at the other topics, as well.

 **TA DA!**

Constellations in Action!

Live Space Show—http://www.slooh.com. This is SO neat and you can have seven days free. Get online and watch the constellations each night for a week. Create a journal to record what you are seeing. Join as many missions as you can. You will be hooked! We guarantee it.

Experiment

Begin a Star Log right away. Each time you "watch" the stars, log what you see. It is very important to keep a calendar, since different constellations are seen at different times of the year. You can refer to your journal in future years and see how much you have learned. Look at the constellations and their location in the sky before you go outside. Use these Web sites: http://clevermedia.com/arcade/ const.html and http:// www.kidsastronomy.com/astroskymap/constellation_ hunt.htm

In the Classroom

A large collection of lesson plans for the study of astronomy—http:// www.teach-nology.com/teachers/lesson_plans/science/astronomy/

Make Your Own Constellation and write a myth to go with it—http://www. lessonplanspage.com/ScienceLAMakeYourOwnConstellationMyth5.htm. Cross curriculum.

ET, Phone Home!

EXTRATERRESTRIAL LIFE

New Words

Aliens
Flying Saucers
Mars *Voyager*
SETI—Search for Extraterrestrial Life
UFO—Unidentified Flying Objects

What Is Extraterrestrial Life?

Many people, even many scientists, wonder if there is really intelligent life on other planets. If there is, is that life sophisticated enough to send spaceships to Earth to explore our planet? People have pondered this for centuries. Some believe that there are signs on Earth of earlier visitors. Crop circles and unidentified flying objects (UFOs) may indicate more recent visits. Other people think those signs are a hoax.

Is it possible that life exists on other planets, even if that life is not sending spaceships to Earth? That is what the National Aeronautics and Space Administration (NASA) is trying to learn with the Mars Exploration Rover. That is what SETI is trying to learn with its giant sensors. We may never know for sure.

What Can I Write About?

Discuss the conditions necessary for life on other planets.

Examine the Mars *Explorer* and its findings.

Find incidents of UFOs and consider the possible explanations.

Explain why humans could or could not establish a colony outside Earth.

Write about crop circles. What are they? What do people believe? What do scientists say?

Are There Books on Extraterrestrial Life?

We can't begin to tell you the best books. There are many. Use your library catalog. Do not forget the reference area, where you can find background information and statistics.

Asimov, Isaac. He has written several books, including *Extraterrestrial Civilizations*, *Is There Life on Other Planets*, and *Aliens and Extraterrestrials: Are We Alone?*

Melton, J. Gordon, ed. *Encyclopedia of Occultism and Parapsychology.* Detroit: Gale, 2001.

New Book of Popular Science. Vol. 1. Danbury, CT: Grolier, 2004.

World Book Encyclopedia of Science. Vol. 1, *Astronomy.* Chicago: World Book, 2001.

Can the Internet Help?

PBS and NOVA—http://www.pbs.org/wgbh/nova/worlds/morrison.html. Explore the possibility of life on other planets.

The University Corporation for Atmospheric Research—http://www.windows. ucar.edu/tour/link=/cool_stuff/tours_main.html. Explores the atmosphere and geology of other planets and how they would affect life.

See a map of UFO sightings—http://www.larryhatch.net/

The Museum of Unnatural History—http://www.unmuseum.mus.pa.us/ ufo.htm. Explores some of the evidence that ancient aliens explored the earth.

Area 51, a military facility for social phenomena and state of mind—interesting links—http://www.ufomind.com/area51/. Much has been removed.

Crop Circles—http://paloweb.com/Society/Paranormal/Crop_Circles/. Links to several sites that try to explain this phenomenon.

 **TA DA!**

Extraterrestrials in Action!

The Darwin Centre—http://www.nhm.ac.uk/darwincentre/live/archive/extreme. html. Explores the possibility of life on other planets through videos of extreme environments.

HarperCollinsKids—http://www.harperchildrens.com/games/switch/aliens/. Design a space alien.

Experiment

The National UFO Reporting Site—http://www.nuforc.org/. The place to report your sighting of a UFO.

In the Classroom

The RESA Web site—http://www.resa.net/nasa/. Explores life on other planets utilizing Michigan middle school science objectives.

Extraterrestrial lesson plan for middle grades—http://school.discovery.com/ lessonplans/programs/extraterrestrials/

53

Reaching for the Stars.

STEPHEN HAWKING

New Words

Astronomer
Astrophysicist
Big Bang—Black Hole
Cosmology
Lou Gehrig's Disease or ALS
Physics

Who Is Stephen Hawking?

Dr. Stephen Hawking was born in Oxford, England, in 1942, and is considered one of the foremost physicists in all of history. He works on the basic laws that govern the universe. Hawking's book, *A Brief History of Time*, has sold over 10 million copies. Recently, Dr. Hawking revised his black hole theory. He has theorized and written about the Big Bang. One of the nice things for us is that he wrote about his theories in layperson's language, language we can understand. For you future scientists who are interested in the universe, you will enjoy researching this intelligent man who fought an immense physical battle with Lou Gehrig's disease (ALS), while developing his exceptional talents on universal theories.

What Can I Write About?

Write a general biography about this gifted man. Include information about the hardship he faced with his physical disabilities. Be sure to include his theories about the universe.

Research Hawking's recent studies on gravity.

Investigate Hawking's findings on the black hole. He changed his mind about his original theory. Write about both.

Explore Hawking and ALS. He has lived longer than any other person with this disease. This takes you away from astronomy—but to another interesting scientific topic.

Are There Books About Stephen Hawking?

Astronomy reference books and biographical encyclopedias are what you need.

Gjertson, Derek, and Michael Allaby. *Makers of Science.* New York: Oxford, 2002.

Hawking, Stephen. *A Brief History of Time.* New York: Bantam, 1998.

Ryan, Bernard. *Stephen Hawking: Physicist and Educator.* New York: Ferguson, 2004.

Sakurai, Gail. *Stephen Hawking: Understanding the Universe.* New York: Children's Press, 1996.

Strathern, Paul. *Hawking and Black Holes.* New York: Anchor, 1998. (This will represent his earlier theory.)

World of Scientific Discovery. Detroit: Gale, 1994– .

Can the Internet Help?

Psyclops: Stephen Hawking—http://www.psyclops.com/hawking/. Includes biography and links to other sites.

Hawking and his revised black hole theory, from CNN—http://www.cnn.com/2004/TECH/space/07/21/hawking.blackholes.ap/

Stephen Hawking's Page—http://www.hawking.org.uk/home/hindex.html. Includes bio and lectures.

Professor Stephen Hawking—http://members.tripod.com/Barry_Stone/hawking.htm. Web page of a fan.

Stephen Hawking—http://home.cwru.edu/~sjr16/20th_people_hawking.html. Includes accomplishments and a little about ALS, his disease.

Stephen Hawking's Universe—http://www.pbs.org/wnet/hawking/html/home.html

Hawking's Report on Life with ALS—http://www.everydaywarriors.com/adults/stephen_hawking_article.html

 ## TA DA!

Hawking in Action!

Stephen Hawking's Universe is a video in which Hawking presents some of the most astonishing scientific advances in cosmological thought. He interviews other physicists. Local libraries and video stores will have a copy of this video. See Dr. Hawking firsthand.

Experiment

Play space games with NASA—http://spaceplace.nasa.gov/en/kids/live/index.shtml#. Be the first to survive a black hole.

In the Classroom

Black Holes—Lesson Plans—http://school.discovery.com/lessonplans/programs/blackholes/ and http://einstein.stcloudstate.edu/nook/IDEAS/computers/lubben/webpage.html

Close Encounters.

METEORS

New Words

Chondrite—Achondrite
Crater
Fireball—Shooting Star
Irons—Stones—Stony-Irons
Meteor—Meteorite—Meteoroid—Meteor Showers
Simple crater—Complex crater

What Is a Meteor?

Have you ever seen a shooting star? They flash by so quickly that by the time you tell your friend to look, they are gone. When meteors, also known as shooting stars or fireballs, hit the ground, they are called meteorites. They look like stones. When meteorites fall to the ground they make a crater; sometimes it is very large. Why? How?

What Can I Write About?

What is a meteor? What did it come from? If it is so small compared to the big universe, how can we see it? What are these: meteor, meteorite, meteoroid, and meteor showers?

Describe the different types of meteorites, for example, irons, stones, stony-irons.

Discuss the craters made by meteorites. You might select a specific one, like the Barringer crater in Arizona. How large is it? Describe it. How old is it? What meteorites are found there?

Write about The Leonids, an annual meteor shower. What is its history? When is it visible? How do we find it in the sky? Where did it come from? How fast is it?

Write about meteors, comets, or asteroids. Adding color pictures will improve your project.

Are There Books on Meteors and Meteorites?

Aronson, Billy. *Meteors: The Truth Behind Shooting Stars.* New York: Franklin Watts, 1996.

Asimov, Isaac. *Discovering Comets and Meteors.* Milwaukee, MN: Gareth Stevens, 1996.

Littmann, Mark. *Heavens on Fire: The Great Leonid Meteor Storms.* Cambridge, UK: Cambridge University Press, 1998.

Reynolds, Michael. *Falling Stars: A Guide to Meteors and Meteorites.* Mechanicsburg, PA: Stackpole, 2001.

Robinson, Leif. *Astronomy Encyclopedia.* New York: Oxford, 2002.

Can the Internet Help?

Meteorite Central—http://www.meteoritecentral.com/. Take your time. Enjoy the pictures, too.

Earth Impact—http://www.s-d-g.freeserve.co.uk/. Information about meteorites and comets and their encounters with the earth.

Meteor Madness from ThinkQuest: "Asteroids, Meteors, and Comets, Oh My!"—http://library.thinkquest.org/J001812/

Meteors and Meteorites—http://www.solarviews.com/eng/meteor.htm. Includes information about craters

How big is a meteor that makes it to the ground?—http://science.howstuffworks.com/question486.htm. Read, then follow the links.

Sky and Telescope Magazine—http://skyandtelescope.com/observing/objects/meteors/. All about meteors.

CyberSleuth Kids—Meteors—http://cybersleuth-kids.com/sleuth/Science/Space/Meteoroids/. Links to some of the best sites on meteors.

The Leonids—http://comets.amsmeteors.org/meteors/showers/leonid2000.html. All about this meteor shower. View the video and pictures.

Meteorites and Their Properties—http://meteorites.lpl.arizona.edu/. All about meteorites.

 ## TA DA!

Meteors in Action!

At Home Astronomy—Meteoroids and the Craters—http://cse.ssl.berkeley.edu/AtHomeAstronomy/activity_05.html. Make your own.

Experience

Follow Sky and Telescope's manual How to Watch for Meteors—http://skyandtelescope.com/observing/objects/meteors/article_102_1.asp. Record watches.

In the Classroom

Impact Craters—Exploring in the Classroom—http://www.spacegrant.hawaii.edu/class_acts/

Meteorites Don't Pop Corn—http://www.thursdaysclassroom.com/27jul01/corner.html. Articles about meteor showers, with questions and a math lesson.

55

Earth's Night-Light.

THE MOON

New Words

Lunar
Eclipse
Dark Side

What Is the Moon?

When you are outside at night, look up at the moon. Is it a full moon, round and bright? Or a new moon, just a thin crescent in the sky? The whole moon is always there, watching over the earth. Only one side glows, reflecting the light of the sun. The other side is always dark. When part of the dark side faces the earth, it seems to have disappeared. People have been watching the moon since ancient times, trying to understand where it came from and why it changes. The ancient Greeks believed that the goddess Artemis pulled it like a chariot across the sky at night. The Inuits of Greenland believed that the moon was Anningen, chasing his sister, the sun. The Chinese believed that there were 12 moons, one for each month.

What Can I Write About?

There are three main scientific theories about how the moon was formed. Discuss the pros and cons of each and come up with your own theory.

Research the exploration of the moon. You might want to also describe the moon and explain the dark side.

The moon and the earth have profound effects on each other. Learn what those effects are. Consider what would change on Earth if the moon were not there.

Look into the three types of lunar eclipse and share what you have learned.

Are There Books About the Moon?

We can't begin to tell you the best books. There are many. Use your library catalog. Do not forget the reference area, where you can find background information and statistics.

Gatland, Kenneth. *Illustrated Encyclopedia of Space Technology.* 2d ed. New York: Orion, 1989.

Lerner, K. Lee, and Brenda Wilmoth Lerner, eds. *Gale Encyclopedia of Science.* 3d ed. Detroit: Gale, 2004.

New Book of Popular Science. Vols. 1 & 2. Danbury, CT: Grolier, 2004.

Newton, David E., Rob Nagel, and Bridget Travers, eds. *UXL Encyclopedia of Science.* Detroit: UXL, 1997.

World Book Encyclopedia of Science. Chicago: World Book, 2001.

Can the Internet Help?

World Almanac—http://www.worldalmanacforkids.com/explore/space/moon. html. Basic facts about the moon for kids.

NASA—http://kids.msfc.nasa.gov/Earth/Moon/. Interesting facts and news about the moon.

Boat Safe Kids—http://www.boatsafe.com/kids/tides.htm. The moon and the tide.

University of Washington—http://faculty.washington.edu/chudler/moon.html. The moon and behavior.

Moon Mythology from University Corporation for Atmospheric Research— http://www.windows.ucar.edu/tour/link=/mythology/planets/Earth/moon.html

NASA's pages—http://science.nasa.gov/. Search *Moon.* Excellent, up-to-date information.

 **TA DA!**

See the Moon up Close!

NASA—http://www.hq.nasa.gov/office/pao/History/40thann/videos.htm. Audio and video clips of moon exploration.

First Science—http://www.firstscience.com/site/video.asp. Video clips of moon exploration.

Experiment

Observe the moon for a month and chart its changes—http://jfg.girlscouts. org/Why/sciact/Space/moonf/moonchar.htm

In the Classroom

NASA—Exploring the Moon Teacher Guides—http://www.nasa.gov/audience/ foreducators/k-4/multimedia/index.html and http://science.nasa.gov/ (Receive their e-mail). Use keyword.

Harvard Smithsonian Center for Astrophysics—http://www.learner. org/teacherslab/pup/. "A Private Universe" including in-class activities and a discussion forum.

Astronomical Society of the Pacific—http://www.astrosociety.org/education/ activities/astroacts.html. A variety of solar system projects.

56

Storms on the Sun.

SOLAR FLARES AND SUNSPOTS

New Words

Aurora
Corona
Geomagnetic Storms
Northern Lights
Solar Wind
Sunspots—Solar Maximum

What Are Solar Flares and Sunspots?

The sun, 93 million miles from Earth, has been a source of fascination for as long as people have existed. Every ancient culture had a story about how the sun came to be up there in the sky. People have always known they needed the sun to grow crops, but only in recent years, with powerful telescopes and satellites, have we been able to learn just how much the sun affects us. The sun, pretty much the same from day to day to our eyes, is really a place full of massive storms or solar flares, cool areas or sunspots, and a shower of particles called the solar wind.

Although the sun is so far away, those solar flares, sunspots, and solar wind have big effects on Earth. Just what are those effects?

What Can I Write About?

Discuss the consequences of solar flares and geomagnetic storms for communications systems.

What is an aurora, and how is it related to solar flares?

How are scientists able to study the sun? Discuss at least three methods.

Describe the solar cycle. What happens during solar peaks, and what effect do they have on Earth?

Explain cosmic rays.

Are There Books on Solar Flares?

Try searching the catalog for *sunspots* or *solar flares.* If there are no entire books, find books on the sun or the heavens.

Magill, Frank N., ed. *Magill's Survey of Science: Physical Science Series.* Vol. 5. Pasadena, CA: Salem, 1992.

New Book of Popular Science. Vols. 1 & 2. Danbury, CT: Grolier, 2004.

World Book Encyclopedia. Chicago: World Book, 2005.

Can the Internet Help?

The National Weather Service—http://www.crh.noaa.gov/fsd/astro/sunspots. htm. Offers an explanation of solar flares and sunspots.

NASA—http://science.nasa.gov/ssl/pad/solar/sunspots.htm. Explains the sunspot cycle.

Stanford Solar Center—http://solar-center.stanford.edu/weather.html. Chart of the sun's effects on earth.

NASA's Goddard Space Center—http://hesperia.gsfc.nasa.gov/sftheory/ toc.htm. Solar flare theory.

Goddard Space Center—http://www-spof.gsfc.nasa.gov/Education/wsolwind. html. The solar wind is explored at this Web site.

Solar Max—http://www.exploratorium.edu/solarmax/. Excellent information about the sun cycle.

**TA DA!**

Solar Flares in Action!

View a video clip of a solar flare—http://www.astro.uva.nl/demo/sun/ vlammen.htm

Experiment

Mimic Galileo's experiment that proved the existence of sunspots—http:// solar-center.stanford.edu/sunspots/galileo.html

Observe the sun yourself, safely—http://solar-center.stanford.edu/observe/

In the Classroom

NASA—http://www.thursdaysclassroom.com/index_09mar00.html. Connects the latest research with the classroom environment, this time concerning sunspots and solar flares.

Educational Resources on the Sun, from TRACE, a NASA Small Explorer Project—http://vestige.lmsal.com/TRACE/Public/eduprodu.htm

Data and Activities for Solar Learning—http://eo.nso.edu/dasl/. Hands-on activities at all grade levels.

57

Nine Planets.

SOLAR SYSTEM

New Words

Astronomy
Light Year
Galaxy
Telescopes
Milky Way

What Is the Solar System?

In the vast universe, our solar system is just one little speck, and yet our solar system is billions of miles across. Long ago, people believed that the earth was at the center of the universe, and the sun, moon, and stars revolved around it. With the invention of telescopes, they began to realize how much more there was to the universe. Even most of the planets have only been discovered recently. Long ago, brave explorers set out in ships, defying the belief that the earth was flat. Now, brave astronauts venture into space to discover just what is out there.

What Can I Write About?

If you could travel to one planet, which would it be, and why?

Choose one planet and write all about it, or compare and contrast two planets.

Discuss Galileo and his contributions to understanding the solar system.

Describe *Voyager*'s journeys.

Identify the great telescopes of the world and discuss what makes them great.

Explain what is known about other solar systems.

Are There Books on the Solar System?

We can't begin to tell you the best books. There are many. Use your library catalog. Do not forget the reference area, where you can find background information and statistics.

Magill, Frank N., ed. *Magill's Survey of Science: Physical Science Series.* Vol. 5. Pasadena, CA: Salem, 1992.

Moore, Sir Patrick. *Firefly Atlas of the Universe.* Buffalo, NY: Firefly, 1994.

New Book of Popular Science. Danbury, CT: Grolier, 2004.

Ridpath, Ian. *Facts on File Atlas of Stars and the Planets.* New York: Facts on File, 1993.

World Book Encyclopedia. Chicago: World Book, 2005.

World Book Encyclopedia of Science. Vol. 1, *Astronomy.* Chicago: World Book, 2001.

Can the Internet Help?

NASA—http://starchild.gsfc.nasa.gov/docs/StarChild/solar_system_level2/solar_system.html. Presents the facts about the solar system through Star Child.

The Nine Planets for Kids—http://kids.nineplanets.org/intro.htm. Designed by a Cal Poly student for upper elementary grades.

Science Monster—http://www.sciencemonster.com/planets.html. Explains the solar system.

Astronomy for Kids—http://www.dustbunny.com/afk/planets/. Gives details about each of the nine planets.

 **TA DA!**

The Solar System in Action!

NASA—http://starchild.gsfc.nasa.gov/docs/StarChild/solar_system_level2/solar_system.html. Shows the solar system in action.

NASA's Solar System Simulator—http://space.jpl.nasa.gov/. Lets you choose the views.

Solar System—http://www.solarsystem.nasa.gov/kids/index.cfm. Exploration for kids.

Experiment

Although many models of the solar system can be found, this one illustrates the relative distances—http://homepage.ntlworld.com/mark.pollock/ssmodel.htm

In the Classroom

ProTeacher—http://www.proteacher.com/110066.shtml. Gives you links to several solar system lesson plans at different levels.

Space Theme lessons for A to Z Teachers Stuff—http://atozteacherstuff.com/Themes/Space/

Build a Red Rover as a classroom project, and drive it over the surface of Mars!—http://planetary.org/rrrr/school.html

Receive the e-mail edition of Science at NASA Update—http://science.nasa.gov/

Schaaf, Fred. *Seeing the Sky: 100 Projects, Activities and Explorations in Astronomy.* New York: Wiley, 1990.

58

Beam Me Up, Scotty!

SPACE EXPLORATION

New Words

> Heat Shields, Rocket Boosters,
> High Vacuum and Microgravity
> Orbit, Apogee, Parabola
> Payload
> Space Shuttle, Space Lab

What Is Space Exploration?

Nothing is cooler than outer space. Rockets, satellites, astronauts, robots, gravity! People have always wondered about the unknown. We have mentioned several possible topics below. Satellites also study space. See jumpstart 96, "Weather Satellites." Up, up, and away!

What Can I Write About?

Write about the history of space exploration. Don't forget to mention the earlier scientists who figured out the equations that make modern rocketry possible.

Write about the science of Robert Goddard, the father of modern rocketry, or another important person. You may even choose one of the early astronauts, like John Glenn.

Choose one of these space missions and write about it: Atlantis, Columbia, or Endeavor. Or describe the space shuttle, the space station, the spacecraft orbiting Saturn, or the Mars rover.

Write about satellites and the research they do in space. How is information sent and received? What happens to satellites when they no longer send messages?

What is it like, living in space? What training would you need? What would you need to take along? Wear? Eat? What jobs might you have on the spacecraft? Experiments?

Are There Books or Videos on Space Exploration?

Use the library catalog and the librarian's assistance to find the books on your topic.

Beyer, Mark. *Space Exploration.* Danbury, CT: Children's Press, 2002.

Carruthers, Margaret W. *The Hubble Space Telescope.* True Books. New York: Franklin Watts, 2003.

Furniss, Tim. *The Atlas of Space Exploration.* New York: Friedman, 2002.

Nagel, Rob. *Space Exploration: Almanac.* Detroit: UXL, 2004.

Space Exploration. Space Science in Action. [videorecording]. Wynnewood, PA: Schlessinger, 1999.

Stott, Carole. *Space Exploration.* New York: DK Publishing, 2004.

Can the Internet Help?

Space News—http://spaceflight.nasa.gov/home/index.html and http://www.discovery.com/stories/science/iss/iss.html. Take your time on these pages. Your answers are here—including live pictures and videos, research, the space station, and exploration of the planets, and you can take a space walk.

Space Exploration Merit Badge—http://my.execpc.com/~culp/space/space.html. Designed for boy scouts, but excellent links and information for everyone.

How Space Shuttles Work—http://science.howstuffworks.com/space-shuttle.htm. Explore the table of contents for more topics.

Space Missions—http://www.cnn.com/TECH/space/shuttle.html

Space Explorers—http://www.enchantedlearning.com/explorers/space.shtml. Information about the astronauts.

Sea and Sky: Space Exploration—http://www.seasky.org/sky5.html

The Space Shuttle—http://seds.lpl.arizona.edu/~ssa/docs/Space.Shuttle/index.shtml. Take your time here. This site answers many questions.

Living in Space—http://spaceflight.nasa.gov/living/index.html. Everything you need to know, just in case . . .

 **TA DA!**

Spacecrafts in Action!

The Space Place for Kids—from NASA—http://spaceplace.nasa.gov/en/kids/. Experiments, projects, games, videos, and much more for fun.

Experience

For fun, find the TV series *Lost in Space* (from the 1960s) at the video store and watch a few episodes. Then, write a story about what you think it would be like to be lost in space today. Visit this Web site: http://www.lostinspacetv.com/

In the Classroom

NASA—http://quest.arc.nasa.gov/. Educators' site.

59

Great Balls of Fire!

SUN AND STARS

New Words

Astronomy
Constellations
Galaxy
Nova—Supernova

What Are Stars?

There are so many kinds of stars: novas and supernovas, white dwarfs and brown dwarfs, pulsars, red giants and black holes. Our sun, while far brighter to us than anything else in the universe, is just a star. It appears big and bright because it is so close to us. People have always seen the sun and the stars, wondered about them, and made up stories about them. The ancient Romans believed that the sun was a glowing chariot driven slowly across the sky. Brave warriors were thought to be rewarded in death by becoming a new star. Theories about the sun and the stars always had to be hypotheses or guesses. No one could go there and find out how they were formed or what they are made of. New scientific discoveries, however, have made hypotheses more accurate.

What Can I Write About?

Would you like to travel in space? Describe your journey in detail.

Choose a constellation and compare the folklore about it.

Discuss navigation by the stars.

Discuss light pollution and its effects on astronomy.

What is a star? Explain how a star is born.

Are There Books on the Sun and the Stars?

There are many on astronomy and the sun and stars. Use your library catalog.

Darling, David. *The Universal Book of Astronomy from the Andromeda Galaxy to the Zone of Avoidance.* Hoboken, NJ: Wiley, 2003.

Parker, Sybil P., and Jay M. Pasachoff, eds. *McGraw-Hill Encyclopedia of Astronomy.* New York: McGraw-Hill, 1992.

Ridpath, Ian. *Facts on File Atlas of Stars and Planets: A Beginner's Guide to the Universe.* New York: Facts on File, 1993.

World Book Encyclopedia of Science. Vol. 1, *Astronomy.* Chicago: World Book, 2001.

Can the Internet Help?

NASA's Observatorium—http://observe.arc.nasa.gov/nasa/exhibits/stellarbirth/opening1.html. Tells how stars are born.

NASA—http://observe.arc.nasa.gov/nasa/exhibits/sun/sun_1.html. Some interesting facts about the sun.

Sea & Sky—http://www.seasky.org/sky.html. Sky news, astronomy resources, and a tour of the cosmos are offered here.

Astronomy for Kids—http://www.dustbunny.com/afk/index.html. Sky maps and constellations.

ThinkQuest—http://library.thinkquest.org/25763/. Explores the stars.

National Geographic—http://www.nationalgeographic.com/features/97/stars/. Examines the constellations.

Solar Max—http://www.exploratorium.edu/solarmax/. All about the cycle of the sun. The topics and links here may offer new information.

TA DA!

Stars in Action!

NASA—http://www.solarviews.com/cap/sun/sunb.htm. A video clip that discusses the sun's corona.

Experiment

Kids Involved Doing Science and Union College—http://www.union.edu/PUBLIC/KIDS/fsnCannedConstellations.htm. Make your own constellation viewers and learn to identify the constellations.

In the Classroom

University of Wisconsin—http://whyfiles.org/011comets/crecipe.html. Make a comet in the classroom.

Girl Scouts of America—http://scoutingweb.com/scoutingweb/Program/Science.htm#Astronomy. Astronomy ideas and projects.

NASA—http://www-spof.gsfc.nasa.gov/stargaze/Lintro.htm. Lesson plans.

The Fourth Dimension

TIME

New Words

Atomic Clock
Longitude—Dava Sobel
Pendulum
Solar Time

What Is Time?

Tick tock, tick tock. A grandfather clock keeps time with the steady beat of a pendulum swinging back and forth. A wind-up watch slowly unwinds to mark the passage of time. Newer watches and clocks are silent because batteries keep track of time. Ancient people didn't have watches or clocks, but they still kept track of time, using sundials, the movement of the moon and the tides, and the change of seasons. When it's noon here, it is midnight on the other side of the world.

Time zones change as we travel. It's 12:00 just to the west of a certain longitude. Step to the east and it becomes 1:00. Before the invention of trains, accurate time wasn't too important. Telling time by the sun was sufficient. But trains moved so fast, they would pass through a time zone in hours instead of days, and train engineers had to know exactly what time it was. If you live close to a time zone change, you may travel nearby and arrive before you leave! And what about traveling by airplane across continents? You might arrive yesterday.

What Can I Write About?

Explain time zones and their purpose. Make a chart of places you would like to travel and times.

Compare two calendars, such as the Islamic lunar calendar, the Chinese lunisolar calendar, the Mayan calendar, the Gregorian calendar, and the Julian calendar. Or choose one and explain it.

Build a sundial. Make a chart of the time on a sundial compared to an accurate watch, and report on your findings.

What do longitude and latitude have to do with time? What is Greenwich Mean Time?

Are There Books on Time?

Use your library catalog. *Time and space* are the effective key words.

New Book of Popular Science. Danbury, CT: Grolier, 2004.

Parker, Sybil P., and Jay M. Pasachoff, eds. *McGraw-Hill Encyclopedia of Astronomy.* New York: McGraw-Hill, 1992.

Sobel, Dava. *Longitude: The True Story of a Lone Genius Who Solved the Greatest Scientific Problem of His Time.* New York: Walker, 1995.

Can the Internet Help?

The Earthdial Project—http://planetary.org/mars/earthdial/index.html. A network of sundials around the world.

Mr. Dowling—http://www.mrdowling.com/601-daylight.html. Explains time and space at a middle school level.

NASA—http://www-spof.gsfc.nasa.gov/stargaze/Slatlong.htm. Learn what latitude and longitude have to do with time.

Is time travel possible? PBS explores the possibility—http://www.pbs.org/wgbh/nova/time/

What time is it anywhere in the world? Two sites—http://www.whattimeisit.com/ and http://www.timeanddate.com/worldclock/

 **TA DA!**

Time in Action!

Science Museum of Minnesota—http://www.playingwithtime.org/. Time-lapse photography shows the blink of an eye, slowly, and building construction, quickly.

PBS—http://www.pbs.org/wgbh/nova/time/sagan.html. Listen to Carl Sagan discuss time travel.

Orbitor Space Flight Simulator—http://www.medphys.ucl.ac.uk/~martins/orbit/orbit.html. Download a free space-time simulator, but be forewarned, this takes a lot of time!

Experiment

University of California, Berkeley Lawrence Hall of Science—http://www.lhs.berkeley.edu/StarClock/starclockprintout.html. Tell time by the stars! Make your own star clock.

In the Classroom

Lockheed—http://www.lmsal.com/YPOP/Classroom/Lessons/Sundials/sundials.html. Make sundials as a classroom project! Instructions are at various levels, some using protractors, sine, and tangent.

NASA—http://www-spof.gsfc.nasa.gov/stargaze/Llatlong.htm. Lesson plan on timekeeping for upper level students.

MATTER

What is matter? The dictionary says it is "that which has mass and occupies space; an atom is the smallest indivisible unit of matter." If that is the case, then matter matters! Matter is everywhere, except in a vacuum. Matter is everything. Chemistry is the study of matter and how it changes and interacts with other matter. It has four states—which you already know. Learn more about the chemistry that makes up our world.

Anatomy of a Burn.

ACIDS AND BASES

New Words

Litmus
Acid
Base
Alkali
Neutral
Ions
Salt

What Are Acids and Bases?

Almost every liquid is either an acid or a base. The few exceptions, such as distilled water, are considered neutral. But the strength of an acid or base will vary. It is measured on a pH scale, with scores between 0 and 14. If the pH is very low, the liquid is an acid. If it is high, the liquid is a base. And, of course, if the pH is right in the middle, at 7, the material is neutral. Just what does the pH scale measure? The number of H ions that have broken loose. Yikes! Read and learn.

What Can I Write About?

Explain the pH factor. Include how to test and how to change the pH.

Describe what happens when you combine bases and acids.

Compare and contrast acids and bases. Why are they so important?

Discuss some of the early theories of acids and bases. Evaluate the scientific techniques of the time.

Are There Books on Acids and Bases?

We can't begin to tell you the best books. There are many. Use your library catalog. Do not forget the reference area, where you can find background information and statistics.

Lerner, K. Lee, and Brenda Wilmoth Lerner, eds. *Gale Encyclopedia of Science.* 3d ed. Vol. 1. Detroit: Gale, 2004.

New Book of Popular Science. Vol. 3. Danbury, CT: Grolier, 2004.

Newton, David E., Rob Nagel, and Bridget Travers. *UXL Encyclopedia of Science.* Vol. 1. Detroit: UXL, 1998.

Tocci, Salvatore. *Chemistry Around You.* New York: Arco, 1985.

Can the Internet Help?

ChemTutor—http://www.chemtutor.com/acid.htm. Explains acids and bases for older students.

Vision Learning—http://www.visionlearning.com/library/module_viewer.php?mid=58. A more simple explanation of acids and bases.

University of British Columbia—http://www.chem.ubc.ca/courseware/pH/index.html. This very thorough tutorial not only explains the nature of acids and bases but quizzes you on each chapter. Go slowly and you will "get it."

Chem4Kids—http://www.chem4kids.com/files/react_acidbase.html. Offers the most basic explanation of acids and bases.

The pH Scale—http://www.ec.gc.ca/water/en/manage/qual/e_ph.htm. A table to help you understand. Also, information about pH and water quality.

 **TA DA!**

Acids and Bases in Action!

GEMS Alien Juice Bar game, from the Lawrence Hall of Science at University of California Berkeley—http://sv.berkeley.edu/showcase/flash/juicebar.html. Has virtual experiments with acids and bases.

Interactive Science Tutor—http://www.glencoe.com/sec/science/Science600/co/617.php?iRef=617. Play an acids and bases matching game.

Experiment

KidzWorld—http://www.kidzworld.com/site/p601.htm. Write a secret message in invisible ink! This site shows you three ways to do it.

About.com—http://chemistry.about.com/od/demonstrationsexperiments/ss/appleenzyme.htm. The browning of apples can demonstrate acids and bases in this experiment.

In the Classroom

The PH Factor, from the Miami Museum of Science—http://www.miamisci.org/ph/default.html. Activities to excite students about acids and bases.

Teach-nology—http://www.teach-nology.com/teachers/lesson_plans/science/chemistry/reactions/. Offers several lesson plans on chemical reactions, including acids and bases.

Elementary, My Dear Watson.

CHEMICAL ELEMENTS

New Words

Atomic Number
Chemistry
Electron
Elements
Melting Point
Mendeleyev
Periodic Table

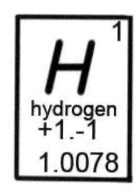

What Is an Element?

Chemical elements are the building blocks from which all matter is composed. When a substance cannot be reduced further, it is an element. Right now, there are 110 known elements. Some of these elements are very familiar to us. Chemists hope to find out what things are made of by breaking them down to their lowest form and putting them back together again. (H_2O = water) Love chemistry? Love to experiment? If so, make this your topic!

What Can I Write About?

What are chemical elements? Who studies this topic? How do they find information?

Explain the history of the study of elements—add a time line. Discuss only two or three important periods.

Discuss the history of the periodic table. Who created it? What led to this creation?

Choose one of the elements to learn about, for example, helium. Don't forget the health and environmental effects of this element. Choose one of the elements we all know.

Are There Books on Elements?

Use your library catalog. Do not forget the reference area and books on your topic.

Brandolini, Anita. *Fizz, Bubble & Flash: Element Explorations and Atom Adventures for Hands-on Science Fun!* Charlotte, VT: Williamson, 2003.

Knapp, Brian. *Elements.* Danbury, CT: Grolier, 2001.

Stockley, Corinne. *The Usborne Illustrated Dictionary of Science: A Complete Reference Guide to Physics, Chemistry and Biology.* Tulsa, OK: EDC, 2002.

Stwertka, Albert. *A Guide to the Elements.* New York: Oxford, 2002.

Zannos, Susan. *Dmitri Mendeleyev and the Periodic Table.* Hockessin, DE: Mitchell Lane, 2005.

Can the Internet Help?

Web Elements—http://www.webelements.com/. The most complete site—with sound and short videos; includes discovery, history, and uses.

An Interactive Chemical Elements Table—http://www.chemicalelements.com/. Basics, atomic structure, isotopes, and Internet links.

Chem4Kids—http://www.chem4kids.com/files/elem_intro.html. One of the easiest sites to understand. Basics, plus 18 elements defined.

Lenntech Periodic Table—http://www.lenntech.com/periodic-chart.htm. Good information including health and environmental effects.

History of the Periodic Table—http://www.ausetute.com.au/pthistor.html. Study of elements.

Periodic Table of the Elements—http://pearl1.lanl.gov/periodic/default.htm. Another site with easy to understand explanations and pictures.

Visual Elements—http://www.chemsoc.org/viselements/pages/periodic_table.html

Timeline of Element Discovery—http://chemistry.about.com/library/weekly/aa030303a.htm. Also take the "tour" of other sites.

 **TA DA!**

Chem Comics in Action!

The Periodical Table—http://www.uky.edu/Projects/Chemcomics/. As used in comic books! What fun!

Games—http://www.syvum.com/squizzes/chem/ and http://education.jlab.org/indexpages/elementgames.html. Quizzes, activities, and games. Includes several on the elements.

In the Classroom

Discovery School lesson—http://school.discovery.com/lessonplans/programs/elements/. Grades 6–8.

SMILE Program—http://www.iit.edu/~smile/cheminde.html. Chemistry index of activities and labs.

Science You Can Eat!

COOKING WITH SCIENCE

New Words

Calories
Carbohydrate
Food Chemistry
Food Science
Glucose
Leavening
Lipids
Proteins

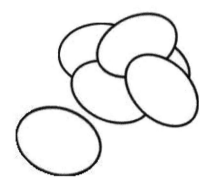

What Does Cooking Have to Do with Science?

Foods are chemical compounds, and a recipe is a formula. If you had to eat everything raw and without spices, food would be pretty dull. Cooking creates a chemical reaction, changing the food into different substances. The appearance, feel, and taste may all change. When you take a little oil and a little flour and an egg and yeast, none of them looks very exciting. But mix them together and bake, and all of a sudden you have bread! Adding certain ingredients or changing temperature by boiling or freezing may preserve foods. Think about a strawberry. If you leave it out, it will get moldy in just a couple of days. Cook and can it and it can last for years. Cooking may seem like an everyday activity, but it is science.

What Can I Write About?

Explore the magic of eggs! Write about their many properties and changing states.

Identify at least three leaveners and discuss what they do.

Explain calories, where they come from and how they work.

Discuss several methods of food preservation and the science behind them.

Identify some food additives. Find out just what they are. Write about their purpose and their drawbacks.

Are There Books on Cooking Science

Use your library catalog, searching *cooking science*. Encyclopedias will have information.

Maynard, Chris. *Kitchen Science.* New York: DK Publishing, 2001.

Morgan, Sally. *Superfoods: Genetic Modification of Foods.* Science at the Edge. Chicago: Heinemann Library, 2002.

Tocci, Salvatore. *Chemistry Around You.* New York: Arco, 1985.

Can the Internet Help?

Yummy Physics—http://www.geocities.com/yummyphysics/. Shows the physics of cooking.

About.com—http://chemistry.about.com/cs/sciencefairideas/a/aa041503a.htm. Food and cooking chemistry, including science fair project ideas.

BBC site on Cooking Chemistry—http://www.bbc.co.uk/science/hottopics/cooking/chemistry.shtml. Explores such questions as, "Did cooking make us human?"

Eggs Science from Alberta Egg Producers—http://www.eggs.ab.ca/kids/Egg%20Science/splash.htm

Science of Cooking from Exploratorium—http://www.exploratorium.edu/cooking/. Examine the scientific processes of cooking.

**TA DA!**

Cooking in Action!

Watch a Webcast of cooking science from Exploratorium—http://www.exploratorium.edu/cooking/webcasts/index.html. You can view the science of bread, the science of chocolate, and the science of cheese, among others.

Experiment

Exploratorium—http://www.exploratorium.edu/cooking/eggs/kitchenlab.html. Helps you experiment with eggs, from dissolving the shell through chemistry to using physics to tell whether an egg is hard-boiled.

The Entomology Department of the University of Iowa—http://www.ent.iastate.edu/misc/insectsasfood.html. Recipes for cooking with insects.

In the Classroom

Science Friday from PBS—http://www.sciencefriday.com/kids/sfkc20041224-1.html. Audio programs, discussion, and activities on cooking science.

Cook and Eat Chemistry from the State of Utah—http://www.uen.org/utahlink/lp_res/nutri375.html. A curriculum guide.

Food Science lesson plans gathered by Penn State—http://www.foodscience.psu.edu/outreach/fun_food_science.html and http://www.sciencenetlinks.org/lessons.cfm?BenchmarkID=8&DocID=396

Underlying Structure.

CRYSTALS

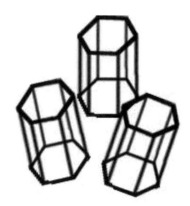

New Words

Lattice
Solute
Solvent
Amorphous Solids
Crystallography

What Is a Crystal?

A crystal is the backbone of just about any solid. The exceptions, glass and plastics, are often considered not to be true solids but amorphous solids. There are seven types of crystals, each named for its geometric shape. Look at the shapes with a microscope if you can, or see pictures in books and on the Web sites. They are beautiful! Some crystals, such as salt and sugar, are large enough that you can see them with your eyes. To see them even better, use a magnifying glass.

Many types of crystals are formed when molten minerals cool. The slower they cool, the larger the crystals. If you try making your own, you might try letting some cool quickly and others in a warmer area to see the difference.

What Can I Write About?

What is a crystal? How is it formed?

Grow your own crystals and record and discuss their development.

Find three uses for crystals and explain them. Or compare and contrast diamonds and graphite.

Explain the lattice as it relates to crystals.

Describe what happens to crystals when their substance melts, and when it hardens again.

Are There Books on Crystals?

Use your library catalog. Do not forget the reference area, where you can find background information and statistics.

Erickson, Jon. *An Introduction to Fossils and Minerals.* New York: Facts on File, 2000.

Magill, Frank N. *Magill's Survey of Science: Physical Science Series.* Pasadena, CA: Salem, 1992.

New Book of Popular Science. Danbury, CT: Grolier, 2004.

Stagl, Jean. *Crystals and Crystal Gardens You Can Grow.* New York: Franklin Watts, 1990.

Can the Internet Help?

Kiwi Web of New Zealand—http://www.chemistry.co.nz/crystals_defined.htm. What is a crystal? Shapes, colors, and crystal gardens.

How Stuff Works—http://www.howstuffworks.com/diamond1.htm. The origin of diamonds.

The Science Museum of Virginia—http://www.smv.org/prog/xtaldsc.htm. Gives a brief introduction to crystals.

Mindat.org—http://www.mindat.org/. This mineralogy Web site allows you to search by crystal system or specific mineral. It provides chemical data, hardness, and photographs.

Crystallography—http://mathforum.org/alejandre/workshops/crystal.html. How crystals form, the seven systems, good links.

Photonic Crystals—http://ab-initio.mit.edu/photons/. Research—some difficult, but plenty of information for most students.

TA DA!

Crystals in Action!

Florida State University—http://micro.magnet.fsu.edu/moviegallery/chemical crystals/liquidcrystals/. Video clips of liquid crystals.

Experiment

National Geographic Kids—http://www.nationalgeographic.com/ngkids/trythis/tryfun1.html. Try growing emeralds, rubies, and sapphires.

The San Diego Museum of Natural History—http://www.sdnhm.org/kids/minerals/grow-crystal.html. Shows you how to grow your own salt crystals.

In the Classroom

Yale-New Haven Teachers' Institute—http://www.yale.edu/ynhti/curriculum/units/1989/6/89.06.04.x.html. Crystals: What are they?

Discover the Science of Diamonds, a lesson plan from CNN—http://cnnstudentnews.cnn.com/2001/fyi/lesson.plans/11/20/diamond.science/

The Smithsonian Institution—http://www.smithsonianeducation.org/educators/lesson_plans/minerals/minerals_crystals.html. Lesson plans about crystals and gems.

It Feels Like It Weighs a Ton!

DENSITY

New Words

Float
Mass
Sinking
Weight

What Is Density?

You spend all your life understanding the world around you, and then science comes along and confuses everything! For instance, would you rather be hit by a ton of bricks or a ton of feathers? You know a feather is lighter, but a ton is a ton, of course! If you drop a brick and a feather, which one will hit the ground first? You think again; of course, the brick will. But astronauts tried a similar experiment on the moon with surprising results. When they dropped a feather and a hammer, they hit the ground at the same time!

We tend to think of density and weight as the same thing. Often they behave the same. But as you explore density, you will learn about the very important differences.

What Can I Write About?

Explain the differences between weight and density.

Write about Archimedes and his discoveries concerning density.

Explain how a submarine sinks and floats. You might want to compare it to scuba divers or dolphins and whales.

Discuss density as it relates to gases.

How can density help you to identify an element?

Write about the effects of gravity on density, and what that means on the moon or other planets.

Are There Books on Density?

We can't begin to tell you the best books. There are many. Use your library catalog. Do not forget the reference area, where you can find background information and statistics.

Clark, John O. E. *Physics Matters! Matter.* Vol. 1. Danbury, CT: Grolier, 2001.

Cooper, Christopher. *Matter.* Eyewitness Science and Nature. New York: Dorling Kindersley, 2000.

Dispezio, Michael. *Awesome Experiments in Force and Motion.* New York: Sterling, 1998.

New Book of Popular Science. Vol. 3. Danbury, CT: Grolier, 2004.

Can the Internet Help?

Edinformatics—http://www.edinformatics.com/math_science/mass_volume_density.htm. Mass, volume, and density are explored on this page.

Beyond Books—http://www.beyondbooks.com/psc91/4e.asp. The difference between mass and weight is explained.

Density Notes from Science by Jones—http://www.sciencebyjones.com/density_notes.htm. Gives the density of many different materials.

Vision Learning—http://www.visionlearning.com/library/module_viewer2.php?mid=37&l=&let1=Gen. Tells about Archimedes and density.

How Stuff Works—http://www.howstuffworks.com/question663.htm. Explains how density makes the Galileo Thermometer work.

Bone Density in Athletes—http://depts.washington.edu/bonebio/bonStrength/exercise/sports.html. Look at each sport, then follow Next⟩ to more information.

 **TA DA!**

Density in Action!

EOA Scientific—http://www.eoascientific.com/campus/science/multimedia/weight_mass/view_interactive. Interactive demonstration of density and gravity.

Experiment

Try this for fun!—http://www.nationalgeographic.com/ngkids/trythis/tryfun4.html. Layered liquids make a rainbow because of the different densities.

In the Classroom

Kids Union—http://www.kids.union.edu/blocksWithADifference.htm. Density demonstration for grades 3–6.

The density of sugar is demonstrated with diet soda—http://www.middleschoolscience.com/dietcoke.htm

National Geographic—http://www.nationalgeographic.com/xpeditions/lessons/14/g68/trythisoil.html. Offers a more complex demonstration of density relating to oil.

UCLA Physics Department—http://www.physics.ucla.edu/k-6connection/Mass,w,d.htm. Suggestions and an activity on teaching density to kids.

It's All Relative.

ALFRED EINSTEIN

New Words

E = MC^2
Physics
Theory of Relativity
Time, Light, Energy, Gravity

Who Was Alfred Einstein?

What is light? How does it travel? How fast can it go? Is time the same for everyone? Does the rate at which time flows depend on where you are and how fast you are traveling? How would a house painter experience gravity if he fell off a roof? Would he be weightless during his fall? Einstein considered all of these questions and gave us new answers. Einstein lived during the early twentieth century. He was a poor student, but he excelled at math and science. The thoughts he had about physics are being used today. Many of our inventions are the result of the answers to his questions. Einstein explained his theory about relativity: "When you sit with a nice girl for two hours, it seems like two minutes. When you sit on a hot stove for two minutes, it seems like two hours. That's relativity."

What Can I Write About?

Write a biography of Albert Einstein's life, including his contributions to science and math.

Einstein's General Theory of Relativity proposed that matter causes space to curve. Read more about this and explain it by giving examples.

Choose just one area of Einstein's scientific contributions—his work with time, light, or energy. How did he think of these ideas? Try to explain in your own words.

Write about the inventions we have today because of Einstein's theories. Or, for older students, write about challenges to Einstein's theories.

Are There Books About Albert Einstein?

We can't begin to tell you the best books. There are many. Use your library catalog.

Biography Today: Scientists & Inventors Series : Profiles of People of Interest to Young Readers. Detroit: Omnigraphics, 1996– .

Brallier, Jess M. *Who Was Albert Einstein?* New York: Grossett & Dunlap, 2002.

Hammontree, Marie. *Albert Einstein: Young Thinker.* New York: Aladdin, 1986.

McPherson, Stephanie. *Ordinary Genius: The Story of Albert Einstein.* Minneapolis, MN: Carolrhoda, 1995.

Parker, Steve. *Albert Einstein and Relativity.* New York: Chelsea House, 1995.

Can the Internet Help?

Albert Einstein Home Page—http://www.humboldt1.com/~gralsto/einstein/einstein.html. This information put together by a student is a good start.

Time Magazine—100 Most Important People of the Century—http://www.time.com/time/time100/poc/magazine/albert_einstein5a.html

Albert Einstein—http://www.westegg.com/einstein/. Links to some of the best sites on the Internet.

Center for History of Physics—http://www.aip.org/history/einstein/. Good biographical information. One of the best sites.

American Museum of Natural History—http://www.amnh.org/exhibitions/einstein/light/index.php. Excellent information and easy to understand.

Einstein for Kids—http://www.albert-einstein.org/.index6.html. Be sure to browse the multimedia to see and hear Einstein.

Einstein's Legacy—http://www.colorado.edu/physics/2000/applets_EL.html. What inventions do we have today because of Einstein's theories?

 **TA DA!**

Think Like Einstein!

PBS activities—http://www.pbs.org/wgbh/nova/time/think.html

Experiment

Time Traveler Game from NOVA—http://www.pbs.org/wgbh/nova/einstein/hotsciencetwin/index.html

Light Traveler—http://www.pbs.org/wgbh/nova/einstein/hotsciencelight/index.html

In the Classroom

NOVA Online Teacher's Guide to Einstein—http://www.pbs.org/wgbh/nova/teachers/programs/2311_einstein.html

Einstein Archives Online—http://www.alberteinstein.info/. Digitized manuscripts and picture gallery.

What Goes Up, Must Come Down.

NEWTON'S LAWS

New Words

Acceleration
Gravity
Inertia
Inertia
Momentum

What Are Newton's Laws?

Isaac Newton didn't change anything about force and motion. Gravity, inertia, and acceleration existed before Isaac Newton came along, and they are still here hundreds of years later. What he did was think about these things, and then explain them in a way that has helped science develop. His first law, the Law of Inertia, says that it takes some sort of force to start things in motion, and behind every motion is some sort of force. The second law is Acceleration = force/mass. Simply put, things move faster if they're hit harder. In his third law of motion, Conservation of Momentum, Newton explained that for every action there is an equal and opposite reaction. In other words, when you kick a ball, that ball also strikes your foot.

What Can I Write About?

Describe one of your favorite activities such as skiing, baseball, or bicycling, using the concepts of force and motion.

Try an experiment using force or motion. Some are suggested in the "Experiment" section below, and you may find others. Explain your assumptions before the experiment and what you learned from it.

Use Newton's Third Law to illustrate how birds fly and how airplanes stay up in the air.

Compare centripetal force to centrifugal force using Conservation of Momentum.

Explain how a moon stays in orbit around a planet, using the concepts of Newton's Third Law.

Are There Books on Newton's Laws?

We can't begin to tell you the best books. There are many. Use your library catalog. Do not forget the reference area, where you can find background information and statistics.

Clark, John E. E. *Physics Matters!* Danbury, CT: Grolier, 2001.

Magill, Frank N., ed. *Magill's Survey of Science: Physical Science Series.* Pasadena, CA: Salem, 1992.

New Book of Popular Science. Vols. 3 & 4. Danbury, CT: Grolier, 2004.

Can the Internet Help?

Fear of Physics—http://www.fearofphysics.com/index.html. All sorts of examples of gravity, friction, and acceleration.

The Physics Classroom from Glenbrook High School—http://www.glenbrook. k12.il.us/gbssci/phys/Class/1DKin/U1L1a.html. A great site for motion and vectors.

The Physics Classroom—http://www.physicsclassroom.com/Class/newtlaws/ U2L4a.html. Explains Newton's Third Law.

NASA—http://www.grc.nasa.gov/WWW/K-12/airplane/newton.html. Explains the Laws of Motion and specifically how they affect airplanes.

All World Knowledge—http://www.allworldknowledge.com/newton/. Lighthearted explanations of Newton's Laws.

 **TA DA!**

Newton's Laws in Action!

NASA—http://quest.nasa.gov/space/teachers/liftoff/newton.html. View a 12-minute video showing Newton's Laws in space.

An interactive game illustrating force and velocity—http://www. interactivestuff. org/sums4fun/ projectile.html

Newton's 3 Jet Engine

Experiment

PBS—http://pbskids.org/zoom/activities/sci/. Experiments and activities using force and motion.

In the Classroom

Classroom activities demonstrating force and motion—http://wings.avkids. com/Curriculums/Forces_Motion/

With a few supplies, you can create a hovercraft to demonstrate the Conservation of Momentum—http://www.darylscience.com/Demos/Hovercraft.html

Illinois Institute of Technology—http://www.iit.edu/~smile/physinde.html. This collection of physics lesson plans includes several on Newton's Laws of Motion.

Goddard Space Center and Sonoma State University—http://swift. sonoma.edu/education/. Posters and lesson plans.

Ions on the Loose!

RADIOACTIVITY

New Words

> Alpha, Beta, and Gamma Rays
> Geiger Counter
> Half-Life
> Isotopes
> Nuclear

What Is Radioactivity?

Radiation results when the nucleus of an atom loses some of its protons and neutrons. It surrounds us, coming from some types of rocks such as granite and from cosmic rays from the sun. It is a powerful force that can be harnessed for use by humankind. Radioisotopes are used in medical tests, nuclear power runs submarines that stay underwater for months at a time, and nuclear power plants provide electricity in many parts of the country. Carefully controlled radiation can treat tumors. It can even be used to date antiquities. But when it is concentrated, such as a leak from a nuclear power plant or radon gas collecting in a basement, it becomes a problem. Too much radiation can cause radiation sickness.

What Can I Write About?

> Choose one of the pioneers of radiation research—Henri Becquerel, Madame Marie Curie, or C. T. R. Wilson—and write about his or her discoveries.

> Compare alpha, beta, and gamma radiation.

> Describe how radiation is harnessed in a nuclear power plant or a nuclear submarine.

> Look into carbon dating and explain how it works.

> What are some of the problems caused by radiation? Consider one thoroughly, or compare some.

> If radon is a problem in your area, discuss its causes and what can be done about it.

Are There Books on Radioactivity ?

> Use your library catalog. Do not forget the reference area, where you can find background information and statistics.

Bortz, Fred, and Alfred Bortz. Library of Subatomic Particles Series. New York: Rosen. Includes these titles—*Electron, Proton, Neutron, Neutrino, Quark,* and *Photon*—all published in 2004.

Clark, John O. E. *Physics Matters!* Danbury, CT: Grolier, 2001.

McGrath, Kimberly A., ed. *World of Physics.* Detroit: Gale, 2001.

Pasachoff, Naomi. *Madame Curie and the Science of Radioactivity.* New York: Oxford University Press, 1996.

Can the Internet Help?

NIEHS Kids Page—http://www.niehs.nih.gov/kids/uranium.htm. Positive uses of radioactivity.

The ABC's of Nuclear Science, from the Lawrence Berkeley National Laboratory—http://www.lbl.gov/abc

Electricity from Nuclear Power, from the Tennessee Valley Authority—http://www.tvakids.com/electricity/nuclear.htm

FactMonster—http://www.factmonster.com/ce6/sci/A0860622.html. The discovery of radioactivity.

Nuclear Fuel Waste Bureau—http://www.nfwbureau.gc.ca/english/View.asp?pf=1&x=627#Radiation. What is radiation?

How X-rays Work, from How Stuff Works—http://science.howstuffworks.com/x-ray.htm

Cleveland Museum of Natural Science—http://www.uhrad.com/kids.htm. X-rays for kids.

The Discovery of Radioactivity—http://www.accessexcellence.org/AE/AEC/CC/radioactivity.html. Basic, understandable information. List of radioactive materials.

**TA DA!**

Learn More on Your Own!

American Institute of Physics—http://www.aip.org/history/curie/brief/index.html. Interactive story of Madame Curie and the science of radioactivity.

Experiment

The Lawrence Berkeley National Laboratory—http://www.lbl.gov/abc/Contents.html#experiment. Offers nine experiments with radiation. Don't worry; online is a safe way to experiment with radiation!

In the Classroom

Radioactivity lesson plans for grades 6–12—http://www.curriculum.edu.au/maths300/download/m300bits/007pradi.htm and http://www.thirteen.org/edonline/ntti/resources/lessons/radioactive/

Everything Matters.

SOLIDS, LIQUIDS, AND GASES

New Words

Mass
Molecules
Physical Changes
States of Matter
Solids, Liquids, Gases, Plasmas

What Are Solids, Liquids, and Gases?

Everything is composed of matter, and matter is divided into three classes: solids, liquids, and gases. So, if you write about solids, liquids, and gases you will be writing about everything. Or you will be writing about the materials that everything consists of. Confusing? Yes, but very interesting. Everyone knows the example of the three states of water: ice (solid), water (liquid), and steam (gas). See if you can understand more about this topic.

What Can I Write About?

Identify the states of matter and then write about each. Be sure to describe clear examples. This is a project where your class would benefit by seeing and experiments.

Why does some matter change? Write about the influence temperature has on matter. Give good examples of change caused by temperature. Give some examples of materials in different states.

Choose just one state, for example solids. Explain the chemical makeup of this state and give good examples. Be sure to explain whether or not it can be changed.

Are There Books or Videos on Solids, Liquids, and Gases?

Use your library catalog to search for "matter". Reference books will get you started.

Ballard, Carol. *Solids, Liquids, and Gases: From Ice Cubes to Bubbles.* Heineman, 2003.

Berger, Melvin. *Solids, Liquids and Gases: From Superconductors to the Ozone Layer.* New York: Putnam, 1989.

Cooper, Christopher. *Matter.* Eyewitness Science and Nature. New York: DK Publishing, 2000.

Gardner, Robert. *Science Projects about Solids, Liquids, and Gases.* Berkeley Heights, NJ: Enslow, 2000.

Osborne, Louise, and Carol Gold. *Solids, Liquids, and Gases.* Buffalo, NY: Kids Can, 2000.

Oxlade, Chris. *States of Matter.* Chemicals in Action series. Chicago: Heinemann, 2000.

Can the Internet Help?

Chemistry for Kids: Matter—http://www.chem4kids.com/files/matter_intro. html. Basic information about the chemical properties of matter.

Matter—Physical science—http://www.usoe.k12.ut.us/curr/science/sciber00/ 8th/matter/sciber/intro.htm. Experiments and explanations.

Matter—http://www.mcwdn.org/Physics/Matter.html. Try the quiz. This will help you know whether you understand or not.

Matter—http://ippex.pppl.gov/interactive/matter/default.htm. Properties of matter and the states of matter.

Matter—http://www.school-for-champions.com/science/matterstates.htm. This site will answer several of your questions.

States of Matter—http://www.chem.purdue.edu/gchelp/atoms/states.html. Easy to understand and has a table that explains the behavior of matter.

ChemTutor—States of Matter—http://www.chemtutor.com/sta.htm

 **TA DA!**

Matter in Action!

The Strange Matter Exhibit—http://www.strangematterexhibit.com/index. html. Have fun and experience STRANGE matter.

Take a break with these games about matter—http://www.gamequarium. com/matter.html

Experiment

Matter—http://www.harcourtschool.com/activity/states_of_matter/. Try your own experiment after studying this one.

In the Classroom

Hogue, Lynn. *Investigating Solids, Liquids, and Gases with Toys.* New York: McGraw-Hill, 1997.

States of Matter Lesson Plans—http://www.teach-nology.com/teachers/lesson_ plans/science/chemistry/matter/

Matter: Properties of Matter and States of Matter—http://www.emints.org/ ethemes/resources/S00001504.shtml. Exercises and plans.

MEDICINE AND HEALTH

This is one area we should all be interested in. Medical treatment is changing all the time. Researchers are finding ways to keep us alive much longer than previous generations. Some of the deadly diseases of the past are no longer a great concern. But there are new diseases discovered every day, and treatments change. Select one of these topics or another—viral or bacterial diseases may be a topic you would like to learn about. Our person this time is Antonia Novello. She was responsible for the government's big campaign against teen smoking and drinking. Today she works with children with AIDS. There are other important medical researchers, including biotechnologists. This is an important field. Find out more.

Quackery or Cure?

ALTERNATIVE MEDICINE

New Words

Acupuncture
Chiropractics
Complementary Medicine
Herbal Medicine
Holistic Methods
Meditation and Yoga

What Is Alternative Medicine?

Just about any health treatment besides traditional medicine can be considered alternative medicine. It can include something as simple as having a cup of chamomile tea to help you relax or a cup of chicken soup when you have a cold. It can also be a form of medicine practiced in other parts of the world such as acupuncture or massage therapy. When alternative medicine is used along with traditional medicine, it is considered complementary medicine.

What Can I Write About?

Identify several forms of alternative medicine and compare them.

Choose one form of alternative medicine and discuss it in depth.

Discuss the pros and cons of herbal medicine.

Choose an illness or disease such as a cold or cancer. Compare traditional and alternative treatments.

Are There Books on Alternative Medicine?

Use your library catalog. Do not forget the reference area and the librarian.

Krapp, Kristine M., and Jacqueline L. Longe, eds. *Gale Encyclopedia of Alternative Medicine.* Detroit: Gale, 2000.

Lerner, K. Lee, and Brenda Wilmoth Lerner, eds. *Gale Encyclopedia of Science.* 3d ed. Vol.1 . Detroit: Gale, 2004.

Levinson, David. *Health and Illness: A Cross-Cultural Encyclopedia.* San Francisco: ABC-CLIO, 1997.

New Book of Popular Science. Vol. 5. Danbury, CT: Grolier, 2004.

Schlager, Neil, ed. *Science and Its Times: Understanding the Social Significance of Scientific Discovery*. Vol. 7, *1950–Present*. Detroit: Gale, 2000.

Can the Internet Help?

KidsHealth—http://kidshealth.org/parent/system/medicine/alternative_medicine. html. Discusses the pros and cons of alternative medicine. It mentions many forms.

The Center for Complementary and Alternative Medicine from the National Institutes of Health—http://nccam.nih.gov/health/whatiscam/. Detailed information and statistics. It's written for adults, so some of the language may be difficult.

Holistic Kids—http://www.holistickids.org/overview_therapies/bioenergetic. html. Explanations of several forms of alternative medicine, including acupuncture, healing touch, and Reiki.

The Chiropractics Association of Australia—http://www.chiropractors.asn.au/ aboutchiro/faq/faqchiro.html. Explains how chiropractic works.

The Holistic Approach to Chronic Illness, from Healthy Child—http://www. healthychild.com/database/the_holistic_approach_to_chronic_illness.htm

A Different Way to Heal, from Scientific American Frontiers—http://www.pbs. org/saf/1210/. See if the series is in your area—and look for good articles on alternative medicine.

 **TA DA!**

Alternative Medicine in Action!

Most libraries have yoga videos for kids. Try your library catalog to find one.

Experiment

Try some yoga poses and see how they make you feel. Get a book from the library for the best explanations, or try this site from the Yoga Garden—http:// www.theyogagarden.com/poses.html

Try Meditation for Kids from the Online Family Buddhist Center—http://www. idsl.net/heather/onlinebuddhistcenter/meditationhall/Meditationsforkids.html

In the Classroom

The Alternative Fix, from PBS—http://www.pbs.org/wgbh/pages/frontline/ shows/altmed/. Includes background and a teacher's guide.

The Alternative Medicine Homepage, from the University of Pittsburgh—http:// www.pitt.edu/~cbw/altm.html. Has links to a wide variety of Web pages, listed by disease.

Rebel Cells.

CANCER

New Words

Benign—Malignant
Chemotherapy
Leukemia
Radiation Therapy
Tumor

What Is Cancer?

You have millions of cells in your body. They reproduce, or make new cells just like themselves, regularly to replace old cells and to help you grow. But when those cells go out of control and create abnormal cells, they can crowd out normal cells. As a result, the cancer makes you sick. There are many types of cancer. Some, such as brain or breast cancer, seem to be genetic. Some, such as leukemia, particularly affect children. Others, such as skin cancer and lung cancer, are often caused by lifestyle.

What Can I Write About?

Discuss the cancers that are affected by smoking or by breathing secondhand smoke.

Choose one type of cancer. It may be one that affects you or someone you know. Examine the causes, treatment, and prognosis.

Compare and contrast radiation therapy and chemotherapy.

Examine cancer trends. Are certain types increasing or decreasing? Evaluate your findings.

Discuss preventative measures to decrease cancer risk with lifestyle changes.

Are There Books on Cancer?

Use your library catalog and ask the librarian to help with specific types of cancer.

Alagna, Magdalena. *Everything You Need to Know About Chemotherapy.* Need to Know Library. New York: Rosen, 2001.

Benowitz, Steven I. *Cancer.* Diseases and People. Berkeley Heights, NJ: Enslow, 1999.

Bunch, Bryan, ed. *Diseases.* Danbury, CT: Grolier, 1997.

Encyclopedia of Family Health. New York: Marshall Cavendish, 1998.

New Book of Popular Science. Danbury, CT: Grolier, 2004.

Olendorf, Donna, Christine Jeryan, and Karen Boyden, eds. *Gale Encyclopedia of Medicine.* Detroit: Gale, 1999.

Can the Internet Help?

KidsHealth—http://kidshealth.org/kid/health_problems/cancer/cancer_kinds.html. Some kinds of cancer kids get.

Cancersource—http://www.cancersourcekids.com/. Explains many different kinds of cancer that affect kids.

The National Cancer Institute—http://www.cancer.gov/cancer_information/. Detailed information about types of cancer and treatments.

Tobacco and Cancer, from the American Cancer Society—http://www.cancer.org/docroot/PED/ped_10_1.asp?sitearea=PED

Advocate Lutheran Hospital—http://www.advocatehealth.com/lgch/services/cancer/braintumor/kids.html. Explains treatments for brain tumors. Included are descriptions of chemotherapy and radiation therapy that can apply to any type of cancer.

How Cancer Works, from How Stuff Works—http://health.howstuffworks.com/cancer.htm

Texas A&M University—http://coolshade.tamu.edu/index1.html. Skin cancer facts and statistics.

 **TA DA!**

Cancer in Action!

Leukemia patient Ben Durkin wanted to make a video game about childhood cancer to help other kids—http://www.makewish.org/ben. The Make a Wish Foundation helped him.

Biology in Motion—http://biologyinmotion.com/index.html. Animated illustrations of normal cell division and of cell evolution and mutation.

Experiment

In some ways, your life is an experiment in cancer research. But read about one student's experience in a cancer research laboratory—http://www.vanderbilt.edu/exploration/students/students_richmond_lab.htm

In the Classroom

Lesson plans and background information—www.cancer.org/ (The American Cancer Society) and http://www.leafy-greens.org/lessonplans.html (National Leafy Greens Council).

We Care!

ENVIRONMENTAL HEALTH

New Words

Epidemiology
Environmental Health
Toxic
Pesticides
Hazardous—Danger—Warning—Caution

What Is Environmental Health?

Many people are concerned about children and the effects of the environment on their health. Air pollutants, pesticides, lead, and mercury are all known to be harmful. Mobile phones may even be harmful. Research is now showing that asthma, cancer, autism, diabetes, and even attention deficit disorder are somehow linked to the environment. Baby colic has even been tied to smoking. This is a big, broad subject, so be sure to talk with your teacher about your plan. Narrow your subject so that you can do a good job.

What Can I Write About?

What do we mean when we say environmental health? Describe two or three of the environmental issues that can affect health.

Write about the labels used on products to indicate they are harmful. What do they mean? Who puts the labels on these products? Give examples.

What is a toxic substance? Write about several. What harm do they cause?

Write about an illness that can be ascribed to the environment. Find medical research that shows this.

What are some of the causes of environmental allergies? Write about treatment.

Are There Books on Environmental Health?

We can't begin to tell you the best books. There are many. Use your library catalog. Do not forget the reference area, where you can find background information and statistics.

Collman, James. *Naturally Dangerous: Surprising Facts About Food, Health, and the Environment.* Sausalito, CA: University Science, 2001.

The Human Body & the Environment: How Our Environment Affects Our Health. Westport, CT: Greenwood, 2003.

Schneider, Dona. *Children's Environmental Health: Reducing Risk in a Dangerous World.* Atlanta, GA: American Public Health Association, 2000.

Can the Internet Help?

National Institute of Environmental Health—http://www.niehs.nih.gov/kids/hottopics.htm. Take your time on these pages. There is a lot here.

EPA's page for kids—Learn about Chemicals at Home—Pesticides, Toxic Substances, Labels—http://www.epa.gov/kidshometour/index.htm

How Stuff Works—Lungs——http://science.howstuffworks.com/lung5.htm. Look at the many topics and see whether they are what you need.

Safety and Health Policy Center—http://www.nsc.org/ehc.htm. Poisons, air quality, radiation, sun, secondhand smoke.

National Center for Environmental Health—http://www.cdc.gov/nceh/kids/99kidsday/default.htm

Childhood Allergies—http://allergies.about.com/od/childrenallergies/. Search for *environment—indoor and outdoor allergy triggers.*

Environment, Health and Safety Online—http://www.ehso.com/contents.php. Excellent topics to select and fact sheets—for older students.

 **TA DA!**

Green Squad in Action!

Green Squad at School—http://www.nrdc.org/greensquad/intro/intro_1.asp. Check out your school to find out whether it is environmentally safe.

Learn about chemicals in your home—http://www.epa.gov/kidshometour/

Experiment

Fact Sheet—How Do You Study Environmental Health—http://www.niehs.nih.gov/oc/factsheets/fshow.htm

In the Classroom

National Institute of Environmental Health Sciences—http://www.niehs.nih.gov/science-education/teachers/home.htm. Environmental health topics. Site includes fact sheets, pamphlets, brochures, booklets, news, flyers, and videos.

Chip Off the Old Block.

GENES AND HEREDITY

New Words

DNA—Cloning
Dominant—Recessive
Genetics—Heredity
Mutations—Traits

What About Genes and Heredity?

Can you curl your tongue? Raise one eyebrow? Wiggle your ears? Do you have blue eyes? Are you tall or short? Who do you look like in your family? Maybe your great-grandmother or great-grandfather? Traits like these and many others are passed on to you by your parents. Is there anyone on earth exactly like you? What about your identical twin? What are "inheriting traits?" Learn about your gene pool!

What Can I Write About?

Define genes. Where do these genes get their marching orders? What about heredity?

Research DNA. Explain chromosomes, genes, proteins, cells. Where do your chromosomes come from? How do they make you what you are? Are all cells the same?

Chromosomes are interesting to learn about. Do all creatures (including us) have the same number of chromosomes? What is special about chromosomes? What is their job?

What is a genetic disorder? Write about mutations that cause the cell to behave differently. Are they inherited or acquired? Name and describe a genetic disorder. Can they be predicted? How?

Are There Books or Videos on Genes and Heredity?

Use the library catalog to search for *DNA, genetics,* or *heredity.*

Dorling Kindersley Illustrated Family Encyclopedia. New York: Dorling Kindersley, 2002.

Gallant, Roy. *The Treasure of Inheritance.* New York: Benchmark, 2002.

Human Body in Action Genes and Heredity. [videorecording]. Wynnewood, PA: Schlessinger, 2001.

Johnson, Rebecca. *You and Your Genes.* Washington, DC: National Geographic Society, 2003.

Reilly, Philip. *Is It in Your Genes? The Influence of Genes on Common Disorders and Diseases That Affect You and Your Family.* Cold Spring Harbor, NY: Cold Spring Harbor Laboratory Press, 2004.

Snedden, Robert. *Cell Division and Genetics.* Chicago: Heinemann, 2003.

Can the Internet Help?

The Gene Scene—http://ology.amnh.org/genetics/index.html. Understanding DNA and genes.

Designer Genes—ThinkQuest—http://library.thinkquest.org/18258/noframes/intro.htm. The Site Outline will make it easier to find what you need.

The Basics and Beyond—http://gslc.genetics.utah.edu/units/basics/. Take the tour and learn about DNA, genes, heredity, and traits.

DNA from the Beginning—http://www.dnaftb.org/dnaftb/. A primer on DNA, genes, and heredity. Take your time.

The Gene School—http://library.thinkquest.org/19037/general_info.html. Heredity information here is easy to understand.

Kids Genetics—DNA, Genes, Heredity—Inherited diseases—http://genetics.gsk.com/kids/heredity01.htm. Easy. Videos included.

You and Your Genes—from the National Institutes of Health—http://www.niehs.nih.gov/kids/genes/home.htm

Genetic Disorders—http://gslc.genetics.utah.edu/units/disorders/. Mutations.

 **TA DA!**

Heredity in Action!

Learn some fun factoids about genes—and surprise your friends—http://genetics.gsk.com/kids/index_kids.htm and http://www.uga.edu/srel/kidsdoscience/kidsdoscience-fun.htm (Code Puzzle is fun.).

Experiment

Create a pedigree chart for your family from your grandparents to today. Include aunts, uncles, cousins, and your own family. Find the information at the site listed here. (Watch the *More About Heredity* film to make sure you understand the format and symbols to use.)—http://genetics.gsk.com/kids/heredity01.htm and http://domin.dom.edu/faculty/craigdav/N%20SC160/pedigree.html (trait list).

In the Classroom

Genes and Heredity Lesson Plans—http://www.kumc.edu/gec/lessons.html. We like *Children Resemble Their Parents.*

74

An Ounce of Prevention.

IMMUNIZATIONS

New Words

Antibodies
Antigens
Immunity
Vaccinations

What Is Immunity?

Immunity is your body's ability to fight off disease. Each time you are exposed to a virus or bacteria, your body creates antibodies to fight off that disease. If you never received any vaccinations or immunizations, you would have to receive all of your antibodies the hard way by being sick first. With vaccinations, your body is exposed to an illness, but not enough to make you ill. The antibodies your body creates will remain in your system in case the real disease comes along.

What Can I Write About?

Write about the development of the smallpox vaccine and compare it to the development of vaccines in general.

Compare and contrast acquired immunity versus immunity from vaccinations.

Discuss the standard childhood vaccinations and the reasons you might need others as well.

There are several vaccinations that have almost eliminated once deadly childhood diseases. Choose one and find out what a difference it has made in the world.

Discuss how a vaccine is made. How does it get tested and put on the market for use? Who distributes it?

Are There Books on Immunity?

We can't begin to tell you the best books. There are many. Use your library catalog. Do not forget the reference area, where you can find background information and statistics.

Bunch, Bryan, ed. *Diseases.* Vol. 8. Danbury, CT: Grolier, 1997.

Childcraft: The How and Why Library. Chicago: World Book, 2003.

New Book of Popular Science. Vol. 3. Danbury, CT: Grolier, 2004.

Newton, David E., Rob Nagel, and Bridget Travers. *UXL Encyclopedia of Science.* Vol. 5. Detroit: UXL, 1998.

World Book Student Discovery Encyclopedia. Chicago: World Book, 2003.

Can the Internet Help?

PBS—http://www.pbs.org/wgbh/aso/ontheedge/polio/. Gives a basic, comic book style explanation of Salk's polio vaccine.

Keep Kids Healthy—http://www.keepkidshealthy.com/welcome/immunizations. html. A schedule of childhood vaccines and descriptions of each.

The Centers for Disease Control—http://www.cdc.gov/NIP/publications/fs/ gen/shouldknow.htm. Lists 10 things you should know about immunizations. It includes side effects.

The Centers for Disease Control—http://www.cdc.gov/travel/vaccinat.htm. Explains what additional vaccines you might need if you are traveling to another country.

UNICEF—http://www.unicef.org/immunization/index_polio.html. Data about eliminating polio and other diseases around the world.

British Broadcasting Corporation—http://www.bbc.co.uk/history/discovery/ medicine/smallpox_01.shtml. A history of smallpox vaccination.

All About Vaccines, from the Food and Drug Administration—http://www. fda.gov/oc/opacom/kids/html/vaccines.htm. A kids' page.

 **TA DA!**

The Immune System in Action!

Immunization Action Coalition—http://www.vaccineinformation.org/video/index. asp. Video clips of diseases that can be prevented by immunizations.

Experiment

All Info about Science for Families—http://scienceforfamilies.allinfo-about. com/features/feelingrotten.html. Diseases can spread from one person to another or from one apple to another in this experiment.

In the Classroom

The Immunization Action Coalition—http://www.immunize.org/. Offers free information sheets and detailed information.

State of Massachusetts—http://www.mass.gov/dph/cdc/epii/imm/school_req/ teachers.htm. Recommended immunizations for teachers and staff.

Just Say NO!

ANTONIA NOVELLO

New Words

Campaign
National Institutes of Health (NIH)
National Women's Hall of Fame
Pediatric Nephrologist
Surgeon General

Who Is Dr. Antonia Novello?

Dr. Novello was the first woman and the first Hispanic to become Surgeon General of the United States. She had first worked as a private doctor. Next she worked for the U.S. Health Service, and the first President George Bush (1989–1993) selected her as Surgeon General. She has made women and Hispanics very proud because of her fight against underage drinking and smoking. Dr. Novello has won several awards and has been named to the National Women's Hall of Fame. Today, she works with children who are born with the AIDS virus. It takes a dedicated doctor to work with these young babies born with AIDS. Though she is not well known, there is plenty of information about her, and Dr. Novello will be an excellent choice for writing a biography of an important person in science.

What Can I Write About?

Find out about Dr. Novello's background. Where is she from? What education does she have? How did she become interested in working with babies?

Research Novello's work as Surgeon General. What issues did she support while in this position? What did she do to oppose these issues?

What position does she hold today? What work is she doing? Discuss some of the issues and dangers she faces in her work.

Are There Books About Dr. Novello?

We can't begin to tell you the best books. There are many. Use your library catalog. Do not forget the reference area, where you can find background information and statistics.

Biography Today: Scientists & Inventors Series: Profiles of People of Interest to Young Readers. Detroit: Omnigraphics, 1996– .

Gale Encyclopedia of Medicine. Detroit: Gale, 2001. Biography—Novello, Dr. Antonia,

Hawxhurst, Joan C. *Antonia Novello: U.S. Surgeon General.* Brookfield, CT: Millbrook, 1995.

Marvis, Barbara J. *Contemporary American Success Stories: Famous People of Hispanic Heritage.* Mitchell Lane Multicultural Biography Series. Childs, MD: Mitchell Lane, 1995.

Novello, Antonia. *Youth and Alcohol: Unrecognized Consequences.* Washington, DC: U.S. Dept. of Health and Human Services, 1992.

Can the Internet Help?

Surgeon General's biography of Dr. Novello—www.surgeongeneral.gov/library/history/bionovello.htm. Browse the rest of the site, too.

National Women of Science—http://www.greatwomen.org/women.php?action=viewone&id=1. Biographical information.

Surgeon General's Report for Kids about Smoking—http://www.cdc.gov/tobacco/sgr/sgr4kids/sgrmenu.htm

National Institutes of Health report on Underage Drinking—http://www.niaaa.nih.gov/publications/aa59.htm

Smoking Stinks, from Kid's Health—http://kidshealth.org/kid/watch/house/smoking.html. Good information.

 **TA DA!**

Be an Ad Buster!

Use these cigarette ads or another that you find to launch your own campaign against smoking—http://www.cdc.gov/tobacco/sgr/sgr4kids/adbust.htm

Test Your Tobacco IQ

Centers for Disease Control—http://www.cdc.gov/tobacco/tips_4_youth/quiz.htm. Take the test. See how much you know about tobacco.

In the Classroom

Tobacco Free Kids—http://tobaccofreekids.org/. This site has some very good ideas on no smoking campaigns for your class.

The Great American Smoke Out—Lesson Plans for the Classroom—http://www.education-world.com/a_lesson/lesson034.shtml

You Are What You Eat.

NUTRITION

New Words

Basic Food Groups
Food Pyramid
Vegetarian

What Is Nutrition?

Everything you eat is part of your nutrition, even candy bars and potato chips. But of course, there is good nutrition and bad nutrition. Your goal should be to have good nutrition. Eating well helps you build a strong body and have energy and brain power that you need to succeed.

What Can I Write About?

What is a food pyramid? How does the Food and Drug Administration determine what each layer of the pyramid is? Use the pyramid to plan a week's healthy diet for your family.

Take a food group, such as fruits and vegetables, and check out how your body uses it.

Explain what effects a candy bar has on your body. Be sure to include the good things along with the bad.

Consider a vegetarian diet in terms of the food pyramid. Can vegetarians have a nutritious diet? How? Make a chart showing what they would eat during a day.

If you have an allergy to a certain food such as milk, peanuts, or wheat, investigate the alternatives to still give you a well-balanced diet.

Are There Books on Nutrition?

Use your library catalog. There is lots of information on this topic.

Bellenir, Karen, ed. *Diet and Nutrition Sourcebook.* 2d ed. Detroit: Omnigraphics, 1999.

Bruun, Ruth Dowling, and Bertel Bruun. *The Human Body.* New York: Random House, 1982.

Encyclopedia of Family Health. Vol. 9. New York: Marshall Cavendish, 1998.

Encyclopedia of Foods: A Guide to Healthy Nutrition. San Diego, CA: Academic, 2002.

Gale Encyclopedia of Medicine. 2d ed. Vol. 5. Detroit: Gale, 2002.

Smolin, Lori A., Mary B. Grosvenor, and Richard J. Deckelbaum. *Nutrition for Sports and Exercise.* New York: Chelsea, 2004.

Can the Internet Help?

KidsHealth—http://www.kidshealth.org/kid/stay_healthy/. Tells you how to stay healthy. Scroll down the page for all sorts of information on food.

Tour the Food Guide Pyramid, from Nutrition Explorations—http://www.nutritionexplorations.org/kids/main.asp

Keep Kids Healthy—http://www.keepkidshealthy.com/nutrition/. Tells all about the food pyramid, vegetarian diets, popcorn and peanut butter, and more.

ThinkQuest, Nutrition on the Web for Teens—http://library.thinkquest.org/10991/. For older kids; it includes world nutrition, metabolic rates, and a diet planner.

Kid's Nutrition.org—From Baylor College of Medicine—http://www.kidsnutrition.org/. What to eat to maintain health.

 **TA DA!**

Nutrition in Action!

The Nutrition Café—http://www.exhibits.pacsci.org/nutrition/nutrition_cafe.html. Has games and allows you to evaluate your diet.

Experiment

American Heart Association Kids Cookbook—http://www.healthyfridge.org/kidsrec.html. Try these recipes.

University of Illinois—http://www.ag.uiuc.edu/~food-lab/nat/. Plan a healthy diet for your family for a day. Check to make sure it has all the nutrients you need with this nutrition calculator.

In the Classroom

North Dakota State University—http://www.ext.nodak.edu/food/kidsnutrition/edu-1.htm. Nutrition and food safety teaching materials.

The growers of Washington State apples—http://www.healthychoices.org/. Lesson plans and worksheets.

77

Everything Is Related.

SLEEP DISORDERS

New Words

Bedwetting—Sleep Terrors
Biological Clock
Childhood Apnea
Insomnia
REM—Rapid Eye Movement
Sleep Deprivation—Sleep Debt
Sleep Walking (Somnambulism)—Sleep Talking

What Is a Sleep Disorder?

We spend about one-third of our lives sleeping. We spend another third at school, and the last third is spent playing, doing chores and homework, reading, working, and all the other things we enjoy! When you are over 70 years old, you have already spent about 20 years sleeping, in five years of which you have been dreaming! We all have an internal or biological clock that helps control sleep and wakefulness. Disruption of the rhythms of this clock causes sleeping problems. Find out more.

What Can I Write About?

Write a paper about sleep. How much sleep do kids your age need? How does sleep help you? Describe the sleep cycle.

What are sleep disorders? How common are they? Are they dangerous? What causes them?

Write about *one* of the sleep disorders: sleep walking, sleep talking, snoring, sleep apnea, bedwetting, or restless legs syndrome. Symptoms? Causes? Danger? Treatment? Cure?

Are There Books or Videos on Sleep Disorders?

Use your library catalog. Ask the librarian to help you find reference books on sleep.

Bayer, Linda. *Sleep Disorders*. Philadelphia: Chelsea House, 2001.

Ferber, Richard. *Solve Your Child's Sleep Problems*. Old Tappan, NJ: Fireside, 2005.

Sadeh, Avi. *Sleeping Like a Baby: A Sensitive and Sensible Approach to Solving Your Child's Sleep Problems.* New Haven: Yale, 2001.

Silverstein, Alvin. *Sleep.* New York: Franklin Watts, 2000.

Stewart, Gail. *Sleep Disorders.* San Diego, CA: Lucent, 2003.

Thorpy, Michael J., and Jan Yager. *The Encyclopedia of Sleep and Sleep Disorders.* New York: Facts on File, 2001.

Can the Internet Help?

KidsHealth—http://www.kidshealth.org/. Excellent information. Choose Kids or Teens. Then search SLEEP for lots of good articles by topic, from "How much sleep do I need?" to "Having trouble sleeping?"

Explore Your Sleep and Dreams—http://library.thinkquest.org/C005545/english/index1.htm. Stages of sleep, disorders, theories of dreams.

Children and Sleep Disorders—http://www.stanford.edu/~dement/children.html (for all) and http://www.stanford.edu/~dement/learn.html (for older children).

Sleep Disorders in Children—http://www.aafp.org/afp/20010115/277.html. Sleep time chart included.

Medline—http://www.nlm.nih.gov/medlineplus/sleepdisorders.html. Medical papers and information about sleep disorders. Good links.

Sleep disorders from about.com—http://sleepdisorders.about.com/. Use the links to articles, not offers (to buy).

Sleep for Kids—http://www.sleepforkids.org/. Includes the sleep cycle, why we need sleep, dreams. Includes games.

 **TA DA!**

Sleep Disorders in Action!

Sleep for Kids—http://www.sleepforkids.org/html/games.html. Several games and puzzles you might enjoy.

Experiment

Do you remember your dreams? Keep a SLOG (sleep log). Find the journal worksheets and questions that will help you remember at http://faculty.washington.edu/chudler/chsleep.html. Other sleep activities are there as well.

In the Classroom

Sleep for Kids—http://www.sleepforkids.org/html/habits.html. Information for teachers and parents.

Activities for the classroom and beyond—http://faculty.washington.edu/chudler/experi.html

Bird Flu and Mad Cow Disease.

ZOONOSES

New Words

Rabies
West Nile Virus
Lyme Disease
Mad Cow Disease
Avian Flu or Influenza
Salmonella
Emerging Diseases

What Are Zoonoses?

No, it's not pronounced zoo noses. The word is zo-o-no-ses, and it means diseases that can be spread from animals to humans. You would be surprised at how many there are! Some of them are listed above. Some can be spread through the air. Some are spread by insects like mosquitoes or ticks. Some can even be spread by eating! Your parents are probably already taking precautions against getting zoonoses by taking your pets in for vaccinations, cooking meats thoroughly, and protecting you from mosquitoes.

What Can I Write About?

Find and compare at least three diseases that are carried by mosquitoes or ticks.

Discuss the spread and prevention of rabies. Include both pets and wild animals.

Explore the flu. Include where it comes from, how it spreads, and why it's different every year.

Examine mad cow disease.

Are There Books on Zoonoses?

We can't begin to tell you the best books. There are many. Use your library catalog. Do not forget the reference area, where you can find background information and statistics. Your search may need to include the new words listed above or *pets* or *animals*.

Bunch, Bryan, ed. *Diseases*. Vol. 1. Danbury, CT: Grolier, 1997.

Encyclopedia of Family Health. New York: Marshall Cavendish, 1998.

Kohn, George Childs, ed. *Encyclopedia of Plague and Pestilence from Ancient Times to the Present.* Rev. ed. New York: Facts on File, 2001.

Lerner, K. Lee, and Brenda Wilmoth Lerner, eds. *Gale Encyclopedia of Science.* 3d ed. Vol. 6. Detroit: Gale, 2004.

Can the Internet Help?

Healthy Child—http://www.healthychild.net/articles/sh32zoonoses.html. Several types of zoonoses.

Centers for Disease Control—http://www.cdc.gov/ncidod/dvrd/kidsrabies/. Rabies facts for kids.

KidsHealth—http://kidshealth.org/parent/infections/bacterial_viral/pet_infections. html. Infections that pets carry.

Neuroscience for Kids—http://faculty.washington.edu/chudler/bse.html. Mad cow disease.

The Food and Drug Administration—http://www.fda.gov/oc/opacom/kids/ html/madcow.htm. Explains mad cow disease at a more basic level.

Science Explained—http://www.synapses.co.uk/science/fluvirus.html. Avian flu.

Centers for Disease Control—http://www.cdc.gov/ncidod/dvbid/westnile/q&a. htm. Answers questions about West Nile virus.

 **TA DA!**

Zoonoses in Action!

Centers for Disease Control—http://www.cdc.gov/ncidod/dvbid/westnile/ psa.htm. Watch a video about prevention of West Nile virus.

See what happens when a dog gets rabies. Rent this movie from your local video store: *Old Yeller.* [videorecording]. Burbank, CA: Walt Disney Home Video, 2002 (originally released 1957).

Amrican Museum of Natural History—http://www.amnh.org/nationalcenter/ infection/infectionindex.html. Infection detection and protection.

Experiment

Rather than take a chance on experimenting, immunize your pets against zoonotic diseases like rabies!

In the Classroom

National Geographic—http://www.nationalgeographic.com/xpeditions/lessons/ 18/g912/parasites.html. Parasites and disease.

Lyme Disease Foundation—http://www.lyme.org/communityed.html. Community education materials.

TECHNOLOGY

Technology is the technical means people use to improve their surroundings. It also refers to our knowledge of using tools and machines to do tasks efficiently. Technology helps us control our environment. We use tools and systems to improve our work. Technology helps us to communicate, build better buildings, travel, and play! Imagine what life was like before computers and e-mail. Some technology is changing so quickly that we find our equipment out of date by the time we buy it. We are all part of the age of technology—the digital age.

Help Is Here!

ASSISTIVE TECHNOLOGY

New Words

Artificial Limbs
E-fabrics—Smart Textiles
Wearable Computing
Wheelchair Olympics

What Is Assistive Technology?

If you're lucky, you have 10 fingers to clutch with and 10 toes to wriggle. You can walk, talk, see, and hear. But not everyone is so fortunate! For those who need help, there is assistive technology. Whether it is a wheelchair to make us mobile, artificial hands to aid in holding, a computer to do the talking, or a machine to read aloud, assistive technology offers new solutions to old problems. Imagine wearing a jacket that notices a chill in the air and starts to heat up. Your mom wouldn't have to remind you to wear your coat. Imagine a hat that whispered in your ear, "That's Joe. He is Meg's brother. He likes baseball." You wouldn't need to worry about your poor memory. Imagine gloves that could read sign language and speak the words out loud. What a boon!

What Can I Write About?

Find out about existing assistive technology for one of the challenges listed above. Write about it, explaining its use.

Learn and write about wheelchair Olympics or other sports for physically challenged children.

Evaluate a speech synthesizer that will read to you, such as Magic or Kurzweil, if you have one at your school. Interview a person who has to use it.

Learn how wearable computing can help people with special needs. Write about it.

Are There Books on Assistive Technology?

Use your library catalog. The librarian will help.

Englebert, Phillis. *Technology in Action: Science Applied to Everyday Life: Communication, Electronics and Computers.* Detroit: UXL, 1999.

Lerner, K. Lee, and Brenda Wilmoth Lerner, eds. *Gale Encyclopedia of Science.* 3d ed. Detroit: Gale, 2004.

McGrath, Kimberly A., ed. *World of Invention.* 2d ed. Detroit: Gale, 1999.

Overlook School for the Blind. *Technology for All: Assistive Technology in the Classroom.* Philadelphia: Towers, 2001.

Can the Internet Help?

Abledata—http://www.abledata.com/. Tells about all sorts of assistive technology by product type.

The Centers for Disease Control—http://www.cdc.gov/nchs/fastats/disable.htm. Offers statistics on people with disabilities.

The Nemours Foundation—http://kidshealth.org/parent/system/ill/assistive_tech_p2.html. Just what is assistive technology? This site explains it.

The National Library of Medicine—http://www.nlm.nih.gov/medlineplus/assistivedevices.html. Links to valuable information on wheelchairs, robotic arms, adaptive vehicles, and more.

The International Paralympics—http://www.paralympic.org/release/Main_Sections_Menu/index.html. Shows what disabled persons can do with assistive technology. Choose Winter Sports or Summer Sports.

How Stuff Works—http://www.howstuffworks.com/computer-clothing.htm. How computerized clothing works.

 **TA DA!**

Assistive Technology in Action!

Mark Overmyers—http://www.cs.uu.nl/people/markov/kids/motion.html. Offers free software for a game that helps you understand robotic motion.

Experiment

Bored.com—http://www.talkingonline.com/. In this example of technology for the visually impaired, you can type in the words you want to hear and the computer will talk to you.

MIT—http://www.media.mit.edu/wearables/lizzy/index.html. Are you inspired to create your own wearable computer? This site has some FAQs to help you.

In the Classroom

Special Needs and Technology, from the Teacher Tap—http://www.eduscapes.com/tap/topic80.htm

CNN—http://cnnstudentnews.cnn.com/2001/fyi/lesson.plans/04/11/wearable.computer.da/. A lesson based on "Through a Cyborg's Eyes."

Can You Hear Me Now?

CELL PHONES

New Words

Cellular Phone
Digital
Frequency
Full Duplex and Half Duplex
Liquid Crystal Display (LCD)

What Is a Cell Phone?

A cell phone actually works like a very sophisticated radio. Today, 20 percent of all teens have their own cell phones. Why do their parents buy them? Is it because the parents want to be able to stay in contact with their teens? Why do teens want a cell phone? Is it so they can stay in touch with all of their friends? With a cell phone you can call friends and parents, play a game, search the Internet, maintain a list of tasks and homework, store your phone numbers, text message a friend, take pictures and send them to friends, and record your voice. You have an entire entertainment center right in your hand.

What Can I Write About?

Write about the history of the cell phone. Include a time line for more interest.

Explain the basics of how cell phones work. Discuss different phone services.

Write about the health dangers of using a cell phone. Start at the Food and Drug Administration (FDA) site for this topic.

Write about security risks and cell phone hacking. What can be done?

Write a paper that explains cell phone coverage areas and roaming.

Compare two cell phone companies; discuss services, charges, options. Make a chart.

Are There Books or Videos on Cell Phones?

Use the keyword *telecommunications*, but watch for dates. Use the newest books.

Carlo, George Louis, and Martin Schram. *Cell Phones: Invisible Hazards in the Wireless Age.* New York: Carroll & Graf, 2001.

Macauley, David. *The Way Things Work: Telecommunications.* [videorecording]. Wynnewood, PA: Schlessinger, 2003.

Pachter, Barbara, and Susan Magee. *The Jerk with the Cell Phone: A Survival Guide for the Rest of Us.* New York: Marlow, 2004.

Stetz, Penelope. *The Cell Phone Book: Everything You Wanted to Know About Wireless Telephony (But Didn't Know Who or What to Ask).* Newport, RI: Aegis, 2002.

Can the Internet Help?

How Cell Phones Work—http://www.howstuffworks.com/cell-phone.htm. The best.

FDA's Consumer Information on Wireless Phones—http://www.fda.gov/cellphones/. Are there dangers in having a cell?

How Cell Phones Work—http://www.ee.washington.edu/class/498/sp98/final/marsha/final.html. Easy to understand, helpful drawings.

Useful Cell Phone Information—http://www.cellphoneinfo.com/index.html. Take a little time here. Good information and links.

Wired online magazine reports on the cell phone—http://www.wired.com/news/culture/0,1284,58861,00.html. Read "She's Gotta Have It" and other articles. "Miss Manners" is a good article if you are reporting on cell phone protocol.

Protecting Your Phone from Hackers—http://www.whbf.com/Global/story.asp?S=3016189&nav=0zGnWy80

 **TA DA!**

Cell Phones in Action!

Create a cell phone from sand—http://www.strangematterexhibit.com/index.html. Choose "transform" to find this activity.

Experiment

Create a campaign as part of your research, using posters, flyers, e-mail, or other modes of delivery. You might campaign against (or for) use of cell phones by children. Remember, many sources report that cell phones are dangerous for young kids. Learn and campaign. You might even work with a partner who also reports on the topic and create a debate for the classroom. List your points on both sides of the argument. A good campaign takes planning.

In the Classroom

What Can I Afford—http://www.thirteen.org/edonline/lessons/afford/index.html. Great idea for a math lesson, comparing cell phone plans. Grades 5–8.

Lesson Plan on Communication—http://www.cybersmartcurriculum.org/lesson_plans/45_21.asp. Looks at technology as a means of communicating.

You've Got Mail.

COMMUNICATING ON THE WEB

New Words

Blog—Blogosphere—Wiki—RSS—IM—Oh my!
Bulletin Boards, Listservs, Chat, E-Mail
POP (Post Office Protocol)
Spam

How Do We Communicate on the Internet?

Kids today chat, message, and blog with their friends as easily as they phone them. Most communication today takes place on the Internet using chat, instant messaging, blogs, bulletin boards, Listservs, and e-mail. Kids find it easy to use these new ways to communicate, but do we really understand how they work? Select one type of communication and report on it. Be sure you practice this method, so you can answer all the questions that may occur.

What Can I Write About?

Write about e-mail or another Internet communication topic. How does this method work? Where are the data stored? How are they used?

Write about Internet etiquette (netiquette). What is it? What are some of the rules? Tell why netiquette is important.

List and describe each part of an e-mail message (or a blog or listserv or discussion board.) Show examples with labels in your report. Find scientific data that explain how these messages work.

Find out more about e-mail and write a research paper arguing that e-mail is better than "snail mail" (postal mail.) State both sides of your argument and make a strong case for e-mail.

Are There Books on E-Mail, Chat, and Listservs?

The library catalog will help you serach for *electronic mail systems* or *Internet, juvenile.*

Bell, Mary Ann. *Internet and Personal Computing Fads.* New York: Haworth, 2004.

Gosney, John W. *Blogging for Teens.* Independence, KY: Premier, 2004.

Jordan, Shirley. *From Smoke Signals to E-Mail: Moments in History.* Logan, IA: Perfection Learning, 2000.

Rothman, Kevin F. *Coping with Dangers on the Internet: Staying Safe On-Line.* New York: Rosen, 2001.

Souter, Gerry, Janet Souter, and Allison Souter. *Researching on the Internet: Using Search Engines, Bulletin Boards, and ListServs.* Berkeley Heights, NJ: Enslow, 2003.

Can the Internet Help?

Learn the Net: E-Mail and How It Works—http://www.learnthenet.com/english/html/20how.htm

How Stuff Works—http://computer.howstuffworks.com/. One of the best places we know to get good basic information. Type in your specific search terms, e.g., blog, e-mail, Listserv.

Teaching Kids How to Talk to the World—http://www.youthlearn.org/learning/teaching/email.html. Explanation of each communication type.

History of Email—http://www.multicians.org/thvv/mail-history.html. Includes spam.

Safety while using Web communication tools—http://www.microsoft.com/athome/intouch/keeptabs.mspx. Link to the sites at the right.

TA DA!

Create a Blog!

The newest technology for communicating on the Web is the blog. Create your own and invite your friends. See this URL for directions and a place to post your blog: http://www.blogger.com/start

Want to Have Fun?

Communicate on the Web—http://www.kidscom.com/chat/chat.html. Play games, chat, answer a poll, and more here. Meet a friend.

Internet Safety Game—http://www.kidscom.com/games/isg/isg.html

In the Classroom

Create a blog for your classroom. Why? See examples at http://www.rss-specifications.com/kids-blogging.htm. Get started at http://www.blogger.com/start or see an example at http://dl1.yukoncollege.yk.ca/talog2/addedValuesPI/discuss/msgReader$263

Kids Connection—http://www.ks-connection.org/. This site is excellent to see how kids are connecting. Get a pen pal from anywhere in the world for your class or post a project you are doing.

Modern-Day Piracy.

DIGITAL COPYRIGHT

New Words

Burning CDs
Computer Ethics
Digital Millennium Act
Fair Use
MP3s
Piracy

What Is Digital Copyright?

When your friend has a great new music CD and you would like to listen to it too, do you burn a copy of it on your computer? When you borrow a movie from the video store and aren't finished with it by the due date, do you copy it? Do you buy a new computer program for one computer and use it for two? It is so easy these days to make a copy of electronic information like music, movies, and software that we often don't think twice about making that copy. Sometimes you're allowed to do that, but in many other situations you are not. By learning about electronic copyright, you'll protect yourself from accidentally stealing. Don't be a pirate! Find out more about the law.

What Can I Write About?

What is digital copyright? Whom does it protect? Why is it important that Internet users pay attention to copyright?

Read about the Digital Millennium Act and explain it.

Research the legal ways of downloading music.

What are record companies and software companies doing to keep people from copying their products illegally?

Should copying digital media be legal? Support your views with facts.

Are There Books on Digital Copyright?

Use your library catalog. Do not forget the reference area, where you can find background information and statistics.

American Bar Association. *Family Legal Guide.* 3d ed. New York: Random House, 2004.

Elias, Stephen, and Richard Stein. *Patent, Copyright and Trademark*. 7th ed. Berkeley, CA: Nolo, 2004.

Litman, Jessica. *Digital Copyright: Protecting Intellectual Property on the Internet*. Amherst, NY: Prometheus, 2001.

Can the Internet Help?

The Copyright Association of the United States—http://www.copyrightkids. org/whatcopyframes.htm. Explains the basics of copyright law for kids.

The United States Copyright Office—http://www.copyright.gov/faq.html. Answers commonly asked questions.

This site explains the Digital Millennium Act and tells when you may make a copy of software—http://www.pcstats.com/articleview.cfm?articleID=868

Legal sites for downloading music on the Web—http://www.musicunited.org/

How Stuff Works—http://stuffo.howstuffworks.com/music-licensing.htm. How music licensing works.

 **TA DA!**

Copyright in Action!

Business Software Alliance—http://www.playitcybersafe.com/kids/games/index. cfm. Games that help make you more aware of copyright.

Cornell University—http://www.cit.cornell.edu/oit/ucpl/debate.html. Watch a debate about copyright.

Experiment

Take a survey. How many of your friends have copied a CD? Did they know it was illegal? How many are using legal music downloading services? Make a graph of your findings.

In the Classroom

The Business Software Alliance—http://www.playitcybersafe.com//cybercrime/ index.cfm. Offers curriculum and guidelines to avoid cyber crime.

A copyright lesson plan for ages 8–11—http://www.multiage-education.com/ russportfolio/curriculumtopics/assurecopyrightlesson.html

83

Whodunit?

FORENSIC SCIENCE

New Words

Forensic Science
Fingerprints
DNA
Evidence

What Is Forensic Science?

There are new and fascinating ways used by scientists to solve crimes. Forensic science is any science that relates to the law. Forensic science includes analyzing fingerprints, DNA, and handwriting; computer animations; and profiling. It also includes looking through trash at a crime scene—or conducting autopsies and experiments. If you are a *Law and Order* fan, you may want to do a little sleuthing regarding forensic science.

What Can I Write About?

What is forensic science? Describe several scientific methods law enforcement officers use to solve crimes.

Write about one of the forensic sciences, like fingerprinting, handwriting, or DNA evidence. Include its history, an explanation of the science, and examples of real-life solutions.

Conduct your own scientific investigation and write up your methodology and findings in your report: See samples at http://school.discovery.com/lessonplans/programs/whodidit/. (Get your teacher's permission.)

Are There Books on Forensic Science?

Do not forget the reference area, where you can find background information.

Campbell, Andrea. *Forensic Science: Evidence, Clues, and Investigation.* New York: Chelsea House, 2000.

Donkin, Andrew. *Dead Giveaways: How Real Life Crimes Are Solved by Amazing Scientific Evidence, Personality Profiling and Paranormal Investigations.* Scranton, PA: Element, 1998.

Fridell, Ron. *DNA Fingerprinting: The Ultimate Identity.* New York: Franklin Watts, 2001.

Innes, Brian. *Search for Forensic Evidence.* Milwaukee, WI: Gareth Stevens, 2005.

Pentland, Peter, and Pennie Stoyles. *Forensic Science.* Philadelphia: Chelsea House, 2003.

Wiese, Jim. *Detective Science: 40 Crime-Solving, Case-Breaking, Crook-Catching Activities for Kids.* New York: Wiley, 1996.

Can the Internet Help?

Forensic Science—http://home.earthlink.net/~thekeither/Forensic/forsone.htm. Good basic information—follow the links on this site.

Exploring Forensics—http://library.thinkquest.org/TQ0312020/

Genetics: Gateway to the Future—http://library.thinkquest.org/17109/. Basic DNA information.

The Why Files—http://whyfiles.org/014forensic/. A fun way to learn about different methods of forensic science.

How Stuff Works—http://people.howstuffworks.com/. Use the search screen, "Forensic Science"; you will find topics such as How DNA Works, Fingerprinting, Autopsies, Unsolved History, and more.

Genes and DNA—http://www.genecrc.org/site/ko/index_ko.htm. Basic understanding of DNA. Includes a glossary.

Virtual Museum—http://www.virtualmuseum.ca/Exhibitions/Myst/en/index. html. Has an exhibit to test your deduction skills.

 **TA DA!**

FBI in Action!

Take the FBI Challenge!—http://www.fbi.gov/kids/6th12th/6th12th.htm or http://www.fbi.gov/kids/k5th/kidsk5th.htm. Use your forensic knowledge in FBI cases.

Experiment

Solve any of these mysteries—http://www.yesnet.yk.ca/schools/wes/webquests_ themes/mysteries_theme/mystery.html. Become a forensics expert.

In the Classroom

Whodunnit—http://www.cyberbee.com/whodunnit/crime.html. Have fun in your classroom with exercises and experiments for the forensic scientist.

Science Friday Kids' Connection™ DNA fingerprinting—http://www. sciencefriday.com/kids/sfkc20030411-1.html. Building critical thinking.

Crime Scene Investigations—http://gouchercenter.edu/jcampf/ForensicScience. htm and http://school.discovery.com/lessonplans/programs/whodidit/. The scientific investigation method—and fun, too.

Let's Google!

THE INTERNET

New Words

Domain
Internet
Links—URL (Uniform or Universal Resource Locator)
Search Engine
World Wide Web (WWW)

What Is the Internet?

The Internet is made up of computers all over the world that are linked or webbed together. That is why it is called the World Wide Web. Different industries have different domains (.edu, .gov, .com, .org). When you navigate the Internet, you can get help for your homework, dig up a recipe, find the phone number of friends, read about the past, learn about inventions, play a game, view a movie, read a book, chat with friends around the world, take an online course, listen to music, research your school assignments, join a Listserv on a topic you love, read a bulletin board, and much more. There seems to be no end to the amount of information on the Internet. But you must be careful. Since anyone can post things to the Internet, not everything you read is true. Also, there are many sites that are unsuitable for kids. Learn more about this powerful tool.

What Can I Write About?

Write a good paper explaining what the Internet is and how we use it to find information and communicate with others.

Write about the history of the Internet or the World Wide Web. Make a time line.

If you want to get technical, choose some aspect of the Internet for your report: like domain name servers, broadband, cable modems, routers, privacy, viruses, or streaming video.

Describe search engines and tell how they work. Include a comparison of two or more.

Are There Books or Videos About the Internet?

Leebow, Ken. *300 Incredible Things for Kids on the Internet.* Marietta, GA: VIP Publishing, 1998.

Loughran, Donna. *Using the Internet Safely.* Austin, TX: Raintree Streck-Vaughn, 2003.

Parks, Peggy J. *The Internet.* San Diego, CA: KidHaven, 2004.

Roza, Greg. *The Incredible Story of Computers and the Internet.* New York: Powerkids, 2004.

Can the Internet Help?

Introduction to the Internet—http://www.burlco.lib.nj.us/Classes/Intforkids/. Very simple explanation of the Internet for kids. Basic information only.

What is the Internet?—http://wings.avkids.com/SPIT/internet.html. This site is very good.

ThinkQuest Complete Guide to the Internet—http://library.thinkquest.org/10043/. ThinkQuest guides are created by young people.

How Stuff Works—http://computer.howstuffworks.com/internet-infrastructure.htm. An explanation of the Internet infrastructure. Other topics are available.

About Networking and Listservs and more—http://www.ifla.org/I/training/listserv/lists.htm

Just for Kids—http://www.ftc.gov/bcp/conline/edcams/kidzprivacy/kidz.htm. Privacy on the Internet.

 **TA DA!**

Make It Yourself!

Make your own Web page—Here are three sites that will help: http://www.smplanet.com/webpage/webpage.html, http://www.surfnetkids.com/webpage.htm, and http://webmonkey.wired.com/webmonkey/kids/

Cyberchase Internet Games—http://pbskids.org/cyberchase/games/bargraphs/bargraphs.html. Learn about "bugs" on the Internet.

Experiment

Join a science Listserv and interact with other kids around the country—http://directory.coollist.com/science/. Choose your topic from this list.

In the Classroom

For math class, have the students compare the several different search engines. This is a good project for evaluating and charting data.

Look around the Internet and find many sites created by students. Have your students post their reports. (The local colleges or high schools may take this on as a project. Then your site will be very neat indeed.) An example is this site: http://www.siec.k12.in.us/~west/online/

The Image of Perfection

PHOTOGRAPHY

New Words

Aperture
Exposure
F Stop
Focal Length
Lens

What Is Photography?

Do you enjoy having your picture taken, seeing beautiful photographs in a magazine, or looking through family photo albums and reminiscing? Admiring pictures can make you want to create your own. People have felt the same way for hundreds of years! The original camera was called a "camera obscura." In a darkened room, a pinpoint of light cast an inverted image. An artist traced around it on a canvas. Cameras have come a long way since then. Now you only have to point a camera, click, and you have an image on film or on a digital camera.

What Can I Write About?

Discuss the difference between single lens reflex and rangefinder cameras.

Explain how cameras work. Consider speed, aperture, film, and developing.

Explore the inventions that came together to create photography.

What is digital photography? How does it work? Compare it with film photography.

What differences has photography made in the world and how we view it?

Create or discover examples of "faking" with pictures and discuss the techniques.

Are There Books on Photography?

Find the newest books on digital photography. The catalog will help.

Johnson, Neil. *National Geographic Photography Guide for Kids.* Washington, DC: National Geographic, 2001.

Longe, Jacqueline L., ed. *How Products Are Made: An Illustrated Guide to Product Manufacturing.* Vol. 4. Detroit: Gale, 1997.

Schmittroth, Linda, Mary Reilly McCall, and Bridget Travers. *Eureka!* Vol. 5. New York: UXL, 1995.

World Book Student Discovery Encyclopedia. Chicago: World Book, 2003.

Can the Internet Help?

U.S. Patent Office—http://www.uspto.gov/web/offices/ac/ahrpa/opa/kids/ponder/ponder5.htm. Photography time line.

Classic cameras, pictures, and descriptions of over 100 old cameras—http://210.226.164.37/camera/index_e.html

How Stuff Works—http://money.howstuffworks.com/camera.htm and http://money.howstuffworks.com/digital-camera.htm. Explains film cameras and digital cameras.

Adobe—http://www.adobe.com/education/digkids/tips/photo/on_the_road.html. Gives tips and ideas for using a digital camera.

The Photonhead Beginners Guide to Photography—http://www.photonhead.com/beginners/. Gives history, how cameras work, and exposure and flash information.

Photo Foolery, the Fake-out Game from National Geographic—http://www.nationalgeographic.com/ngkids/0104/foolery/tips.html

Kodak's site—www.kodak.com. Select Taking Great Pictures. Kodak has the "know-how."

 **TA DA!**

Cameras in Action!

Adobe—http://www.adobe.com/education/digkids/training/tt/main.html. These video clips show how to get maximum use of a digital camera.

Experiment

Kodak—http://www.kodak.com/global/en/consumer/education/lessonPlans/pinholeCamera/pinholeCanBox.shtml. Shows how to make a pinhole camera!

In the Classroom

Kids With Cameras project from Australia—http://www.gigglepotz.com/kidswithcameras.htm. Has ideas, examples, and lesson plans. Lots of fun!

Adobe—http://www.adobe.com/education/digkids/lessons/main.html. Offers lesson plans and ideas for using cameras in the classroom. Not all of them require Adobe software.

86

I'm Stuck on You!

STICKY STUFF

New Words

Adhesive—Cohesive
Art Fry or George de Mestral
Masking Tape, Scotch™ Tape, Velcro™
Post-It™ Notes
Pressure-sensitive materials

What Do We Mean by Sticky Stuff?

Most inventions are created to fill a need. Sticky stuff certainly fits into this category. Wouldn't it be fun to write about the invention of things that are sticky? For example, write about Velcro or Post-It notes or even double-sided tape. Why were they invented? What are their uses? How have they developed since their invention? What is their impact? We think this would be fun to learn about. Inventions always are.

What Can I Write About?

Select a single sticky thing and write about its history and present uses. The new uses of surgical tape may be interesting.

Choose two sticky things and compare them. Give a little background and then compare when you would use one or the other. You might make a chart comparing strength and other factors.

Write a biography of the inventor and why or how he or she came up with the idea for the invention.

Write about adhesives in general. What are they? How do they work? What are their different qualities? What are they made of? You might write about their effects on the environment.

Are There Books on Sticky Stuff?

Do not forget the reference area when looking for scientific inventions.

McGrath, Kimberly A., ed. *World of Invention*. 2d ed. *Detroit: Gale, 1999.*

Proulx, Earl, ed. *Vinegar, Duct Tape, Milk Jugs and More: 1,001 Ingenious Ways to Use Common Household Items to Repair, Restore, Revive, or Replace Just About Everything in Your Life.* Emmaus, PA: Rodale, 2004.

Roberts, Royston. *Lucky Science: Accidental Discoveries from Gravity to Velcro, with Experiments.* New York: Wiley, 1994.

Walker, Kate. *Sticky Stuff.* Southwood, 2002.

Can the Internet Help?

Velcro—http://www.velcro.com/kidzone.html. How it works and its inventor. Be sure to use the links.

Duct Tape, Scotch Tape, Masking Tape, and Post-It Notes History—http://www.ideafinder.com/history/inventions/ducttape.htm, http://www.ideafinder.com/history/inventions/story031.htm, http://www.ideafinder.com/history/inventions/cellophanetape.htm, and http://www.ideafinder.com/history/inventions/maskingtape.htm. And other adhesives. Good links to other information.

Why Sticky Stuff Sticks—http://www.signweb.com/vinyl/cont/stickystuff.html

This to That—http://www.thistothat.com/. What type of adhesive do you need to glue one material to another?

History of Adhesives—http://www.henkelca.com/student/history.asp

Recycling Hotline—http://wlapwww.gov.bc.ca/epd/epdpa/mpp/pubs/bcrhsa1.html. Handling glues and adhesives safely.

Sticky Stuff—http://www.courier-journal.com/foryourinfo/111003/111003.html. Go all the way through—good and simple.

 **TA DA!**

Adhesives in Action!

Activities and art projects with adhesives—http://www.ed.gov/pubs/parents/Science/sticky.html

Download computer "sticky notes" for your own computer—http://www.3m.com/market/office/postit/com_prod/psnotes/download_lite.html. Fun and helpful.

Experiment

Create your own Flubberagoo—http://www.primaryteachers.org/sticky_stuff.htm. Sticky stuff.

In the Classroom

Chewed Paper and Sticky Stuff—http://www.clover.okstate.edu/fourh/aitc/lessons/intermed/pinata.pdf. Lesson plan activities—the nature of paste.

Experiment: The Scientific Method Using Adhesives—http://www.rohmhaas.com/company/plabs.dir/htmldocs/Teaching.html. Classroom fun.

87

Wireless Communication.

TELEVISION AND RADIO

New Words

> Cathode Ray Tube
> Telegraph
> Wireless Transmission

What About Television and Radio?

Before radio, long-distance communication was done using the telegraph, which only sent dots and dashes. On Christmas Eve, 1906, when shipboard telegraph operators were listening for their dots and dashes, to their surprise they heard a violin playing *O Holy Night*. It was heard from Massachusetts to Virginia! Today television is an ordinary part of our daily lives. Almost every household in the United States has one. But that was not always true. Like so many great inventions, television was not the brainchild of only one inventor. Did you know that a moving picture, such as a movie or a television show, is not really moving at all, but a series of still images? As one image appears, the old one is still in your mind, so you see motion. It's the same idea as a flip book.

What Can I Write About?

> Discuss the invention of the television or radio. You might choose one of the many inventors and write about his or her contributions to the media, or include all of them.

> Consider the future of television. What changes would you make, and why?

> Explain how a television or a radio works, or you could compare television and radio.

> Imagine how the world would be different without television.

> Discuss the importance of wireless transmission. Or discuss satellite and high definition television.

Are There Books on Television and Radio?

> Try a search for *communication technology.*

> Considine, Glenn D. *Van Nostrand's Scientific Encyclopedia.* New York: Wiley-Interscience, 2002.

Krapp, Kristine M., and Jacqueline L. Longe, eds. *How Products Are Made: An Illustrated Guide to Product Manufacturing*. Detroit: Gale, 1998.

Langone, John. *The New How Things Work: Everyday Technology Explained*. Washington, DC: National Geographic, 2004.

New Book of Popular Science. Danbury, CT: Grolier, 2004.

Can the Internet Help?

The Federal Communications Commission—http://www.fcc.gov/omd/history/. Explains the history of wireless communication.

PBS—http://www.pbs.org/wgbh/aso/tryit/radio/#. Teaches about radio transmission.

How Stuff Works—http://entertainment.howstuffworks.com/tv.htm. Shows how a television works, part by part.

Panasonic—http://www.discovery.panasonic.co.jp/en/lab/lab01tv/. Explains television in simpler terms.

Ideafinder—http://www.ideafinder.com/history/inventions/story085.htm. Television history.

History of Radio and Television—http://history.acusd.edu/gen/recording/radio-television0.html

How Television Works—http://www.radiodesign.com/tvwrks.htm

 **TA DA!**

Television in Action!

Farnovision—http://www.farnovision.com/. See the first television, patented in 1927, in this video.

Listen to some historical radio broadcasts from as far back as 1931—http://www.hpol.org/

Experiment

Make a radio yourself and demonstrate it to your class—http://antiqueradio.org/econmain.htm, http://www.midnightscience.com/project.html, and http://www.hunkinsexperiments.com/themes/themes_electricity.htm

In the Classroom

Media Awareness lessons—http://www.media-awareness.ca/english/teachers/index.cfm

The Federal Communications Commission—http://www.fcc.gov/cgb/kidszone/teachersguide.html. A guide for teaching children about telecommunications.

88

I Feel It! I See It!

VIRTUAL REALITY

New Words

3-D Graphics
Artificial Reality
Computer Simulations
Immersive and Non-Immersive Virtual Reality
Virtual Environments
VRML (Virtual Reality Modeling Language)

What Is Virtual Reality?

Like science fiction? This topic may be for you. Virtual reality (VR) has become more a tool than a novelty. Immersive reality requires equipment and allows the user to become fully involved in a three-dimensional virtual environment. Newer are the non-immersive VRs, which have uses for doctors, pilots, machinists, real estate agents, architects, teachers, scientists, and many others. Using the Internet, visit a 360-degree panorama of your hotel room, take a virtual tour of the museum, learn about safety, or see a football replay virtually.

What Can I Write About?

What is virtual reality? Include the history of VR. A time line enhances reports.

Write about some of the uses of virtual reality in the workplace. How can it help with training?

Write about immersive virtual reality. Describe the equipment needed. Describe the sensations. Or write about non-immersive VR and tell about its uses in one occupation.

Research virtual reality uses for science and medicine. How can it be helpful? How can it change the way we now research and practice science or medicine?

Are There Books or Videos on Virtual Reality?

Use your library catalog. Unless you are researching history, watch copyright dates and find the newest information.

Baker, Christopher W. *Virtual Reality: Experiencing Illusion.* Brookfield, CT: Millbrook, 2000.

Cefrey, Holly. *Virtual Reality.* New York: Children's Press, 2002.

Darling, David. *Computers of the Future: Intelligent Machines and Virtual Reality.* New York: Dillon, 1995.

Wyborny, Shiela. *Virtual Reality.* San Diego, CA: Blackbirch/Thomson, 2003.

Yount, Lisa. *Virtual Reality.* Detroit: Lucent, 2005.

Can the Internet Help?

Virtual Reality—http://en.wikipedia.org/wiki/Virtual_reality. This is the best overall site to begin with. Be sure to follow the links.

Augmented Reality—http://www.technologyreview.com/articles/05/02/wo/wo_delio021505.asp?p=1. The newest virtual reality. Good article; type in URL carefully.

Virtual Reality Products—http://www.vrealities.com. Learn about the paraphernalia needed.

The History of Virtual Reality—http://archive.ncsa.uiuc.edu/Cyberia/VETopLevels/VR.History.html

What Is Virtual Reality?—http://www.museum.state.il.us/qtvr/about_whatisvr.html. Simple explanation with a good example.

Virtual Reality Lab at University of Michigan—http://www-vrl.umich.edu/. Good information and demonstrations of projects.

How Stuff Works—http://geoweb.tamu.edu/faculty/herbert/bigbend/intro/index.html. Our favorite—Search "Virtual Reality" and find several topics to explore.

 **TA DA!**

Find Out More—Visit the Best!

Hot Virtual Reality Sites—List made by National Institute of Standards in Technology—http://www.itl.nist.gov/iaui/ovrt/hotvr.

Experience

Experience VR on the Web—http://www.thetech.org/events/vre/. View the robotics display and the 360-degree panoramas.

Find a place in your town that has VR; try it.

Virtual tour of the Louvre museum—http://www.louvre.fr/louvrea.htm

In the Classroom

Virtual Reality in Education—http://www.mindspring.com/~rigole/vr.htm. Good background and information about VR's use in education.

Virtual Reality Lesson—http://www.ozedweb.com/infotech/virtual_reality_lesson_1.htm. Be sure to view the PowerPoint presentation. Consists of three lessons.

WEATHER

Weather is the atmosphere's heat or cold, wetness or dryness, calm or storm, clearness or cloudiness. It includes temperature, pressure, humidity, clouds, wind, precipitation, and fog. We always have weather. Meteorologists prepare forecasts or predictions and warnings. We sometimes have fun joking about the weatherperson being wrong—but that job is a science, with many instruments that help. Predicting hurricanes and gales by weather forecasters has saved many lives. Weather is an interesting topic that can also be useful.

 **89**

Castles in the Sky.

CLOUDS

New Words

Stratus
Altostratus
Cumulus
Cumulominbus
Cirrus—Nimbus

What Are Clouds?

When you fly in an airplane, you will often fly through a cloud. It seems wispy and insignificant, like it is not really there, but if the flight gets bumpy, you sure feel it! If you go outside on a foggy morning, you can walk through a cloud. Looking at something close, you can see just fine, but when you look off at a distance, the fog can block your view. When you gaze up at clouds, you might see a dinosaur flying through the sky. As you watch, it slowly transforms into a pirate ship. Clouds can help you create interesting stories, but they also hold valuable information about the weather. As you learn about clouds, you will be able to predict rain or snow and estimate the temperature. You just need to learn to tell cirrus from nimbus.

What Can I Write About?

Describe how clouds form and explain their significance

Choose one type of cloud and tell all about it.

Learn about seeding the clouds. Who does this? How does it work?

Explain how to predict the weather by looking at clouds.

Keep a journal recording cloud types and weather changes, and report on your findings.

Are There Books on Clouds?

Use your library catalog and ask the librarian for help.

Allaby, Michael. *Encyclopedia of Weather and Climate.* New York: Facts on File, 2002.

Allaby, Michael. *Facts on File Weather and Climate Handbook.* New York: Facts on File, 2002.

Ludlum, David M. *Audubon Society Field Guide to North American Weather.* New York: Knopf, 1995.

New Book of Popular Science. Vol. 2. Danbury, CT: Grolier, 2004.

World Book Student Discovery Encyclopedia. Chicago: World Book, 2003.

Can the Internet Help?

Web weather for kids—http://www.ucar.edu/educ_outreach/webweather/cloudhome.html. Explains how clouds form and shows the different types.

Boat Safe Kids—http://www.boatsafe.com/kids/weather1.htm. Explains the different types of clouds and their relation to the weather.

USA Today—http://www.usatoday.com/weather/resources/askjack/wjack3.htm. Ask Jack specific questions about the weather.

Clouds and Precipitation, from the University of Illinois—http://ww2010.atmos.uiuc.edu/(Gh)/guides/mtr/cld/home.rxml. Gives information about cloud development and cloud types.

How are clouds named? Who named them?—http://www.wrh.noaa.gov/fgz/science/clouds.php

 **TA DA!**

Clouds in Action!

University of Iowa—http://www.pals.iastate.edu/carlson/main.html. Pictures of cool clouds.

Clouds R Us—http://www.cloudsrus.com/. All sorts of activities, including making your own barometer.

Experiment

Create a portable cloud—http://www.ucar.edu/educ_outreach/webweather/cloudact2.html

In the Classroom

The Weather Notebook, a radio show about the weather, from Mt. Washington, New Hampshire, offers Teacher Feature—http://www.weathernotebook.org/teacher/index.php

The Educators Reference Desk—http://www.eduref.org/Virtual/Lessons/index.shtml#Search. Several lesson plans for clouds, but you'll have to use the search feature.

Teachers.Net—http://www.teachers.net/lessons/posts/14.html. Make your own clouds, a fourth-grade lesson plan.

The Dust Bowl.

DROUGHT

New Words

Precipitation
Climate
Famine
Hydrologic Cycle

What Is a Drought?

Drought is a shortage of water, usually from too little rain or snowfall, over an extended period of time. Because average precipitation varies in different climates, drought is not defined by a certain amount of rainfall. Instead, it is considered a drought when the amount of rainfall is less than expected for such a long period of time that it affects the quality of life in the area. Farmers can't grow their crops, and rivers and wells run low or even dry. In some parts of the world, it can mean famine.

What Can I Write About?

Explain the causes of drought. How are they predicted? Use examples from your area.

What happens to areas of the world where droughts occur? Select a country (Afghanistan, Ethiopia) and find out more.

Explain the hydrologic cycle, including cause and effect of drought.

Can people make it rain? Look into cloud seeding.

Are There Books on Drought?

Use your library catalog. Ask the librarian if you need help. Reference books on weather can be helpful. Or find books on parts of the world that often have droughts, and they will likely cover your topic.

Allaby, Michael. *A Chronology of Weather.* Dangerous Weather. New York: Facts on File, 2004.

Allaby, Michael. *Encyclopedia of Weather and Climate.* New York: Facts on File, 2002.

Lerner, K. Lee, and Brenda Wilmoth Lerner, eds. *Gale Encyclopedia of Science*. 3d ed. Vol.2 . Detroit: Gale, 2004.

Mongillo, John, and Linda Zierdt-Warshaw. *Encyclopedia of Environmental Science*. Phoenix, AZ: Oryx, 2000.

Newton, David E., Rob Nagel, and Bridget Travers. *UXL Encyclopedia of Science*. Vol. 3. Detroit: UXL, 1998.

Can the Internet Help?

The National Drought Mitigation Center—http://www.drought.unl.edu/kids/. Explains drought.

U.S. Department of the Interior—http://www.usbr.gov/mp/watershare/resources/waterlearn.html. Water management and conservation.

From ThinkQuest—http://library.thinkquest.org/C003603/english/droughts/whatsadrought.shtml. What is a drought?

Drought Information for Kids from the New Jersey Drought Relief Center—http://www.state.nj.us/drbc/drought/kids_droughtinfo.htm

Pitara Kids Network—http://www.pitara.com/discover/5wh/42.htm. Cloud seeding to make it rain.

Natural Hazards: Causes and Effects—Droughts—http://dmc.engr.wisc.edu/courses/hazards/BB02-07.html

Early Warning System for Droughts—http://www.fews.net/. Countries in drought or on alert.

 **TA DA!**

Drought in Action!

Environmental Protection Agency—http://www.epa.gov/safewater/kids/kids_4-8.html. Water games.

Experiment

Louisiana Deparment of Environmental Quality—http://www.deq.state.la.us/assistance/educate/aquifer2.htm. Build your own aquifer.

Science Court—http://www.teachtsp.com/products/productextras/SCISCI/watercycle.html. End the drought in your kitchen. Make it rain!

In the Classroom

The U.S. Geological Survey, *Water Science for Schools*—http://ga.water.usgs.gov/edu/. Water basics, the water cycle, and activities.

Lesson plans—http://www.usbr.gov/mp/watershare/resources/lessonplans.html (government), http://www.nytimes.com/learning/teachers/lessons/20030128tuesday.html?searchpv=learning_lessons (*New York Times*).

Swelling and Upwelling.

EL NIÑO

New Words

> Southern Oscillation
> ENSO
> Monsoon
> Upwelling

What Is El Niño?

Trade winds in the southern Pacific Ocean usually blow toward the west. These winds bring cooler water to South America and monsoons to Southeast Asia and northern Australia in the first months of the year. Every few years, though, the trade winds weaken, and the weather all over the world is affected. Deserts flood, and rain forests face drought. This condition is called El Niño. But the opposite can also happen. Some years, the cooling is stronger than usual. That is called La Niña. In the continental United States, during El Niño years, temperatures in the winter are warmer than normal in the North and cooler than normal in the South. During a La Niña year, winter temperatures are warmer than normal in the Southeast and cooler than normal in the Northwest.

What Can I Write About?

> What happens when El Niño arrives? Discuss the consequences of El Niño on the weather in the United States.

> Consider the consequences of El Niño on the weather in South America. Compare that with what happens in Asia.

> Compare El Niño and La Niña.

> Discover what scientists are doing to understand and predict El Niño.

Are There Books on El Niño?

> Use your library catalog. Search *weather and El Niño.*

> Allaby, Michael. *A Chronology of Weather.* Dangerous Weather. New York: Facts on File, 2004.

> Allaby, Michael. *Encyclopedia of Weather and Climate.* New York: Facts on File, 2002.

Arnold, Caroline. *El Niño: Stormy Weather for People and Wildlife.* New York: Clarion, 1998.

Bredeson, Carmen. *El Niño and La Niña: Deadly Weather.* Berkeley Heights, NJ: Enslow, 2002.

Englebert, Phillis. *Dangerous Planet: The Science of Natural Disasters.* Vol. 2. Detroit: UXL, 2001.

Can the Internet Help?

National Oceanic and Atmospheric Administration—http://elnino.noaa.gov/. The facts about El Niño and La Niña.

The Why Files—http://whyfiles.org/050el_nino/1.html. Explains El Niño for younger kids.

NASA—http://kids.earth.nasa.gov/archive/nino/. Explanation of El Niño and Southern Oscillation.

University Corporation for Atmospheric Research—http://www.ucar.edu/ communications/factsheets/elnino/. The basics and anatomy of El Niño.

University of Illinois—http://ww2010.atmos.uiuc.edu/(Gh)/guides/mtr/eln/ home.rxml. Explains the significance of El Niño and La Niña from an economic point of view.

Pacific Marine Environmental Lab—http://www.pmel.noaa.gov/tao/elnino/ nino-home.html. Impact and benefits of El Niño and La Niña.

 TA DA!

El Niño in Action!

El Niño cartoons collected by COAPS—http://www.coaps.fsu.edu/lib/ climatoons/

NASA—http://topex-www.jpl.nasa.gov/elnino/index.html. View satellite images to see what is happening with El Niño this year.

Experiment

ThinkQuest—http://www.preservice.org/T0300830/ELNINO.htm. This experiment shows why water temperatures matter.

In the Classroom

Exploring the Environment has a module on El Niño—http://www.cotf. edu/ete/modules/elnino/elnino.html

National Oceanic and Atmospheric Administration—http://www.elnino.noaa. gov/edu.html. Links to El Niño educational sites.

A Web Inquiry Project for students from San Diego State University—http:// edweb.sdsu.edu/wip/examples/elnino/

Well, Blow Me Down!

HURRICANES

New Words

Hurricane Hunters
Meteorologist
Natural Disaster
Saffir-Simpson Hurricane Scale
Eye—Center—Eyewall

What Is a Hurricane?

A hurricane is a tropical storm with winds blowing at 74 mph or faster. These winds blow in a large spiral around a calm center known as the eye. August and September are peak months during the hurricane season, which lasts from June 1 through November 30. If you have ever experienced a hurricane, you won't forget it. It can devastate a large area along the coast—and then rush inland to do damage there. Find out more about nature's deadliest storm.

What Can I Write About?

How does a hurricane develop? What are its characteristics? Damage?

Write about the role of one of the hurricane reporting centers. Examples include the National Hurricane Center, Federal Emergency Management Agency (FEMA), and the National Oceanic and Atmospheric Administration (NOAA).

Write about a specific hurricane. Find out all you can about it. Find pictures, statistics.

Write about the hurricane hunters or others who research hurricanes. How do they go about their research? What scientific equipment do they use?

Write about the Saffir-Simpson Hurricane Scale. Why was it developed? How does it help hurricane watchers? Give examples of different storms for each intensity.

Are There Books on Hurricanes?

Cosgrove, Brian. *Weather.* DK Eyewitness. New York: DK, 2004.

Lauber, Patricia. *Hurricanes: Earth's Mightiest Storms.* New York: Scholastic, 1996.

Palm Beach Post. *Mean Season: Florida's Hurricanes of 2004.* Atlanta, GA: Longstreet, 2004.

Richards, Julie. *Howling Hurricanes.* Broomall, PA: Chelsea House, 2001.

Sheets, Bob, and Jack Williams. *Hurricane Watch: Forecasting the Deadliest Storms on Earth.* New York: Vintage, 2001.

Can the Internet Help?

Excellent videos about hurricanes—http://media.dsc.discovery.com/news/videogallery/hurricanegallery.html. You'll have to watch the ads first, but this information is worth the wait.

National Geographic—http://www.nationalgeographic.com/eye/hurricanes/hurrintro.html. Videos and information about hurricanes.

National Hurricane Center—http://www.nhc.noaa.gov/. Histories, information about preparedness, charts, and FAQ section.

Find out about the Hurricane Hunters and their work—http://www.hurricanehunters.com/ and http://www.nationalgeographic.com/ngkids/0308/hurricane/

Go to Accuweather's Hurricane School—http://www.accuweather.com/wx/school/hurricane.htm. Lots there to learn.

Hurricane Awareness—http://www.nws.noaa.gov/om/hurricane/index.shtml. Understanding, preparing, research centers, and tracking charts.

Saffir-Simpson Hurricane Scale—http://www.aoml.noaa.gov/general/lib/laescae.html. Scale used to describe the intensity of a storm.

 ## TA DA!

Hurricanes in Action!

How are hurricanes named?—http://kids.mtpe.hq.nasa.gov/archive/hurricane/names.html. Are the names ever retired? Find out!

Tracking Hurricanes—http://www.miamisci.org/hurricane/instructions.html. Have fun tracking several big hurricanes of the past.

Experience

Movie Catalog of Hurricanes, from NASA—http://rsd.gsfc.nasa.gov/rsd/movies/movies.html. Watch them and draw conclusions.

In the Classroom

Theme pages from CLN—http://www.cln.org/themes/tsunamis.html. Links to educational resources by subject.

The Eye of the Hurricane—http://www.nationalgeographic.com/xpeditions/lessons/07/g35/trythishurricane.html. Lesson for the Cyberflight.

Takes Both Rain and Sunshine to Make One.

RAINBOWS

New Words

Atmospheric Optics
Chromatic Dispersion
Halos—Glories—Coronas
Primary Bow, Secondary Bow, Supernumeraries
Rainbow Wheel
Reflection—Refraction

What Is a Rainbow?

One of the best gifts nature offers is the rainbow. Its beauty is hard to describe. Bright sun to your back and rain clouds off in the distance in the direction of your shadow are the conditions you are looking for to spot a rainbow. Other places you may see rainbows are in the mist from garden hoses, lawn sprinklers, and fountains. Remember, only when a mist or rainfall is around and the sun is out can you see a rainbow. We hear there is gold at the end of the rainbow. Choose rainbows as your topic. If you can spot more rainbows because you understand more, your research will pay off. Right?

What Can I Write About?

What are rainbows? What causes rainbows? How are they formed?

Describe the differences in primary and secondary rainbows, double rainbows, and supernumerary ones.

What are the colors in the rainbow? Are they always in the same order? Make a rainbow for your class. Explain. Use this site: http://www.exploratorium.edu/science_explorer/reflecting_rainbows.html

You may want to write about one or two other atmospheric optics, like halos or coronas.

Are There Books on Rainbows?

We can't begin to tell you the best books. There are many. Use your library catalog. Do not forget the reference area, where you can find background information and statistics.

Ahrens, Donald D. *Meteorology Today: An Introduction to Weather, Climate and the Environment.* Independence, KY: Thomson Learning, 2002.

Bower, Miranda. *Experiment with Weather.* Minneapolis, MN: Lerner, 1994.

Dickinson, Terence. *Exploring the Sky by Day: An Equinox Guide to the Weather and the Atmosphere.* Camden East, ON: Camden, 1988.

Gallant, Roy. *Rainbows, Mirages, and Sundogs: The Sky as a Source of Wonder.* New York: Macmillan, 1987.

Weather. Pleasantville, NY: Reader's Digest, 1997.

Can the Internet Help?

First, look at this key to terms you need to know to identify types of rainbows— http://www.sundog.clara.co.uk/rainbows/key.htm

About Rainbows—http://my.unidata.ucar.edu/content/staff/blynds/rnbw.html. What makes the bow? What makes the colors? What are supernumerary arcs?

Atmospheric Optics—http://www.sundog.clara.co.uk/atoptics/phenom.htm. Many kinds of rainbows are explained. Beautiful pictures.

Light and Optics—http://ww2010.atmos.uiuc.edu/(Gh)/guides/mtr/opt/wtr/ rnbw/frm.rxml. What makes a rainbow and other color optics?

How Rainbows Form—http://www.greatestplaces.org/book_pages/iguazu/ rainbows.html. Look at other topics in The Joy of Visual Perception.

Rainbows: How Stuff Works—http://science.howstuffworks.com/rainbow.htm. Follow the other links, also.

Rainbows, Halos, and Coronas—http://www.wxdude.com/Rainbows.html

The Physics of a Rainbow—http://www.phy.ntnu.edu.tw/java/Rainbow/rainbow. html

All the Sky—Atmosphere—http://www.allthesky.com/atmosphere/atmosphere. html. Photos and brief explanation of atmospheric phenomena.

 **TA DA!**

Rainbows in Action!

Get your camera out the next time you see a rainbow and get a few color shots. Lucky you, if you get a double rainbow. Look here for inspiration: http://www. rainbowmaker.us/

Experiment

The Mathematics of Rainbows—http://www.geom.uiuc.edu/education/calc-init/ rainbow/

In the Classroom

Share these with students!—http://www.rainbowmaker.us/ and http://www. iit.edu/~smile/ph9203.html

To Everything There Is a Season.

SEASONS

New Words

> Earth's Axis
> Elliptical Orbit
> Equinox
> Hemispheres—Solstice

What Is a Season?

Summer, fall, winter, and spring. Many of us live in places where the four seasons are easy to identify. When spring comes, we think, "This is my favorite season." When fall arrives, we think, "Oh, I love fall. It is my favorite season." This is natural, because each season has its own beauty. The seasons are the result of the tilt of the earth's axis.

What Can I Write About?

Explain the four seasons. What causes them? What are some of their characteristics?

Compare seasons in the northern and southern hemispheres. Why are they different?

Write about a single season: spring, summer, winter, or fall. Explain the tilt of the earth's axis that brings this season. What are the characteristics of this season? Discuss plant and animal behavior during your selected season.

Astronomers can tell us exactly when a new season begins. How? Explain the solstice and equinox.

Are There Books About the Seasons?

The library catalog will help you find the books on seasons in your library.

Aguardo, Edward, and James Burt.. *Understanding Weather and Climate.* 3d ed. Englewood Cliffs, NJ: Prentice Hall, 2003.

Gold-Dworkin, Heidi. *Learning About the Changing Seasons.* New York: McGraw-Hill, 2000.

New Book of Popular Science. Danbury, CT: Grolier, 2004.

Newton, David E., Rob Nagel, and Bridget Travers, ed. *UXL Encyclopedia of Science*. Detroit: UXL, 1997.

Stewart, David. *Seasons*. New York: Franklin Watts, 2002.

Wagner, Ronald L., and Bill Adler. *The Weather Sourcebook: Your One-Stop Resource for Everything You Need to Feed Your Weather Habit*. Old Saybrook, CT: Globe Pequot, 1994.

Weather, Seasons, and Time. [videorecording]. Wynnewood, PA: Schlessinger, 2004.

Can the Internet Help?

The Seasons—in the northern and southern hemispheres—http://csep10. phys.utk.edu/astr161/lect/time/seasons.html

Seasons of the Year, from NASA—http://www-spof.gsfc.nasa.gov/stargaze/ Sseason.htm. Good basic information.

What Causes the Seasons?—http://howstuffworks.com/question165.htm

Earth's Seasons—a video from NASA—http://kids.msfc.nasa.gov/earth/seasons/ EarthSeasons.asp

The Seasons—http://lectureonline.cl.msu.edu/~mmp/applist/seasons/cd190b. htm. Online applet showing the year.

The Reasons for the Seasons—http://www.astronomy.org/programs/seasons/

 **TA DA!**

Seasons in Action!

Enjoy the seasons of the year in a wildlife garden—http://flood.nhm. ac.uk/cgi-bin/wgarden/

Orisinal has many seasonal games—http://www.ferryhalim.com/orisinal/. This is truly a neat site!

Reasons for the Seasons—http://www2.worldbook.com/features/seasons/ html/seasons.htm

Experiment

Track the sun and see the reasons for the seasons—http://dana. ucc.nau.edu/~jcd48/

In the Classroom

Art and music classes can listen to Vivaldi's *Four Seasons*—while they draw their feelings about each season—http://w3.rz-berlin.mpg.de/cmp/vivaldi_ op8_1to4_four_seasons.html. Discuss the music suggesting each season.

Seasons of the Year—http://www.phy6.org/Stargaze/Lseason.htm and http://faldo.atmos.uiuc.edu/w_unit/LESSONS/seasons.html. Lesson plans and exercises.

Light Shows and Boom!

THUNDERSTORMS

New Words

Hail
Benjamin Franklin
St. Elmo's Fire
Updraft
Multi Cell, Single Cell, Supercells

What Is a Thunderstorm?

We have all experienced a violent storm. The rain pounds, lightning cuts across the sky, and thunder booms. It's like the earth shudders. When you are safely indoors, a thunderstorm can be a magnificent thing to watch. You wonder what causes this powerful storm. A big boom might send you hiding under the covers. But don't worry. As thunderstorm researcher Karl B. Eachron has said, "If you hear the thunder, the lightning did not strike you. . . . If it did strike you, you would not have known it."

What Can I Write About?

Explain the components of a thunderstorm. What is needed to create a thunderstorm?

Explain the causes of lightning and thunder. (See if Karl Eachron was right.) Why are there more thunderstorms in the summer?

Compare types of lightning such as streak lightning, ball lightning, heat lightning, and St. Elmo's Fire.

Write about safety precautions you should follow in a thunderstorm.

Describe the three types of thunderstorms. Include drawings. Your own photographs?

Don't forget about Ben Franklin's experiments with lightning. Write about them.

Are There Books on Thunderstorms?

Use your library catalog. Try *thunderstorms; weather.*

Allaby, Michael. *Encyclopedia of Weather and Climate.* New York: Facts on File, 2002.

Ludlum, David M. *National Audubon Society Field Guide to American Weather.* New York: Knopf, 1995.

Sipiera, Paul, and Diane Sipiera. *Thunderstorms.* A True Book. New York: Children's Press, 1999.

World Book Student Discovery Encyclopedia. Chicago: World Book, 2003.

Can the Internet Help?

UCAR, the University Corporation for Atmospheric Research—http://www.ucar.edu/communications/infopack/lightning/basics.html. Lightning basics.

How Stuff Works—http://science.howstuffworks.com/lightning.htm. How lightning works.Follow the additional links.

National Geographic—http://www.nationalgeographic.com/lightning/. Gives the science and history of lightning.

National Weather Service—http://www.crh.noaa.gov/mkx/owlie/anvil.htm. Tells all about lightning and thunder.

FEMA—http://www.fema.gov/kids/thunder.htm. Explains thunderstorms in basic terms.

University of Chicago—http://ww2010.atmos.uiuc.edu/(Gh)/guides/mtr/svr/home.rxml. Dangers, types, and components of thunderstorms.

Thunderstorms—http://weather.cod.edu/sirvatka/ts.html. A good explanation of the three types of thunderstorms.

 **TA DA!**

Thunderstorms in Action!

NASA's KSNN explains lightning in this video clip—http://ksnn.larc.nasa.gov/videos_low.cfm?unit=lightning

Experiment

Web Weather for Kids—http://www.ucar.edu/40th/webweather/lightng/light.htm. Make lightning with a pie tin and a piece of wool.

In the Classroom

Interactive lesson on lightning from WeatherEye—http://weathereye.kgan.com/cadet/lightning/teachers.html

CLS's Lightning Theme Page—http://www.cln.org/themes/lightning.html. Links to lesson plans and other Web pages about lightning.

The National Weather Service—http://www.lightningsafety.noaa.gov/teachers.htm. Activities and lesson plans on lightning safety.

Tracking Hurricanes.

WEATHER SATELLITES

New Words

Latitude—Longitude
Orbit
Payload
Solar panels
Trajectory
Wavelength

What Is a Weather Satellite?

A satellite is any object that orbits or revolves around another object. For example, the moon is a satellite of Earth. Man-made satellites are used for communication, spying, search and rescue, scientific research, meteorology, navigation, and space exploration. Weather satellites help meteorologists predict the weather and help to monitor both day-to-day weather conditions and longer term climatic change around the world.

What Can I Write About?

What is a weather satellite, and what does it do?

Write about the history of weather satellites. In what ways have they improved?

Choose one of the weather satellites, like TIROS, and discuss its "job." What are some of the measuring instruments onboard used to help meteorologists predict and understand the weather?

Describe the anatomy of a weather satellite. Why does it stay in orbit? What happens to it when it stops working?

Are There Books on Weather Satellites?

Books about *satellites* or *weather* will include weather satellites.

Cobb, Allan B. *Weather Observation Satellites*. New York: Rosen, 2003.

Day, John A., and Vincent Schaefer. *Peterson First Guide to Clouds and Weather.* Boston: Houghton Mifflin, 1991.

Dickinson, Terence. *Exploring the Sky by Day: An Equinox Guide to Weather and the Atmosphere.* Camden East, ON: Camden, 1988.

Kahl, Jonathan. *National Audubon Society First Field Guide: Weather.* New York: Scholastic, 1998.

Parker, Steve. *Satellites.* Austin, TX: Raintree Steck-Vaughn, 1997.

Can the Internet Help?

Tech Museum—Satellites—http://www.thetech.org/exhibits_events/online/satellite/

Satellites—http://collections.ic.gc.ca/satellites/english/. Excellent information and images.

How Satellites Work—http://octopus.gma.org/surfing/satellites/

Satellites that predict the weather, and information about each—http://www.met.fsu.edu/explores/Guide/satguide.html

Space Information from Japan—http://spaceinfo.jaxa.jp/index_e.html. Basic information and video about satellites.

National Weather Service—http://www.nws.noaa.gov/. Predicts the news using several systems, including satellites.

Unisys Weather—http://weather.unisys.com/. For the professional and beginner. Collects weather data via several systems, including satellite, radar, and surface data (ground reports from around the world). Interesting.

 **TA DA!**

Satellites in Action!

Launch a Satellite—http://octopus.gma.org/surfing/satellites/launch.html

Build a Satellite, from Science for Families—http://scienceforfamilies.allinfo-about.com/features/satellites.html

Experiment

The Falcon's Nest—http://home.earthlink.net/~w0dfi/2nd.html. For the real space lovers, this site lets you track satellites, get updates from NASA, and more.

In the Classroom

Lesson plans for teaching students to read satellite images—http://school.discovery.com/lessonplans/programs/satelliteimages/, http://members.tripod.com/exworthy/weather.htm, or http://www.atmos.uiuc.edu/courses/atmos100/gen_exercises/satellite.pdf. Fun and educational—several ages.

Red Sky at Night, Sailor's Delight . . .

WEATHER VERSUS CLIMATE

New Words

Jet Stream
Atmosphere
Barometer
Temperature

What Is the Difference Between Weather and Climate?

Hawaii is generally warm and sunny with a generous sprinkling of rain, Arizona is hot and dry, and Minnesota is cold. Although at any given time, these statements might not be true, they do describe the climates of each of the states. But there are days when you might shiver in Honolulu. It does rain in Arizona, and in Minnesota the temperature once reached 114 degrees (in 1936.) Weather is the state of the atmosphere at any given time and place, while climate is how the weather acts over many years.

What Can I Write About?

What is the difference between weather and climate? Explain thoroughly. Give an example using the area of the country where you live.

Compare the climate and the recent weather in your area.

Discuss the jet stream and how it relates to weather and climate.

Study changes in climate over a period of time.

Discuss weather forecasting.

Are There Books on Weather and Climate?

Use your library catalog. Do not forget the reference area, where you can find background information.

Allaby, Michael. *How the Weather Works.* Pleasantville, NY: Reader's Digest, 1999.

Childcraft: The How and Why Library. Chicago: World Book, 2003.

Lerner, K. Lee, and Brenda Wilmoth Lerner, eds. *Gale Encyclopedia of Science.* 3d ed. Vol.4 . Detroit: Gale, 2004.

Mongillo, John, and Linda Zierdt-Warshaw. *Encyclopedia of Environmental Science.* Phoenix, AZ: Oryx, 2000.

Tanacredi, John T., and John Loret, eds. *Experiment Central.* Vol. 4. Detroit: UXL, 2000.

World Book Student Discovery Encyclopedia. Chicago: World Book, 2003.

Can the Internet Help?

National Oceanic and Atmospheric Administration—http://www.ncdc.noaa.gov/oa/climate/research/monitoring.html. Weather and climate data for the past five years.

National Drought Mitigation Center—http://www.drought.unl.edu/whatis/climographs.htm. Climographs of some U.S. cities.

Dan's Wild Wild Weather Page—http://www.wildwildweather.com/. Forecasting, weather maps, satellites, and more.

National Center for Atmospheric Research—http://www.eo.ucar.edu/basics/index.html. Explore weather and climate.

The Science of Jet Streams, from the Academy of Science of St. Louis—http://www.jracademy.com/%7Ewotawaj/index.html

Weather vs. Climate—http://weathereye.kgan.com/cadet/climate/. Simple explanations of differences. Explains seven regional climates.

 **TA DA!**

Weather in Action!

Scholastic—http://www.scholastic.com/kids/weather/. You can control the weather.

Listen to Weather Meteorology! From Nick Walker, the Weather Dude—http://www.wxdude.com/guide.html

Experiment

Southwest Regional Climate Center—http://www.dnr.state.sc.us/climate/sercc/education/education.html. Make your own anemometer or barometer.

In the Classroom

National Oceanic and Atmospheric Administration—http://www.oar.noaa.gov/k12/html/teacherinfo.html. Weather teaching materials and activities.

National Center for Atmospheric Research—http://www.eo.ucar.edu/educators/index.html. Weather research at various grade levels.

Scholastic's teacher site about the weather—http://teacher.scholastic.com/researchtools/articlearchives/weather/index.htm

40 Percent Chance of Precipitation.

THE WEATHERPERSON

New Words

Air Masses, Air Pressure
Doppler Radar
Forecasting—Predicting
Meteorological, Meteorologist
UV Rays

What Is a Weatherperson?

In forecasting the weather, the weatherperson uses his or her own language: words like *fronts* and *air masses, high and low air pressure, precipitation, humidity, UV index, wind,* and *temperature.* He or she reads maps, graphs, and weather map symbols and uses conversion charts to tell us how hot or cold it feels outside—not just how hot or cold the temperature is. Learn more about the weather, and you will have fun watching and interpreting the maps and charts on the weather channel. How can the weatherperson have so much equipment to help him or her and still occasionally be wrong?

What Can I Write About?

The meteorologist or forecaster predicts and helps us understand the weather around the world. Meteorology is an interesting and important scientific career. Forecasting and predicting the weather—how does the weatherperson do this? Write about this job.

Understanding weather instruments—What about the thermometer, barometer, anemometer, hydrometers, rain gauge, wind meters, radios, and more?

Reading weather maps—Can you understand symbols, charts, maps, and graphs the weatherperson uses? Explain.

Write about weather calculations: temperature, moisture, pressure, and wind conversions. What are they? Can you do the math?

Are There Books About the Weatherperson?

Use your library catalog. Ask the librarian to help you find specific topics.

Breen, Mark. *Kids' Book of Weather Forecasting: Build a Weather Station, "Read" the Sky and Make Predictions!* Charlotte, VT: Williamson, 2000.

Dickinson, Rosemary. *Meteorology : Observing, Understanding, and Predicting Weather.* Tucson, AZ: Zephyr, 2002.

Pipe, Jim. *Weather.* Mankato, MN: Stargazer, 2005.

Weather. My First Pocket Guide. Washington, DC: National Geographic, 2001.

Wills, Susan. *Meteorology: Predicting the Weather.* Minneapolis, MN: Oliver, 2004.

Can the Internet Help?

Predicting the Weather—http://www.weather.com/education/index.html

The Weather Dude—http://www.wxdude.com/. Read about the weather and listen to his songs!

The Weather Classroom, for Students—http://www.weatherclassroom.com/home_students.php. Excellent information about what happens.

What Is Weather?—http://www.ussartf.org/predicting_weather.htm

Weather Conversion Charts—http://www.crh.noaa.gov/pub/metcon.shtml. Try them. Also, follow the other links for more information.

Cyber Bee Weather Destinations—http://www.infotoday.com/MMSchools/mar98/cybe0398.htm. Explanations and links.

Weather World 2010 Project—http://ww2010.atmos.uiuc.edu/(Gh)/guides/mtr/fw/home.rxml. Use the index to find most of the topics.

Weather Symbols Chart—http://www.teachervision.fen.com/tv/printables/WeatherSymbols.pdf

Doppler Radar from *USA Today*—http://www.usatoday.com/weather/wdoppler.htm

Weather Topics—http://www.stteresa.net/weather.htm and http://www.42explore.com/weather.htm

 **TA DA!**

Weatherpersons in Action!

Weather activities for kids—http://www.ucar.edu/educ_outreach/webweather/ and http://www.weatherwizkids.com/WxExperiments.htm. Enjoy these games, riddles, and experiments.

Track the weather for two weeks. Measure the rain and track the temperature. Compare each day to the weatherperson's forecast.

In the Classroom

National Severe Storms Room lessons—http://www.nssl.noaa.gov/edu/. Activities and information.

FEMA for Teachers—http://www.fema.gov/kids/tch_links.htm

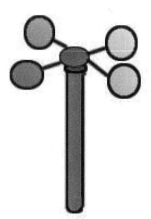

Who Has Seen the Wind?

THE WIND

New Words

Anemometer
Air Pressure
Bird Migration
Jet Stream—Gulf Stream
Wind Chill Temperature Index

What Is the Wind?

Christina Rossetti wrote a famous poem about the wind, "Who has seen the Wind?" Other poets have written about it, too. Try to find their poems on the Internet. The wind is one of the forces that influences our weather. Without wind there would be little or no change in the weather. A winter storm can become deadly if it is accompanied by strong winds. Find out where wind comes from and how we measure it. How can it help us?

What Can I Write About?

Write a paper about the wind. Where does it come from? Does it influence weather?

Write about wind chill. What is it? Explain how it is measured, the instrument used, and how it works. Tell how wind chill affects real temperature for humans and animals.

Have fun. Write about the wind and flying kites. Make a kite and test your information.

Write about the Beauford Wind Scale (or another wind instrument.) Who was Beauford? What does his scale measure? Describe the scale and use it in your own experiments.

Describe and explain the types of winds you encounter locally (sea breezes, land breezes, mountain breezes, etc.).

How can the wind be used to help us? What is wind power? Explain.

Are There Books About the Wind?

Use your library catalog. Ask the librarian to help you find specific topics.

Onish, Liane. *Wind and Weather: Climates, Clouds, Snow and How Weather Is Predicted.* Scholastic, 1995.

Parker, Steve. *Wind Power*. Milwaukee: Gareth Stevens, 2004.

Petersen, Christina. *Wind Power*. New York: Children's, 2004.

Pipe, Jim. *Weather*. Mankato, MN: Stargazer, 2005.

Wills, Susan. *Meteorology: Predicting the Weather*. Minneapolis: Oliver, 2004.

Can the Internet Help?

Weatherwizkids—Wind—http://www.weatherwizkids.com/wind1.htm. Get started with this site. Find the basics here.

Wind chill temperature (WCT) explained—http://www.nws.noaa.gov/om/windchill/. Try the wind chill calculator.

Wind! from 42 Explore—http://www.42explore.com/wind.htm. Good links, well defined.

Forces and Wind, from the University of Illinois—http://ww2010.atmos.uiuc.edu/(Gh)/guides/mtr/fw/home.rxml. Excellent information; good site for types of winds.

Wind Power in Colorado—http://www.cogreenpower.org/Wind.htm. Why buy it? What is it? Environmental benefits.

"Forces That Create Winds" and "Local Winds"—chapters from *Physical Geography*—http://www.physicalgeography.net/fundamentals/7n.html and http://www.physicalgeography.net/fundamentals/7o.html

National Wind Technology Center—http://www.nrel.gov/wind/. The wind is harnessed for energy. How?

Professor Kite—http://www.gombergkites.com/howgen.html or http://www.gombergkites.com/nkm/wind1.html. Choosing the right kite for the type of wind. Learn about kite science.

Wild Wild Weather—http://www.wildwildweather.com/wind.htm

Winter Weather Awareness—http://www.nws.noaa.gov/om/winter/index.shtml. Write about the winter storm and the wind.

 **TA DA!**

Wind in Action!

Weather Experiments—http://www.weatherwizkids.com/WxExperiments.htm. Try the wind sock or anemometer, or find out what is in the wind.

Virtual Kite Zoo—http://www.kites.org/zoo/. For fun.

In the Classroom

Lesson plans from the Franklin Institute—http://www.fi.edu/fellows/fellow6/may99/May%20Project/windlessons.html. These include experiments.

BIBLIOGRAPHY

Adams, Charles K. *Nature's Electricity.* New York: McGraw-Hill, 1986.

Aguardo, Edward, and James Burt. *Understanding Weather and Climate.* 3d ed. Englewood Cliffs, NJ: Prentice Hall, 2003.

Ahrens, Donald D. *Meteorology Today: An Introduction to Weather, Climate and the Environment.* Independence, KY: Thomson Learning, 2002.

Algana, Magdalena. *Everything You Need to Know About Chemotherapy.* Need to Know Library. New York: Rosen, 2001.

All About the Brain. The Human Body for Children. [videorecording]. Wynnewood, PA: Schlessinger, 2001.

Allaby, Michael. *A Chronology of Weather.* Dangerous Weather. New York: Facts on File, 2004.

———. *Encyclopedia of Weather and Climate.* New York: Facts on File, 2002.

———. *Facts on File Weather and Climate Handbook.* New York: Checkmark, 2002.

———. *How the Weather Works.* Pleasantville, NY: Reader's Digest, 1999.

Allen, Missy. *Dangerous Plants and Mushrooms.* New York: Chelsea House, 1993.

American Bar Association. *Family Legal Guide.* 3d ed. New York: Random House, 2004.

Animal Adaptations. Animal Life in Action. [videorecording]. VHS FN7782. Wynnewood, PA: Schlessinger Media, 2000.

Animal Life Cycles. [videorecording]. Wynnewood, PA: Schlessinger Media, 1999.

Arnold, Caroline. *El Niño: Stormy Weather for People and Wildlife.* New York: Clarion, 1998.

Aronson, Billy. *Meteors: The Truth Behind Shooting Stars.* New York: Franklin Watts, 1996.

Asimov, Isaac. *Discovering Comets and Meteors.* Milwaukee, MN: Gareth Stevens, 1996.

———. *How Did We Find out About the Atmosphere?* New York: Walker, 1985.

Associated Press Library of Disasters. Vol. 1, *Earthquakes and Tsunamis.* Danbury, CT: Grolier, 1998.

Baker, Christopher W. *Virtual Reality: Experiencing Illusion.* Brookfield, CT: Millbrook, 2000.

Ballard, Carol. *How Do Our Eyes See?* Austin, TX: Raintree Steck-Vaughn, 1998.

———. *Lungs: Injury, Illness, and Health.* Chicago: Heinemann-Raintree, 2003.

———. *Solids, Liquids, and Gases: From Air to Stone.* Orlando, FL: Heinemann-Raintree, 2003.

Bang, Molly. *Chattanooga Sludge: Cleaning Toxic Sludge.* San Diego: Harcourt, 1996.

Bankston, John. *Jacques-Yves Cousteau: His Story Under the Sea.* Bear, DE: Mitchell-Lane, 2003.

Bayer, Linda. *Sleep Disorders.* Philadelphia: Chelsea House, 2001.

Beers, Mark H., et al. *Merck Manual of Medical Information.* 2d ed. Whitehouse Station, NJ: Merck, 2003.

Bell, Mary Ann. *Internet and Personal Computing Fads.* New York: Haworth, 2004.

Bellenir, Karen, ed. *Diet and Nutrition Sourcebook.* 2d ed. Detroit: Omnigraphics, 1999.

Bender, Lionel. *Invention.* Eyewitness Books. New York: Knopf, 1991.

Bennett, David. *Roller Coasters: Wooden and Steel Coasters, Twisters, and Corkscrews.* Edison, NH: Cartwell, 1998.

Benowitz, Steven I. *Cancer.* Diseases and People. Berkeley Heights, NJ: Enslow, 1999.

Berger, Melvin. *Solids, Liquids and Gases: From Superconductors to the Ozone Layer.* New York: Putnam, 1989.

Berger, Melvin, and Gilda Berger. *What Makes an Ocean Wave? Questions and Answers About Oceans and Ocean Life.* New York: Scholastic, 2001.

Beyer, Mark. *Space Exploration.* Danbury, CT: Children's Press, 2002.

Biography Today: Scientists & Inventors Series: Profiles of People of Interest to Young Readers. Detroit: Omnigraphics, 1996- .

Bortz, Fred, and Alfred Bortz. The Library of Subatomic Particles Series. New York: Rosen. Includes these titles—*Electron, Proton, Neutron, Neutrino, Quark, and Photon*—all published in 2004.

Bower, Miranda. *Experiment with Weather.* Minneapolis, MN: Lerner, 1994.

Brailler, Jess M. *Who Was Albert Einstein?* New York: Grossett & Dunlap, 2002.

Brain and the Nervous Systems. Human Body in Action. [videorecording]. Wynnewood, PA: Schlessinger, 2001.

Brandolini, Anita. *Fizz, Bubble & Flash Element Explorations and Atom Adventures for Hands-on Science Fun!* Charlotte, VT: Williamson, 2003.

Bredeson, Carmen. *El Niño and La Niña: Deadly Weather.* Berkeley Heights, NJ: Enslow, 2002.

Breen, Mark. *Kids' Book of Weather Forecasting: Build a Weather Station, "Read" the Sky and Make Predictions!* Charlotte, VT: Williamson, 2000.

Briedahl, Harry. *The Zoo on You: Life on Human Skin.* New York: Chelsea House, 2002.

Brimner, Larry Dane. *Caves.* True Book. New York: Children's Press, 2000.

Bruun, Ruth Dowling, and Bertel Bruun. *The Human Body.* New York: Random House, 1982.

Bryan, Jenny. *Your Amazing Brain: A Fascinating See-Through View of How Our Brain Works.* New York: Random, 1996.

Bryan, Nichol. *Love Canal: Pollution Crisis.* Milwaukee, WI: World Almanac, 2004.

Buckwalter, Stephanie. *Volcanoes: Disaster & Survival.* Berkeley Heights, NJ: Enslow, 2005.

Bunch, Bryan, ed. *Diseases.* Danbury, CT: Grolier, 1997.

Burton, Jane, and Kim Taylor. *The Nature and Science of Colors.* Milwaukee, WI: Gareth Stevens, 1998.

Campbell, Andrea. *Forensic Science: Evidence, Clues, and Investigation.* New York: Chelsea House, 2000.

Carlo, George Louis, and Martin Schram. *Cell Phones: Invisible Hazards in the Wireless Age.* New York: Carroll & Graf, 2001.

Carlson, Shawn, ed.. *Scientific American: The Amateur Scientist: The Complete Collection.* [CD-ROM]. Coventry, RI: Tinkers Guild, 2002.

Carruthers, Margaret W. *The Hubble Space Telescope.* True Books. New York: Franklin Watts, 2003.

Carson, Rachel. *The Sea Around Us.* New York: Oxford, 1951.

———. *The Sense of Wonder.* New York: Harper & Row, 1965.

———. *Silent Spring.* Boston: Houghton Mifflin, 2002. First published in 1962.

Cefrey, Holly. *Virtual Reality.* New York: Children's Press, 2002.

Cheeke, Peter. *Impacts of Livestock Production on Society, Diet, Health , and the Environment*. Danville, Il: Interstate, 1993.

Childcraft: The How and Why Library. Chicago: World Book, 2003.

Clark, John O. E. *Physics Matters!* Danbury, CT: Grolier, 2001.

Cobb, Allan B. *Weather Observation Satellites*. New York: Rose, 2003.

Collman, James. *Naturally Dangerous; Surprising Facts About Food, Health and the Environment*. Sausalito, CA: University Science, 2001.

Considine, Glenn D. *Van Nostrand's Scientific Encyclopedia*. New York: Wiley-Interscience, 2002.

Cook, Nick. *Roller Coasters: Or, I Had So Much Fun I Almost Puked*. Minneapolis, MN: Carolrhoda, 2004.

Cooper, Alan. *Visual Science: Electricity*. London: Silver Burdette, 1985.

Cooper, Ann. *Around the Pond*. Niwot, CO: Roberts Rinehart, 1998.

Cooper, Christopher. *Matter*. Eyewitness Science and Nature. New York: Dorling Kindersley, 2000.

Cosgrove, Brian. *Weather*. DK Eyewitness. New York: DK, 2004.

Cothran, Helen, ed. *Garbage and Recycling: Opposing Viewpoints*. San Diego: Greenhaven, 2003.

Courbon, Paul. *Atlas of the Great Caves of the World*. St. Louis, MO: Cave, 1989.

Cousteau, Jacques. *The Ocean World*. New York: Abradale, 1985.

——. *The Silent World*. Washington, DC: National Geographic, 2004. Originally published in 1953.

Cousteau, Jacques-Yves. *Jacques Cousteau's Calypso*. New York: Harry N. Abrams, 1983.

Cromwell, Sharon. *Why Does My Tummy Rumble When I'm Hungry? And Other Questions About the Digestive System*. Des Plaines, IL: Rigby, 1998.

Curry, Don L. *How Does Your Brain Work?* New York: Children's Press, 2003.

Darling, David. *Computers of the Future: Intelligent Machines and Virtual Reality*. New York: Dillon, 1995.

——. *The Universal Book of Astronomy from the Andromeda Galaxy to the Zone of Avoidance*. Hoboken, NJ: Wiley, 2003.

Davol, Marguerite. *Batwings and the Curtain of Night*. New York: Orchard, 1997.

Day, David. *The Doomsday Book of Animals: A Natural History of Vanished Species*. New York: Viking, 1981.

Day, John A., and Vincent Schaefer. *Peterson First Guide to Clouds and Weather.* Boston: Houghton Mifflin, 1991.

Dearling, Robert, ed. *Encyclopedia of Musical Instruments.* 5 vols. Philadelphia: Chelsea, 2001.

Dickinson, Rosemary. *Meteorology: Observing, Understanding, and Predicting Weather.* Tucson, AZ: Zephyr Press, 2002.

Dickinson, Terence. *Exploring the Sky by Day: The Equinox Guide to Weather and the Atmosphere.* Camden East, ON: Camden House, 1988.

Dispezio, Michael. *Awesome Experiments in Force and Motion.* New York: Sterling, 1998.

Doherty, Paul, and Don Rathjan. *The Magic Wand and Other Bright Experiments on Light and Color.* Chichester, NY: Wiley, 1995.

Donkin, Andrew. *Dead Giveaways: How Real Life Crimes Are Solved by Amazing Scientific Evidence, Personality Profiling and Paranormal Investigations.* Scranton, PA: Element, 1998.

Dorling Kindersley Illustrated Family Encyclopedia. New York: Dorling Kindersley, 2002.

Dubin, Mark. *How the Brain Works.* Malden, MA: Blackwell, 2002.

DuTemple, Leslie A. *Jacques Cousteau.* A&E Biography. Minneapolis: Lerner, 2000.

Earth. E. Explore Series. London: Dorling Kindersley, 2004.

Elias, Stephen, and Richard Stein. *Patent, Copyright and Trademark.* 7th ed. Berkeley, CA: Nolo, 2004.

Elgin, Kathleen. *The Human Body: The Skin.* New York: Franklin Watts, 1970.

Encyclopedia of Family Health. New York: Marshall Cavendish, 1998.

Encyclopedia of Foods: A Guide to Healthy Nutrition. San Diego: Academic, 2002.

Endangered and Extinct Animals. [videorecording]. Wynnewood, PA: Schlessinger, 1999.

Energy for Children: All About Heat. [videorecording]. Wynnewood, PA: Schlessinger Video Library, 2000.

Englebert, Phillis. *Dangerous Planet: The Science of Natural Disasters.* Detroit: UXL, 2001.

————. *Technology in Action: Science Applied to Everyday Life: Communication, Electronics and Computers.* Detroit: UXL, 1999.

Erickson, Jon. *Environmental Geology: Facing the Challenges of Our Changing Earth.* New York: Facts on File, 2002.

———. *An Introduction to Fossils and Minerals.* New York: Facts on File, 2000.

Extinct Species. 10 vols. Danbury, CT: Grolier, 2002.

Facklam, Margery. *Do Not Disturb: The Mysteries of Animals and Sleep.* Boston: Little, Brown, 1989.

Ferber, Richard. *Solve Your Child's Sleep Problems.* Old Tappan, NJ: Fireside, 2005.

Flannery, Tim, and Peter Schouten. *A Gap in Nature: Discovering the World's Extinct Animals.* New York: Atlantic Monthly, 2001.

Fleisher, Paul. *Waves: Principles of Light, Electricity, and Magnetism.* Minneapolis, MN: Lerner, 2002.

Ford, R. A. *Homemade Lightning: Creative Experiments in Electricity.* 3d ed. New York: McGraw-Hill, 2002.

Franceschetti, Donald R. *Biographical Encyclopedia of Mathematicians.* New York: Marshall Cavendish, 1999.

Fridell, Ron. *DNA Fingerprinting: The Ultimate Identity.* New York: Franklin Watts, 2001.

Friedlander, Mark P., and Terry M. Phillips. *The Immune System: Your Body's Disease-Fighting Army.* Minneapolis, MN: Lerner Publications, 1998.

Furgang, Kathy. *My Lungs.* New York: PowerKids, 2001.

Furniss, Tim. *The Atlas of Space Exploration.* New York: Friedman, 2002.

Gale Encyclopedia of Medicine. 2d ed. Detroit: Gale, 2002.

Gallant, Roy A. *Atmosphere: Sea of Air.* New York: Benchmark, 2003.

———. *Rainbows, Mirages, and Sundogs: The Sky as a Source of Wonder.* New York: Macmillan, 1987.

Gardner, Robert. *Science Projects about Solids, Liquids, and Gases.* Berkeley Heights, NJ: Enslow, 2000.

Gatland, Kenneth. *Illustrated Encyclopedia of Space Technology.* 2d ed. New York: Orion, 1989.

Geology of Caves and Caverns. [videorecording]. Maumee, OH: Instructional, 2000.

George, Linda. *Plate Tectonics.* San Diego: Kidhaven, 2003.

Gjertson, Derek, and Michael Allaby. *Makers of Science.* New York: Oxford, 2002.

Godish, Thad. *Air Quality.* 4th ed. Boca Raton, FL: Lewis, 2003.

Gold-Dworkin, Heidi. *Learning About the Changing Seasons.* New York: McGraw-Hill, 2000.

Goodall, Jane. *The Chimpanzee Family Book.* New York: North South Books, 1989.

———. *My Life with the Chimpanzees.* New York: Simon & Schuster, 1988.

Goodman, Susan. *Claws, Coats, and Camouflage: The Way Animals Fit in Their World.* Brookfield, CT: Millbrook, 2001.

Goor, Ron, and Nancy Goor. *Insect Metamorphosis: From Egg to Adult.* New York: Atheneum, 1990.

Gosney, John W. *Blogging for Teens.* Independence, KY: Premier, 2004.

Gray, Samantha. *Ocean.* New York: Dorling Kindersley, 2001.

Grolier Library of North American Biographies: *Entrepreneurs and Inventors.* Vol. 3. Danbury, CT: Grolier, 1994.

Grzimeks Animal Life Encyclopedia. Vol. 3, *Insects.* 2d ed. Detroit: Gale, 2004.

Gurnee, R. H. *Gurnee Guide to American Caves: A Comprehensive Guide to the Caves in the United States Open to the Public.* Teaneck, NJ: Zephyrus, 1979.

Hammontree, Marie. *Albert Einstein: Young Thinker.* New York: Aladdin, 1986.

Harrison, David L. *Caves: Mysteries Beneath Our Feet.* Honesdale, PA: Boyds Mills, 2001.

Hawking, Stephen. *A Brief History of Time.* New York: Bantam, 1998.

Hawxhurst, Joan C. *Antonia Novello: U.S. Surgeon General.* Brookfield, CT: Millbrook, 1995.

Hayhurst, Chris. *The Lungs.* New York: Marshall Cavendish, 2002.

Heifetz, Milton D., and Wil Tirion. *A Walk Through the Heavens: A Guide to the Stars and Constellations and Their Legends.* Cambridge, UK: Cambridge University Press, 1998.

Hickman, Panela. *The Night Book: Exploring Nature after Dark with Activities, Experiments and Information.* Buffalo, NY: Kids Can, 1999.

Hogue, Lynn. *Investigating Solids, Liquids, and Gases with Toys.* New York: McGraw-Hill, 1997.

Hopping, Lorraine Jean. *Jacques Cousteau: Saving Our Seas.* New York: McGraw-Hill, 2000.

Human Body. Eyewitness Books. New York: DK Publishing, 2004.

The Human Body & the Environment: How Our Environment Affects Our Health. Westport, CT: Greenwood, 2003.

Human Body in Action: Genes and Heredity. [videorecording]. Wynnewood, PA: Schlessinger, 2001.

Innes, Brian. *Search for Forensic Evidence.* Milwaukee, WI: Gareth Stevens, 2005.

Jane Goodall's Wild Chimpanzees. [videorecording]. Burbank, CA: Slingshot, 2002.

Johnsen, Carolyn. *Raising a Stink: The Struggle over Hog Farms in Nebraska.* Lincoln, NE: Bison, 2003.

Johnson, Neil. *National Geographic Photography Guide for Kids.* Washington, DC: National Geographic, 2001.

Johnson, Rebecca. *You and Your Genes.* Washington, DC: National Geographic Society, 2003.

Jordan, Shirley. *From Smoke Signals to E-Mail: Moments in History.* Logan, IA: Perfection Learning, 2000.

Kahl, Jonathan. *National Audubon Society First Field Guide: Weather.* New York: Scholastic, 1998.

Kalman, Bobbie. *What Is a Biome?* New York: Crabtree, 1998.

Kampion, Drew. *Waves: From Surfing to Tsunami.* Layton, UT: Gibbs Smith, 2005.

Kehret, Peg. *Escaping the Giant Wave.* New York: Simon & Schuster, 2004.

Kellert, Stephen, ed. *Macmillan Encyclopedia of the Environment.* New York: Macmillan, 1997.

Knapp, Brian. *Elements.* Danbury, CT: Grolier, 2001.

Kohn, George Childs, ed. *Encyclopedia of Plague and Pestilence from Ancient Times to the Present.* Rev. ed. New York: Facts on File, 2001.

Krapp, Kristine M., and Jacqueline L. Longe, eds. *Gale Encyclopedia of Alternative Medicine.* Detroit: Gale, 2000.

———. *How Products are Made: An Illustrated Guide to Product Manufacturing.* Detroit: Gale, 1998.

Krautwurst, Terry. *Night Science for Kids: Exploring the World After Dark.* New York: Lark, 2003.

Lambert, David. *Kingfisher Young People's Book of Oceans.* Boston: Houghton Mifflin, 2001.

Landau, Elaine. *Rachel Carson and the Environmental Movement.* New York: Children's Press, 2004.

Lauber, Patricia. *Hurricanes: Earth's Mightiest Storms.* New York: Scholastic, 1996.

———. *What Do You See and How Do You See It?: Exploring Light, Color, and Vision.* New York: Crown, 1994.

Leebow, Ken. *300 Incredible Things for Kids on the Internet.* Marietta, GA: VIP Publishing, 1998.

Lerner, K. Lee, and Brenda Wilmoth Lerner, eds. *New Gale Encyclopedia of Science.* 3d ed. Detroit: Gale, 2004.

Levinson, David. *Health and Illness: A Cross-Cultural Encyclopedia.* San Francisco: ABC-CLIO, 1997.

Litman, Jessica. *Digital Copyright: Protecting Intellectual Property on the Internet.* Amherst, NY: Prometheus, 2001.

Littmann, Mark. *Heavens on Fire: The Great Leonid Meteor Storms.* Cambridge, UK: Cambridge University Press, 1998.

London, Daniel. *Small Engine Care & Repair.* Chanhassen, MN: Creative, 2003.

Longe, Jacqueline L., ed. *How Products Are Made: An Illustrated Guide to Product Manufacturing.* Vol. 4. Detroit: Gale, 1997.

Loughran, Donna. *Using the Internet Safely.* Austin, TX: Raintree Streck-Vaughn, 2003.

Ludlum, David M. *National Audubon Society Field Guide to American Weather.* New York: Knopf, 1995.

Luhr, James, ed. *Earth.* New York: DK Publishing, 2003.

Macaulay, David. *The Way Things Work.* Boston: Houghton Mifflin, 1988.

———. *The Way Things Work: Telecommunications.* [videorecording]. Wynnewood, PA: Schlessinger, 2003.

Macmillan Health Encyclopedia. Vol. 6, *Sexuality and Reproduction.* New York: Macmillan, 1993.

Magill, Frank N., ed. *Magill's Survey of Science: Physical Science Series.* Pasadena, CA: Salem, 1992.

Magnetism. Physical Science in Action. [DVD]. DVD FV8876. Wynnewood, PA: Schlessinger Media, 2000.

Marsh, Carole. *Heroes & Helpers Adventure Diaries: "Haz" Matt, Hazardous Materials Worker!* Peachtree City, GA: Gallopade, 2002.

Marshall Cavendish Encyclopedia of Health. Terrytown, NY: Marshall Cavendish, 1995.

Marvis, Barbara J. *Contemporary American Success Stories: Famous People of Hispanic Heritage.* Mitchell Lane Multicultural Biography Series. Childs, MD: Mitchell Lane, 1995.

Matero, Robert. *Animals Asleep.* Brookfield, CT: Millbrook, 2000.

Maxwell, Jeffrey. *Engines and How They Work.* New York: Franklin Watts, 2000.

Maynard, Chris. *Kitchen Science.* New York: DK Publishing, 2001.

McGrath, Kimberly A., ed. *World of Invention.* 2d ed. Detroit: Gale, 1999.

———. *World of Physics.* Detroit: Gale, 2001.

McGraw-Hill Encyclopedia of World Biography. New York: McGraw-Hill, 1973.

McNally, Robert. *Skin Health Information for Teens: Health Tips About Dermatological Concerns and Skin Cancer Risks.* Detroit: Omnigraphics, 2003.

McPherson, Stephanie. *Ordinary Genius: The Story of Albert Einstein.* Minneapolis, MN: Carolrhoda, 1995.

Melcher, Gary. *The Audubon Society First Field Guide: Night Sky.* New York: Scholastic, 1999.

Melton, J. Gordon, ed. *Encyclopedia of Occultism and Parapsychology.* Detroit: Gale, 2001.

Midkiff, Ken. *The Meat You Eat: How Corporate Farming Has Endangered America's Food Supply.* New York: St. Martin's Press, 2004.

Mongillo, John, and Linda Zierdt-Warshaw. *Encyclopedia of Environmental Science.* Phoenix, AZ: Oryx, 2000.

Moore, A. D. *Electrostatics: Exploring, Controlling, and Using Static Electricity.* Morgan Hill, CA: Laplacian, 1997.

Moore, George W. *Speleology: Caves and the Cave Environment.* St. Louis, MO: Cave, 1997.

Moore, Sir Patrick. *Firefly Atlas of the Universe.* Buffalo, NY: Firefly, 1994.

Morgan, Sally. *Superfoods: Genetic Modification of Foods.* Science at the Edge. Chicago: Heinemann Library, 2002.

Mosley, John. *The Ultimate Guide to the Sky: How to Find Constellations and Read the Night Sky Like a Pro.* Los Angeles: Lowell, 1997.

Nadeau, Isaac. *Food Chains in a Pond Habitat.* New York: PowerKids, 2002.

Nagel, Rob. *Space Exploration: Almanac.* Detroit: UXL, 2004.

National Geographic Concise Atlas of the World. Washington, DC: National Geographic, 2003.

National Research Council. *Living on an Active Earth: Perspectives on Earthquake Science.* Washington, DC: National Academy, 1999.

New Book of Popular Science. Danbury, CT: Grolier, 2004.

New Illustrated Science and Invention Encyclopedia. Westport, CT: Stuttman, 1989.

Newton, David E., Rob Nagel, and Bridget Travers, eds. *UXL Encyclopedia of Science.* Detroit: UXL, 1997.

Novello, Antonia. *Youth and Alcohol: Unrecognized Consequences.* Washington, DC: U.S. Dept. of Health and Human Services, 1992.

Null, Gary. *Healing with Magnets.* New York: Carroll & Graf, 1998.

Oceans of the World Set. 5 vols. Cleveland, OH: World Almanac, 2004.

Olney, Ross Robert . *The Internal Combustion Engine.* New York: Lippincott, 1982.

Onish, Liane. *Wind and Weather: Climates, Clouds, Snow and How Weather Is Predicted.* Scholastic, 1995.

Osborne, Louise, and Carol Gold. *Solids, Liquids, and Gases.* Buffalo, NY: Kids Can, 2000.

Overlook School for the Blind. *Technology for All: Assistive Technology in the Classroom.* Philadelphia: Towers, 2001.

Oxlade, Chris. *States of Matter.* Chemicals in Action series. Chicago: Heinemann, 2000.

Pachter, Barbara, and Susan Magee. *The Jerk with the Cell Phone: A Survival Guide for the Rest of Us* New York: Marlow, 2004.

Palm Beach Post. *Mean Season: Florida's Hurricanes of 2004.* Atlanta, GA: Longstreet, 2004.

Parker, Steve. *Albert Einstein and Relativity.* New York: Chelsea House, 1995.

———. *Electricity and Magnetism.* New York: Chelsea House, 2004.

———. *Eyewitness: Electricity.* New York: Dorling Kindersley, 2000.

———. *Eyewitness: The Human Body.* New York: DK Publishing. 2004.

———. *Eyewitness: Skeleton.* New York: Dorling Kindersley, 2002.

———. *The Lungs and Respiratory System.* Austin, TX: Raintree Steck-Vaughn, 1997.

———. *Satellites.* Austin, TX: Raintree Steck-Vaughn, 1997.

———. *Skin, Muscles, and Bones.* Milwaukee, WI: Gareth Stevens, 2004.

————. *Wind Power*. Milwaukee: Gareth Stevens, 2004.

Parker, Sybil P., and Jay M. Pasachoff, eds. *McGraw-Hill Encyclopedia of Astronomy*. New York: McGraw-Hill, 1992.

Parks, Peggy J. *The Internet*. San Diego: KidHaven, 2004.

Pasachoff, Naomi. *Madame Curie and the Science of Radioactivity*. New York: Oxford University Press, 1996.

Pearl, Mary Corliss. *Illustrated Encyclopedia of Wildlife*. Lakeville, CT: Grey Castle, 1991.

Pentland, Peter, and Pennie Stoyles. *Forensic Science*. Philadelphia: Chelsea House, 2003.

Perry, Phyllis. *Armor to Venom: Animal Defenses*. New York: Franklin Watts, 1997.

Petersen, Christina. *Wind Power*. New York: Children's, 2004.

Pipe, Jim. *Weather*. Mankato, MN: Stargazer, 2005.

Proulx, Earl, ed. *Vinegar, Duct Tape, Milk Jugs and More: 1,001 Ingenious Ways to Use Common Household Items to Repair, Restore, Revive, or Replace Just About Everything in Your Life*. Emmaus, PA: Rodale, 2004.

Purser, Bruce. *Jungle Bugs: Masters of Camouflage and Mimicry*. Toronto: Firefly, 2003.

Reid, George K. *Pond Life: A Guide to Common Plants and Animals of North American Ponds and Lakes*. Rev. ed. New York: St. Martin's Press, 2001.

Reilly, Philip. *Is It in Your Genes? The Influence of Genes on Common Disorders and Diseases That Affect You and Your Family*. Cold Spring Harbor, NY: Cold Spring Harbor Laboratory Press, 2004.

Rey, Hans Augusto. *Find the Constellations*. Boston: Houghton Mifflin, 1976.

————. *The Stars: A New Way to See Them*. Boston: Houghton Mifflin, 1976.

Reynolds, Michael. *Falling Stars: A Guide to Meteors and Meteorites*. Mechanicsburg, PA: Stackpole, 2001.

Richards, Elise. *Turned on by Electricity*. Mahwah, NJ: Troll, 1997.

Richards, Julie. *Howling Hurricanes*. Broomall, PA: Chelsea House, 2001.

Richardson, Gillian. *Ecosystems: Species, Spaces and Relationships*. Chicago: Raintree, 2003.

Ridpath, Ian. *Facts on File Atlas of Stars and Planets: A Beginner's Guide to the Universe*. New York: Facts on File, 1993.

Roberts, Royston. *Lucky Science: Accidental Discoveries from Gravity to Velcro, with Experiments*. New York: Wiley, 1994.

Robinson, Leif. *Astronomy Encyclopedia.* New York: Oxford, 2002.

Roller Coaster Physics. [videorecording]. Bethesda, MD: Discovery Channel School, 2004.

Roth, Anna. *Current Biography 1951.* New York: Wilson, 1951.

Rothman, Kevin F. *Coping with Dangers on the Internet: Staying Safe On-Line.* New York: Rosen, 2001.

Rourke, Arlene. *Hands and Feet.* Vero Beach, FL: Rourke, 1987.

Roza, Greg. *The Incredible Story of Computers and the Internet.* New York: Powerkids, 2004.

Russell, Sharman Apt. *An Obsession with Butterflies: Our Long Love Affair with a Singular Insect.* Cambridge, MA: Perseus, 2003.

Rutherford, Scott. *The American Roller Coaster.* Osceola, WI: MBI, 2000.

Ryan, Bernard. *Stephen Hawking: Physicist and Educator.* New York: Ferguson, 2004.

Saari, Peggy, ed. *Prominent Women of the 20th Century.* Detroit: UXL, 1996.

Sadeh, Avi. *Sleeping Like a Baby: A Sensitive and Sensible Approach to Solving Your Child's Sleep Problems.* New Haven, CT: Yale, 2001.

Sakurai, Gail. *Stephen Hawking: Understanding the Universe.* New York: Children's Press, 1996.

Sanford, John. *Observing the Constellations.* Old Tappan, NJ: Fireside, 1989.

Sass, Edmund J. *Polio's Legacy: An Oral History.* Lanham, MD: University Press of America, 1996.

Savage, Stephen. *Hands and Feet.* Adaptation for Survival. New York: Thompson, 1995.

Sayre, April Pulley. *Lake and Pond.* New York: Twenty-First Century, 1996.

Schaaf, Fred. *Seeing the Sky: 100 Projects, Activities and Explorations in Astronomy.* New York: Wiley, 1990.

Schlager, Neil, ed. *Science and Its Times: Understanding the Social Significance of Scientific Discovery.* Vol. 7, *1950–Present.* Detroit: Gale, 2000.

Schmittroth, Linda, Mary Reilly McCall, and Bridget Travers. *Eureka!* 6 vols. New York: UXL, 1995.

Schneider, Dona. *Children's Environmental Health: Reducing Risk in a Dangerous World.* Atlanta, GA: American Public Health Association, 2000.

Scientists at Work: Profiles of Today's Groundbreaking Scientists from "Science Times." New York: McGraw-Hill, 2000.

Seymour, Simon. *Icebergs and Glaciers.* New York: HarperTrophy, 1999.

Sheets, Bob, and Jack Williams. *Hurricane Watch: Forecasting the Deadliest Storms on Earth.* New York: Vintage, 2001.

Shin, Linda M., and Karen Bellenir. *Ear, Nose and Throat Disorders Sourcebook.* Detroit: Omnigraphics, 1998.

Silverman, Buffy. *Molds and Fungi.* San Diego: Kidshaven, 2005.

Silverstein, Alvin, Virginia Silverstein, and Robert Silverstein. *Fungi.* New York: Twenty-First Century, 1996.

———. *Sleep.* New York: Franklin Watts, 2000.

———. *Stomachaches.* New York: Franklin Watts, 2003.

Silverstein, Alvin. *Digestive System.* Human Body Systems. New York: Twenty-First Century Books, 1994.

Simon, Seymour. *Bones: Our Skeletal System.* New York: HarperTrophy, 2000.

———. *Earthquakes.* New York: HarperTrophy, 1995.

Simon and Schuster Encyclopedia of Animals: A Visual Who's Who of the World's Creatures. New York: Simon & Schuster, 1998.

Sipiera, Paul, and Diane Sipiera. *Thunderstorms.* A True Book. New York: Children's Press, 1999.

Smith, Roland. *Sea Otter Rescue: The Aftermath of an Oil Spill.* New York: Puffin, 1999.

Smolin, Lori A., Mary B. Grosvenor, and Richard J. Deckelbaum. *Nutrition for Sports and Exercise.* New York: Chelsea, 2004.

Snedden, Robert. *Cell Division and Genetics.* Chicago: Heinemann, 2003.

Sobel, Dava. *Longitude: The True Story of a Lone Genius Who Solved the Greatest Scientific Problem of His Time.* New York: Walker, 1995.

Sootin, Harry. *Experiments with Static Electricity.* New York: Norton, 1969.

Souter, Gerry, Janet Souter, and Allison Souter. *Researching on the Internet: Using Search Engines, Bulletin Boards, and ListServs.* Berkeley Heights, NJ: Enslow, 2003.

Souza, D. M. *What Is a Fungus?* New York: Franklin Watts, 2002.

Space Exploration. Space Science in Action. [videorecording]. Wynewood, PA: Schlessinger, 1999.

Stagl, Jean. *Crystals and Crystal Gardens You Can Grow.* New York: Franklin Watts, 1990.

Stephen Hawking's Universe. [videorecording]. 3 vols. Alexandria, VA: PBS, 1997.

Stephenson, James. *Farm Engines and How to Run Them.* Guilford, CT: Lyons, 2004. (Originally published in 1903.)

Stetz, Penelope. *The Cell Phone Book: Everything You Wanted to Know About Wireless Telephony (But Didn't Know Who or What to Ask).* Newport, RI: Aegis, 2002.

Steward, David. *Seasons.* New York: Franklin Watts, 2002.

Stewart, Gail. *Sleep Disorders.* San Diego: Lucent, 2003.

Stockley, Corinne. *The Usborne Illustrated Dictionary of Science: A Complete Reference Guide to Physics, Chemistry and Biology.* Tulsa, OK: EDC, 2002.

Stott, Carole. *Space Exploration.* New York: DK Publishing, 2004.

Strathern, Paul. *Hawking and Black Holes.* New York: Anchor, 1998.

Stwertka, Albert. *A Guide to the Elements.* New York: Oxford, 2002.

Sutherland, Lin. *Earthquakes and Volcanoes.* Pleasantville, NY: Reader's Digest Children's Publishing, 2000.

Swinburne, Stephen R. *Lots and Lots of Zebra Stripes: Patterns in Nature.* Honesdale, PA: Boyds Mills Press, 1998.

Tanacredi, John T., and John Loret, eds. *Experiment Central.* 5 vols. Detroit: UXL, 2000.

Tanaka, Shelley. *Earthquake On a Peaceful Morning Disaster Strikes San Francisco.* New York: Hyperion, 2004.

Thorpy, Michael J., and Jan Yager. *The Encyclopedia of Sleep and Sleep Disorders.* New York: Facts on File, 2001.

Tocci, Salvatore. *Chemistry Around You.* New York: Arco, 1985.

Trueit, Trudi Strain. *Earthquakes!* New York: Franklin Watts, 2003.

Tsunami: Killer Wave. [videorecording]. Washington, DC: National Geographic, 1997.

Undersea World of Jacques Cousteau. [videorecording]. 10 vols. Los Angeles: Pacific Arts Video, 1989.

U-X-L Encyclopedia of Biomes. Detroit: UXL, 2003.

Van Rose, Susanna. *Volcanoes and Earthquakes.* Eyewitness Books. New York: DK Publishing, 2004.

Vansant, Rhonda, Barbara Dondiego and Claire Kalish. *Nocturnal Animals and Classroom Nights.* Science in Every Sense. McGraw Hill, 1997.

Viegas, Jennifer. *Fungi and Molds.* New York: Rosen, 2004.

Visual Dictionary of the Earth. London: Dorling Kindersley, 1993.

Wade, Mary Dodson. *Texas Plants and Animals.* Chicago: Heinemann, 2003.

———. *Tsunami: Monster Waves.* Berkeley Heights, NJ: Enslow, 2002.

Wagner, Ronald L., and Bill Adler. *The Weather Sourcebook: Your One-Stop Resource for Everything You Need to Feed Your Weather Habit.* Old Saybrook, CT: Globe Pequot, 1994.

Walker, Kate. *Sticky Stuff.* Ontario: Scholastic Canada, 2003.

Walker, Pam. *Ecosystem Science Fair Projects Using Worms, Leaves, Crickets and Other Stuff.* Berkeley Heights, NJ, 2004.

Walker, Pam, and Elaine Wood. *The Digestive System.* San Diego: Lucent, 2003.

Walker, Richard. *Eyewitness Visual Dictionary of the Skeleton.* New York: DK Publishing, 1995.

Warm It Up (Start Your Engines): Small Engines 2. Minneapolis: University of Minnesota Press, 2000.

Weather. Pleasantville, NY: Reader's Digest, 1997.

Weather. My First Pocket Guide. Washington, DC: National Geographic, 2001.

Weather, Seasons, and Time. [videorecording]. Wynnewood, PA: Schlessinger, 2004.

Weilbacher, Mike. *The Magnetism Exploration Kit: Discover One of Nature's Most Astonishing Forces.* Philadelphia: Running Press, 1993.

Whitfield, Paul. *The Human Body Explained: A Guide to Understanding the Incredible Living Machine.* New York: Henry Holt, 1995.

Wiese, Jim. *Detective Science: 40 Crime-Solving, Case-Breaking, Crook-Catching Activities for Kids.* New York: Wiley, 1996.

———. *Roller Coaster Science: 50 Wet, Wacky, Wild, Dizzy Experiments About Things Kids Like Best.* New York: Wiley, 1994.

Williams, Julie. *Skin & Nails: Care Tips for Girls.* Middleton, WI: American Girl, 2003.

Wills, Susan. *Meteorology: Predicting the Weather.* Minneapolis, MN: Oliver, 2004.

Witman, Kathleen L., Kyung Lim Kolasky, and Neil Schlage. *CDs, Super Glue and Salsa.* Series 2. Detroit: UXL, 1996.

Woodford, Chris. *Light.* Routes of Science. Detroit: Blackbirch, 2004.

World Book Encyclopedia. Chicago: World Book, 2005.

World Book Encyclopedia of Science. Chicago, World Book, 2001.

World Book Student Discovery Encyclopedia. Chicago: World Book, 2003.

World of Scientific Discovery. Detroit: Gale, 1994- .

Wyborny, Shiela. *Virtual Reality.* San Diego: Blackbirch/Thomson, 2003.

Young, Robyn V., and Zoran Minderovic. *Notable Mathematicians from Ancient Times to the Present.* Detroit: Gale, 1998.

Yount, Lisa. *Virtual Reality.* Detroit: Lucent, 2005.

Zannos, Susan. *Dmitri Mendeleyev and the Periodic Table.* Hockessin, DE: Mitchell Lane, 2005.

Zemlicka, Shannon. *From Oil to Gas.* Minneapolis, MN: Lerner, 2002.

Zim, Herbert Spencer. *Insects: A Guide to Familiar American Insects.* New York: St. Martin's Press, 2001.

———. *Reptiles and Amphibians.* New York: St. Martin's Press, 2001.

INDEX

ABOUT THE AUTHORS

This is the third in a series by Peggy Whitley and Susan Goodwin, who have worked togther at Kingwood College Library since the early 1990s. The *Jumpstart* series began life as help guides for library students working on current issues assignments. Susan and Peggy have won numerous writing awards for this series and for their creation of the American Cultural History Web sites covering pop culture during the 19th and 20th centuries (kclibrary.nhmccd.edu/decades.html). They have each received the Faculty Exellence Award, quite an accomplishment for a librarian. Recently Susan won 3rd Place, Best of Show, in the Greater Houston Partnership annual photography competition. Peggy was granted a 2005 award by the National Council of Instructional Administrators for *The Scholarship of Teaching*, a special program for faculty development.